ENC 'ER

Including Polymer

Pam West

Vincent Duggleby

First Published		1975
Second	Edition	1980
Third	Edition	1984
Fourth	Edition	1990
Fifth	Edition	1994
Sixth	Edition	2002
Seventh	Edition	2006
Eighth	Edition	2011
Ninth	Edition	2017

British Library Cataloguing in Publication Data
West, Pam and Duggleby, Vincent
English paper money - 9th ed
English banknotes - Collector's guide

ISBN 978-0-9543457-5-4

Edited / Published by

Pam West, British Notes, PO Box 257, Sutton, Surrey SM3 9WW

Front Cover: B414 Polymer £5
Back Cover: B297s A00 000000 £5 Specimen
B345s RA00 000000 £5 Specimen
Page 1: 1842 Submission to the Bank of England

Printed by Pardy & Son Ltd, Ringwood

CONTENTS

FOREWORD by Vincent Duggleby

After 322 years the Bank of England finally took the plunge on 13th September 2016 to switch from paper to polymer and in so doing posed the question: Should English Paper Money change its name? Even when the Jane Austen £10 (scheduled for summer 2017) and the J.M.W. Turner £20 (by 2020) go into circulation, polymer banknotes will make up a tiny fraction of a typical collection. What is perhaps more remarkable is the publicity generated by the Bank of England in the run up to the launch of the Sir Winston Churchill fiver and numerous efforts (illegal?) to destroy them on television, radio and the newspapers.

Gone are the days when the design of a new series was a top secret and the Bank was unwilling to divulge anything to do with security for fear of encouraging forgeries. I well remember being reprimanded for daring to reveal that the Queen's portrait would be "gracefully aged" on the Series D in 1990. An interview with the Chief Cashier would have been out of the question so well done Jonathan Callaway for his interviews with Chris Salmon in the IBNS Journal 2014 (Vol 53, number 1) followed by Victoria Cleland in 2017 (Vol 56 number 1).

Granted it was a good deal easier in the 1960s and 70s to acquire examples of the first run over the counter. But few would argue with the Bank's decision to keep back ultra low numbers of the polymer banknotes and auction them for the benefit of charities. Needless to say that did not deter some people from asking silly prices on the internet. For those with really deep pockets, my vote for the outstanding "discovery" of the last five years goes to the O'Brien 10s D86Z 000001 B271, £1 L64J 000001 B273 and white £5 Y71 000001 B275 dated 17 January 1955. These were sold by Spink for a total of £48,000 plus premium. The Chief Cashier, of course, is in an enviable position and most recently banknotes kept by Sir Jasper Hollom, who died on 29 August 2014, appeared at auction.

Mention must also be made of the indefatigable Tim Lawes who has tracked down the elusive file in the De La Rue printing records. At last, 102 years after the event, we know what really happened (see page 64).

Finally I know that you will join me in congratulating Pam West and her husband Pete for all the hard work they have put in, especially in selecting so many fresh banknotes for the illustrations. It all helps to ensure that the 9th edition of English Paper Money remains the indispensable guide for collectors worldwide.

PREFACE

Vincent Duggleby MBE has always striven to provide superlative information to help collectors achieve their goals and has succeeded in achieving this over seven editions of EPM. As of the 8th Edition, Vincent passed the mantle over to me.

With this the 9th Edition we see the introduction of the polymer £5 banknote featuring Sir Winston Churchill September 2016, signed by Victoria Cleland, which produced a flurry of excitement among collectors and the start of the Polymer Series G. Within the Bank of England charity auction of the low serial numbers of the new £5 were the long awaited low serials and true first prefixes of the Victoria Cleland banknotes which had first been issued March 2015. The £10 polymer featuring Jane Austen is due September 2017 and the £20 featuring JMW Turner due 2020. It is highly likely that the £50 will follow suit. It was thought that the new Boulton and Watt £50 banknote would be a hybrid – a paper banknote with a polymer window, however, the issue was all paper with new security features.

In this edition we have incorporated, for the first time, reverses of all the types of banknotes and introduced many new scans. As usual new discoveries have been made including a B326s £10 Page A00 000000 red hollow overprint specimen, cementing prefix A as the first. Also a B328s £20 Page A00 000000 red hollow overprint specimen. A new replacement has been found B342 MX adding to the already rare MN listing. A group of progressive proofs for the Mahon £1 surfaced in 2016, along with some magnetic serial ribbon trials B283 made in 1960 on pink paper. We have logged more prefixes in Treasury banknotes T3-2 and T3-3. Tim Lawes has researched quantities printed for banknotes from 1957 to 1970, thus, many have been amended, certain prefixes discovered to only be printed up to 960000 instead of 1000000, he also brings new information to the Dardnelles notes.

As 2016 came to a close, Hollom's personal collection of low serial first prefix banknotes were sold at auction. I spoke with his niece after the auction and she mentioned that Jasper's middle name of Quintus followed the fact that he was the fifth son, he had died in 2014. The world banknote collection of Eric P. Newman was sold, which included the rarely seen Harvey £200. J.S.G. Boggs an artist who annoyed the government by creating banknotes in art form died unexpectedly February 2017, having just attended the FUN (Florida United Numismatists) show in Fort Lauderdale.

The banknote collecting world has seen a growth in third party grading companies 'slabbing', especially in America and Asia. The grading standards for each company differs as does the numbering system they use. Generally this has not affected the home market collector, but, overseas collectors often seek a '66' or higher for their English banknotes, something which is certainly attainable with modern banknotes. Though any serious collector of English knows that in some cases a low grade banknote may be the only chance to own one!

Sutton May 2017 Pam West

ACKNOWLEDGEMENTS

Over more than forty-two years of research into English Paper Money, the authors have received help from more individuals and organisations than we could possibly hope to mention here.

Particular thanks for this ninth edition are due to Mike Brill for his research into early white banknote prefixes. Research into Treasury banknotes by Tim Lawes who has spent many hours at The British Library and Mark Ray, both of whom have also helped in other sections with research. A special thanks also go to Tim who has expanded our knowledge of the quantities printed with his enthusiastic indepth mathematical calculation research into the subject. Mark has also assisted with pricing of white banknotes, other sections and provided constructive criticism with his knowledge of Bank of England modern prefix systems and Treasury banknotes prefixes.

Prefix information and scans, in particular by Alan Bungey, Andy Bysouth, Jonathan Callaway, Peter Longmuir, Lou Manzi, Keith McGrath and Mike Sambrook. Support and information from Colin Adams, David Everiss, Kwok Ha, Don Ludwig, Roland Rollins, Stane Straus, Gareth Thomas, Gary Vassallo and Phil Wade.

Along with venerable institutions: The Bank of England museum curator Jennifer Adam, The British Library philatelic department Richard Morel. Auction houses and dealers: Barnaby Faull of Spink, Claire Lobel of Coincraft, Simon Narbeth of Colin Narbeth & Son Ltd, Ian Gradon, Chris Webb and Mike O'Grady of DNW for their constant support and assistance.

To all the 'Collectors' who forwarded new prefixes, scans and general information over the years a big Thank You. My husband Pete for scanning, editing, typing, layout and much more.

Pete and I could not have completed the task without our computer geniuses: Robin Hill (IBNS webmaster) and Steve Smith of Domino Design, an 'InDesign' genius for the programme we use to layout the book.

Treasury Trial (photographic) 1916

CATALOGUE TERMS

Prefix Coding is the combination of letter/s and number/s that precede the actual serial. In most cases this is logical and now not incorporated in the text:

B 99	= letter over number	99 H	= number over letter
X41	= letter number number	R31L	= letter number number letter
28A	= number number letter	AN64	= letter letter number number

Dot, Dash and Squared Dot variants can be found on Treasury banknotes, these are the symbols that appear before the serial Nº., Nº and Nº and depending on the actual banknote may make one type considerably more valuable than its counterpart. Because banknote prefixes are made up of letters as well as numbers, the letters of the alphabet traced for a particular issue are listed. The quantities printed represent the best estimate that can be made calculated from the range of prefixes traced.

Bank of England banknotes since 1940 have incorporated a metal thread as an important safeguard against forgery. The thread shows up clearly when the banknote is held up to the light, in the case of the windowed versions (stardust), it is clearly visible on the surface of the banknote. Because most modern banknotes are multicoloured, the catalogue gives only the predominant colour/s for each type.

All illustrations are a maximum of two-thirds linear size in accordance with Bank of England guidelines. Scans of Series C, D, E, F and G banknotes have been overlaid with the word SPECIMEN in solid black capitals. These should not be confused with genuine Specimen banknotes which are overprinted specimen in red or black by the Bank of England and have all nought prefix/serials.

B390s Specimen AND COMPANY nought prefix/serial

PREFIX & SERIALS

Since the publication of the 8th edition of EPM, extensive sampling of existing Series B & C banknotes has enabled quantities printed and prefixes used to be defined with much more precision than previously. In particular, it has been established that from 1957 to around 1970, all denominations in these two series were printed to a maximum of 960,000 banknotes per prefix, not 1 million. Series A banknotes, Series C after 1970, and later series appear not to have been affected by this restriction. The sampling has also allowed separate estimates to be made for the first time of the number of £5 banknotes printed for Fforde and Page during the period in 1970-71 when the two signatures were randomly mixed. Individual banknote listings in the book have been modified to take account of this new information.

The letters of the alphabet define the way that Bank of England (and Treasury) keeps track of the quantity of banknotes issued and in some cases monitors trials, experiments, replacements, etc. But whereas the Treasury used the whole of the alphabet, except I, the Bank had a more selective approach. From 1928 the 10s and £1 banknotes of Mahon and Catterns use all the letters except I, P and Q (Q used for specimens). From Peppiatt on letters F, G and V were also omitted giving a conveniently round figure of twenty letters available for each issue. When the Portrait Series C banknotes were introduced in 1960, the letter O was dropped and M adopted for replacements. This practice continued into the Pictorial Series D, and was supplemented by L used by itself or in combination for replacements and column sorts in the Historical Series E.

During the Fforde / Page eras there are many overlaps (signature sequence pairs) in certain prefixes. The reason for this was that sheet-fed banknotes were printed in several stages and the sheets have to be stored for drying in between. Because there was a shortage of Page signature blocks, Fforde continued to be used and the two names ran in tandem for several months on different machines. Overlaps between Gill / Kentfield arose from the use of old part printed stock and are considerably rarer, as are those between Page / Somerset and the issues of Lowther / Bailey.

Million Serial, seven digits

PRICING

Prices, in Pounds Sterling (£), are based on a combination of factors: dealer lists, dealer sales, auction realisations, internet site auctions and other deals, which in turn depend on condition and new discoveries. Some dealers price banknotes reasonably whilst others over price giving discounts before you pick the banknote up to look at it. Condition is important, some dealers/auction houses grade conservatively, while others don't, you as the collector must choose carefully. Learn to grade.

Treasury issues are priced in three grades Fine (F), Very Fine (VF) and Extremely Fine (EF). White banknotes up to Bowen are priced in Very Good (VG) Fine and Very Fine, Nairne and Harvey Fine, Very Fine and Extremely Fine. Thereafter prices are for example, in Very Fine, Extremely Fine, and Uncirculated (UNC). Unless they are so rare as to be virtually unobtainable. Specimens, Colour Trials, Cancelled banknotes, etc are usually only found in high grades so look out for grade changes on the same page.

A dealer's price for an uncirculated (100%) banknote will obviously be higher than for one which may not have been in circulation but is not in pristine condition (AUNC). Most pre-war banknotes and even some issued as late as the 1980s are rarely found in 100% and the further back you go the more difficult it becomes. Collectors should remember not all banknotes are obtainable in uncirculated condition.

It has become easier to establish values of pre First World War banknotes simply because of the known quantities of banknotes turning up in auction. The prices quoted should therefore be regarded as an indication of what dealers might charge for the banknotes. It cannot be emphasised too strongly that the price of banknotes the market judges to be scarce can change suddenly with the discovery of a fresh supply. Watch the realisations at auction because at the end of the day a banknote is only worth what someone is prepared to pay for it!

Specific first and last runs are priced in both Treasury and Bank of England, as always there are exceptions where the few surviving examples are in poor condition. Presentation Packs and Errors have pricing policy statements at the beginning of the relevant chapters. Treasury Essays have been priced, this may stimulate demand or not, so prices may vary dramatically.

The word Rare or Scarce in the pricing columns is used if no price can be established. If placed in a grade column that is the known grade of the banknote.

GRADING

Banknotes like coins are collectable in various stages of wear and tear. Ideally, in the case of banknotes from 1900 to 1945 this means at least very fine (VF 75%), from 1945 to 1970 extremely fine (EF 90%) (or VF for first and last prefixes) and thereafter uncirculated (UNC 100%) or about uncirculated (AUNC 98%) with a few exceptions. The main grades are:

UNC	**uncirculated**	**100%**
AUNC	**about uncirculated**	**98%**
EF	**extremely fine**	**90%**
VF	**very fine**	**75%**
F	**fine**	**60%**
VG	**very good**	**55%**
G	**good**	**30%**
P	**poor**	**15%**

It is a matter of subjective judgement as to the precise definition of an uncirculated banknote, and what allowance, for example, should be made for the fact that it has been counted by a bank cashier. The modern production process leaves a small curved indentation (half moon) above or below the thread when guillotining, these banknotes should still be graded as uncirculated. Some dealers use grades such as good extremely fine GEF (95%), about (or near) extremely fine AEF (85%) or good very fine GVF (80%). One problem is that banknotes appear to the inexperienced eye to be perfect are '*slightly off*'. The commonest reason is the habit of cashiers to count a new packet and cause a slight bend in one corner. Very slight edge damage/ marks (felt tip pen) may also occur from cash dispensers. Such banknotes are perfectly acceptable but should be graded AUNC.

With 18th or 19th century banknotes it is unusual to find anything better than VF. Many can only be described as good (G 30%), some banknotes are cut and rejoined due to the practice of posting the two halves separately as a safeguard against theft.

Another pitfall concerns banknotes which have been cleaned/washed/ironed to '*improve*' the grade, which it does not. Examine all banknotes, very carefully for evidence of cleaning/washing as the better grades justify a considerable premium. Unfortunately there are far too many '*laundry jobs*' around. At best this removes the original sheen, UNC banknotes should not be matt, at worst it gives the banknote a washed out faded look destroying its value. Look out for fibres extending from the edges of the banknote.

If in doubt, ask for a written receipt with the condition clearly stated. Defects such as pin holes, tears, dirt, ink marks or hand-stamps (common on white banknotes) should be mentioned separately and taken into account when grading a banknote.

A detailed account of the IBNS (International Banknote Society) method of grading for world paper money will be found on the Society's website, www.theibns.org and www.britishnotes.co.uk, both which the author highly recommends. Diligence will save you from expensive mistakes.

FORMING A COLLECTION

New collectors should aim to keep things as simple as possible to start with. The first step would be to buy a reference catalogue. The second step is to obtain one example of each banknote to illustrate differences in size, type and colour. This will include a white £5 banknote, any 10s and £1 banknote from the Bank of England Series A (Britannia); one of the popular Series B (Helmeted Britannia) £5; one each of the 10s, £1, £5 and £10 Series C (Portrait), the Pictorial Series D from £1 to £50, and the Historical Series E and F (with variants) from £5 to £50. This is called Type Collecting.

By this stage you will be aware of the different Chief Cashier's signatures on the banknotes which will whet your appetite for those signatures you do not have. Some denominations are much harder to find than others and it is probably advisable to stick to what are termed middle series banknotes. You now have a Signature Collection. Add in a few of the commoner replacement banknotes and your collection is acquiring balance.

You will soon realise that the first and last of any series command a premium. Like any first edition these are the most desirable banknotes in any run. The 01 prefixes, the prefixes linking one Chief Cashier to the next, and the last recorded prefixes are elusive. You will need patience and luck to obtain them and a deep pocket for the better grades. You may have to be content with any serial within a given prefix, which falls within the first or last series. You may want an A01 or Z99, but will have to settle for perhaps an A09 and Z74 because they are within your means or available in a better grade.

Some collectors specialise in a particular cashier or series (J.B. Page or Series D) and aim to find an example of every prefix available. This is most readily done when the cashier is in office or the banknotes are in circulation. Others add interest by looking for prefixes which spell words: COIN - SOIL - SIOB - OIL - DO IT - TOIL etc and fun prefixes: NO1 - H2O - IOU etc or adding banknotes with printing errors.

DO IT prefix

Million serial banknotes 1000000 are highly collectable and occasionally appear on the market usually found in lower grades on the Britannia Series, but, other series have been noted including Treasury banknotes. Number One 000001 - Low 000025 - Radar 456654 - Repeater 313131 - Solid 888888 - Ladder 123456 or 012345 or 654321 serial banknotes are also sought after.

Always acquire banknotes in the best possible condition/grade. From 1928 to 1940 this means they will probably have been in circulation, and even then some mid prefixes are very rare. Post Second World War banknotes turn up more frequently AEF to UNC and from about 1970, when the hobby took off, more UNC banknotes were set aside. As far as Treasury and pre-1928 Bank of England banknotes are concerned the best advice is to buy what is available at whatever price you can afford. It is a fact of life that a comprehensive collection of early white fivers (let alone the higher denominations) is now beyond the means of all but the wealthiest. Treasury banknotes have become progressively more expensive in recent years especially in EF or better condition and you may have to be content with an F (fine) examples of some varieties.

Do not economise when storing your collection. Uncirculated banknotes in particular must be handled with great care and certain types of vinyl pocket/wallet/ sleeve can cause banknotes to sweat or buckle so don't compromise when storing your collection. Museums and other institutions use pure polyester products, ask for advice from your dealer and do not begrudge the cost, it will save you money in the long run. Make sure you have clean hands when handling banknotes and use caution when inserting/removing from album pages. Use wallets/sleeves as repeated damage will devalue the collection.

Solid serial

The exciting thing about collecting English Paper Money is that there is always the chance of finding a rarity when cashing a cheque or drawing banknotes from a cash machine. Replacement and experimental banknotes are almost always worth setting aside, especially if they are uncirculated. So check those prefixes carefully and if you spot anything out of the ordinary contact a dealer before you spend them.

TREASURY BANKNOTES 1914 *to* 1928

FIRST (EMERGENCY) ISSUE

The outbreak of the First World War in August 1914 proved to be the end of Britain's 'Golden Age' in more ways than one. Up until that time the gold sovereign and half sovereign had circulated as everyday currency for nearly a century even though the ordinary working man might never have handled them. The white banknotes issued by the Bank of England were legal tender in England and Wales only for amounts of £5 and above. On 5th August 1914 (the day after war was declared) the Currency and Bank Notes Act empowered the Treasury to issue current banknotes of £1 and 10s with full legal tender status and gold convertibility only indirectly through the Bank of England. In fact the Bank had already been working to no avail on a smaller £1 white banknote in the traditional design with the promise to pay 'in standard gold coin' (the so-called 'Gold Note' B208a).

Gold Note Proof

The Government extended the August Bank Holiday for three days until Friday and with the help of the Inland Revenue H.M. Treasury rushed through an emergency design during the weekend of 1st/2nd August. The order for the £1 banknotes went to Waterlow Bros & Layton, who turned to Eyre & Spottiswood for help in preparing the plates (cost £296), to the Royal Mint for a suitable engraved vignette of the King's Head and to Blades, East & Blades for work on numbering. Printing began at Waterlow Bros & Layton's Upper Thames Street factory on the Tuesday morning and continued in round-the-clock shifts. These emergency banknotes were hurriedly and poorly designed, and since there was no ready supply of banknote paper (other than that held by the Bank of England) the printers had to use Royal Cypher (simple) postage stamp paper from stock held at the General Post Office.

According to Lady Atterbury, wife of Sir Frederick Atterbury, Controller of H.M. Stationery Office, he sketched out the design at their home on Hampstead Heath. Sir John Bradbury then signed the notes 'as it was not possible to obtain His Majesty's signature in the extreme haste required by Mr Lloyd George.' In fact Bradbury probably took it upon himself to sign as he was in a similar position of authority at the Treasury to the Chief Cashier at the Bank of England. Minutes of various meetings between Lloyd George and City bankers, show that 2·5 million £1 banknotes were to be ready by Friday morning, the proposed date of issue, with a further 5 million by the same evening. In addition two million pounds worth of postal orders would also become legal tender. When the question of convertibility was raised, Lloyd George came up with an ingenious idea. No one would say they were not convertible. "You can take your £1 banknotes, convert them into Bank of England banknotes and then convert them into gold (but only at the Bank of England)....you do not want to make it easy for the public to get gold!"

The £1 was duly issued on Friday 7th August and on the same day De La Rue were given the go ahead to produce 2·5 million 10s banknotes over the next five days, for issue on Friday 14th August. There are some contradictions in the various statements by Lloyd George as to exactly how many banknotes could be produced in a given time, and the realistic capacity of the printers, but what is not in doubt is the pressure under which they had to operate.

Further examination of the records by researcher, Tim Lawes, has enabled a more accurate estimate to be made of the quantities of the First Issue. These show that Waterlow Bros & Layton were given two separate orders by HMSO for the £1 banknotes. The first (invoiced on 27th August) consisted of 39·8 million individual banknotes in finished form, 4 million numbered banknotes in sheet form and 3·5 million unnumbered in sheet form: a total of just over 47·5 million, of which about 1 million were rejected. The total cost was £20,849. The second order (invoiced on 10th September) was for just over 17 million £1 banknotes and just under 4·5 million 10s banknotes (allowing for rejects).

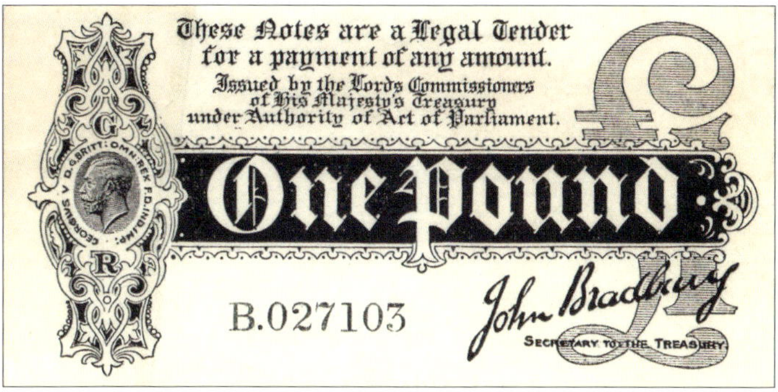

T1 B prefix with full stop

Although De La Rue's invoices are not in the file, the Inland Revenue's vote of credit together with a later memorandum show that the firm printed 22·5 million 10s banknotes in August/September and just over 3 million in November/December 1914: Together with Waterlow Bros & Layton, a total of 30 million banknotes. What has previously not been realised is that two types of paper were used. According to a letter (dated 19th November) from Sir Frederick Atterbury "later issue of the emergency banknotes were printed on paper specially made by Messrs. Joynson under my instructions. It bore, as was necessary, the same watermark, but it was made of materials of a higher class which gave greater strength and a better printing surface." We do not know how long the original GPO stamp paper lasted, or when the new version was delivered, but there was plenty left for De La Rue's later run of the 10s banknotes.

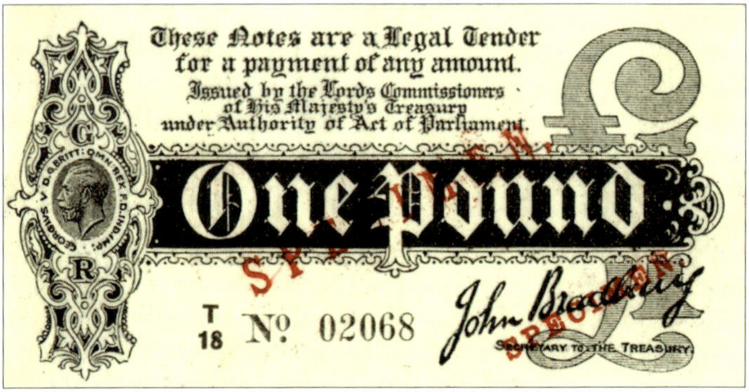

T3s Specimen

What has puzzled collectors over the years is exactly how the prefixes and serials were allocated and the banknotes numbered. The discovery by Tim Lawes of a letter from Waterlow Bros & Layton (dated 26th October) to Sir Frederick Atterbury casts fresh light on the problem. It explains in some detail the extra costs incurred by the firm in meeting the order and the overtime involved in working 168 hours a week (the normal being 50 hours). "Numbering work against time was the most difficult portion of our task and the authorities pressed us to obtain outside assistance in order not to run any possible risk of the banknotes not being produced in the time given us and in the very largely increased numbers notified to us from day to day during the first week as being imperatively required." Sub-contracting numbering work to Blades, East and Blades cost Waterlow Bros & Layton £1,477 but "there were numerous errors which required very special attention to discover and correct".

This may explain the gaps and inconsistencies when trying to reconstruct the survival rate of the different prefixes. The invoices show that 63·6 million £1 banknotes were printed but the weekly returns of currency banknotes prove conclusively that the number issued cannot have exceeded 40 million and was probably around 32 million, which means up to half of them were not needed. In contrast the 10s shows a strong correlation between the number printed and those put into circulation (29·2 million). From this we can deduce that the first De La Rue delivery of 22·5 million used the ornate A1 to A23 prefix followed by six digits, while Waterlow Bros & Layton used the prefixes S and T with six digits, similar to that used for most of the £1 banknotes. This leaves the prefixes B and C with five digits for the second De La Rue printing in December 1914.

Incidentally the first Treasury 10s banknote number A/1 000001 (T9) survives, as do many first series Treasury number one banknotes. The very first £1 A. 000001 (T1) was auctioned twice for the war effort in 1914 (winning bid £222) re-appeared at Spink in 1994 realisation £3,100 and again at DNW 2011 realisation £7,200.

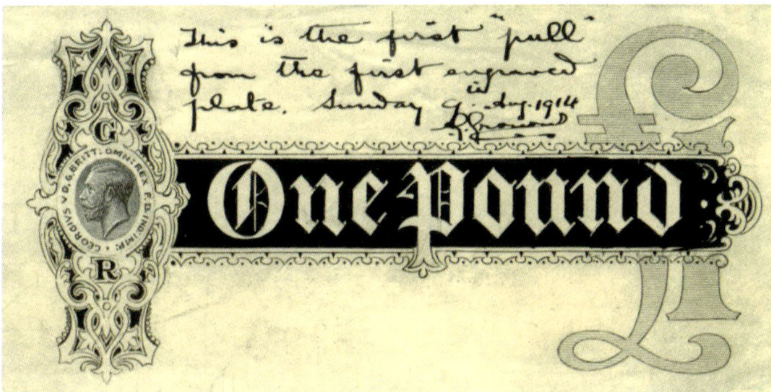

Treasury Proof first pull

Annotated:

'This is the first "pull" from the first engraved plate. Sunday 9th Aug 1914'

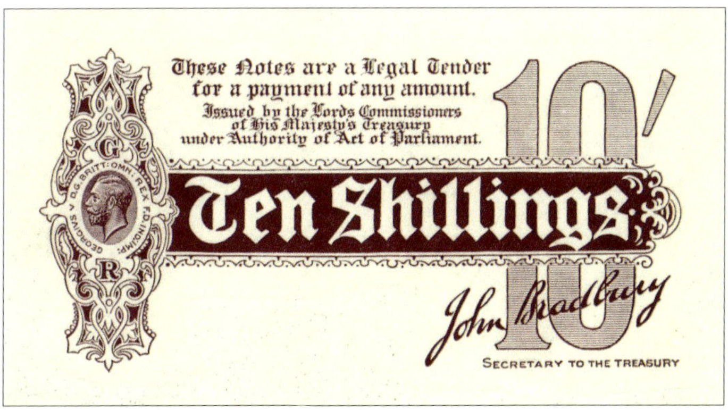

T9ct Colour Trial deep red

SECOND ISSUE

It was only a matter of days after the First Issue appeared that plans were put in hand to produce a more considered and permanent design. Despite strong and colourful competition from the various printers (Bradbury Wilkinson - no connection with Sir John Bradbury - were particularly pressing), the contract for the Second Issue was again divided between De La Rue (£1 and 10s) and Waterlow Bros & Layton (10s only). The designs were those of Mr George Eve (he was paid £126) who also designed some of the George V postage stamps.

On 28th August 1914 they were approved by Lloyd George who had remarked during the second reading of the Currency and Banknotes Amendment Bill the previous day: "The new design will not compare in artistic merit with that of the Scottish banks. We had to consider a good many things and the first thing to consider in a banknote is whether it is easily forgeable or not. If you have a good mass of colour on your banknotes it is not so easy to detect forgery. The simpler a design the more difficult it is to forge, just as the simpler a signature the more difficult it is to forge. Signatures with great flourishes are most easily forged. If you have a simple signature like that on the Bank of England banknote, it is the most difficult thing in the world for the forger. It is much more difficult to imitate flourishes and special adornments. That is the principle on which we have proceeded in the preparation of these banknotes..."

T11ct Colour Trial black

A rather different view was taken (in private) by the Chairman of the Board of Inland Revenue, Sir Matthew Nathan, who said: "The design is not a good one. I preferred the school leaving certificate. But I think we shall get a clear well printed banknote with easily seen and distinctive watermark making forgeries difficult. There will be no undue delay and the cost will not be excessive. When the public abuses the design we will take refuge in it having been made by H.M.'s designer of stamps". The new £1 banknotes duly appeared on 23rd October 1914 and the 10s banknotes on 21st January 1915 without any noticeable complaints!

To calculate the total of Second Issue banknotes, it is necessary to look at the weekly returns for 17th January 1917 (just before the Third Issue £1) and 23rd October 1918 (just before the Third Issue 10s). The totals are 365 million and 482 million respectively which (as Tim Lawes points out) includes the First Issue banknotes. When these are deducted we arrive at a net figure of 333 million for the Second Issue £1 and 453 million for the 10s. In each case this closely matches the recorded alphabetical prefixes and control numbers (1 to 90).

T12-1 M/77 Last

T13s Specimen

THIRD ISSUE

The Treasury, it seems, was still not satisfied and within a few months discussions were under way on yet another change adopting many of the principles which had just been rejected. Judging from the number of surviving essays and trials there was strong competition among the four main security printers. The so called 'Carlton' design which apparently found favour with the Treasury featured St. George and the Dragon, but differed in a number of respects from the issued banknote, credited to Bertram Mackennal. A Treasury memorandum dated March 1916 merely stated that Mackennal had been "good enough to step in the breach" as the only other two possible candidates had gone to the front. Further evidence on this mystery has now been provided by Tim Lawes in the form of a De La Rue invoice for £63 dated 18th April 1916 referring to Carlton Studio, one of the largest firms of commercial art designers and to two of their employees, a Mr. Cooley and Mr. Ernest Wallcousins (1883-1976), a distinguished designer in his day. Were they the two men who had gone to the front?

Study of the progressive Carlton and Mackennal proofs show similar vignettes of St. George and the Dragon, based on the model by Pistrucci used on the sovereign, but the style of lettering is modified and so is the spacing of Bradbury's signature and a different portrait of the King has been used. On the penultimate Bradbury proof is written: "Proof as approved by W. Percy Thompson 19/10/16. George and the Dragon to be lighter top and bottom. Overprint to fit bar. Signature not to impinge."

T30c Cancelled

The new £1 notes were printed in photogravure by Waterlow Bros & Layton despite an attempt by De La Rue to claim breach of contract by the Government. Further research is continuing in an attempt to tie up the loose ends, but De La Rue's frustration can be understood if they had commissioned the original design from Carlton and could argue this was in large part adopted for the issued note. The precise terms of the Third Issue tender have not been located and if there are any contemporary records of Carlton Studio their whereabouts is not known.

In any event, the £1 was issued on 22nd January 1917 and the 10s on 22nd October 1918. The Times commented on the £1: "In design it is an entire departure from the old which as an artistic production it leaves far behind....the most distinctive feature of the note is the splendid likeness of the King on the right hand, which on first glance appears to be embossed owing to the blending of its green and brown....cases have come to light of the imitation of the old issue; it is doubtful whether even the most expert artist in forgery could reproduce the new."

On 27th August 1919 Sir John Bradbury left the Treasury to become Principal British Delegate to the Reparation Commission and was succeeded by Sir Warren Fisher (formerly Chairman of the Board of Inland Revenue). Fisher viewed the currency notes "with a certain temperamental disinclination" but concluded in his memorandum to the Chancellor, Mr Austen Chamberlain, that they should continue to bear the signature of the Secretary to the Treasury. "My signature", he added, "will need some compression!"

T31? / T32? Top prefix has a Dot, bottom prefix has a Dash

There were no more major changes, although collectors will be interested to learn the background of the 'Anchor' banknote formally listed (T16a). In 1923 a new style watermark was introduced into the £1, then in 1927 following the Royal and Parliamentary Titles Act, the heading on both denominations was changed to:

UNITED KINGDOM OF GREAT BRITAIN AND NORTHERN IRELAND

Unfortunately there are no official figures apportioning Bradbury and Fisher banknotes, but on 15th November 1928 total production of the Third Issue was given as 3,624 million £1 banknotes and 1,739 million 10s banknotes plus waste of 356 million and 142 million respectively.

FRACTIONALS

Towards the end of the war, there were serious concerns about a shortage of silver coinage, mainly due to inflation and hoarding, and proposals to remedy this by the issue of 5s banknotes. Bradbury himself was doubtful and the Bank of England totally opposed. “If 5s banknotes are put into circulation, it will very soon become necessary to print banknotes for small denominations” they said (with prophetic accuracy!). Nonetheless the Government pressed ahead with the required bill and were only dissuaded at the very last minute from introducing it on 19th July 1918. In the meantime, designs for even smaller denominations of 2s6d and 1s were prepared and some 5s banknotes had already been printed. Just over a year later, on 31st October 1919, authorisation was given “for the printing of 10 million banknotes of the approved design and bearing the signature of N.F. Warren Fisher in each of the denominations 5s, 2s6d and 1s.” The banknotes were not needed and ordered to be destroyed in 1924, fortunately for collectors a few survived the pulp vats.

T22 / T23 Head Proofs

T23ct Colour Trial blue and green

T22ct Colour Trial brown and blue

T28 2/6 Fisher Fractional

TREASURY ESSAYS

Essays (unissued designs) were submitted by the four main firms of security printing: De La Rue (Carlton Studios), Waterlow Brothers & Layton, Waterlow & Sons and Bradbury, Wilkinson & Co. Ld. Engravers London as early as 1915 for the Treasury Third Issue, but none of them met with the approval of the Chancellor, Reginald McKenna. This resulted in a very long and drawn out process, resulting in complaints from Waterlow Brothers & Layton who had built a new factory in Watford. The Treasury, in the end, did not put the Third Issue designs out to competitive tender, they just agreed terms with Bertram Mackennal something to which De La Rue in particular took strong exception. This may well have been justified as the design the Treasury had commissioned from Carlton Studios by Wallcousins and Cooley, was substantially 'borrowed' by Mackennal, then reworked and may have been one reason why a committee was set up in 1916 to consider future issues. A Treasury circular dated 7th March 1916 states that "The Chancellor proposes to nominate a small committee to consider various questions in connection with the manufacture and issue of currency banknotes and would be obliged if you will nominate a representative of your department to serve on the committee".

Numerous essays were submitted over the years by the security printers. These were held in reserve in the unforeseen event a Treasury Fourth Issue was needed, but the First World War was over and it was only going to be a matter of time before The Bank of England took over the Treasury issues. Although the amalgamation did not happen until 1928, it was being planned in detail as early as 1924.

J. A. C. Harrison, Waterlow & Sons, engraving at his bench

Only three of the essays listed have identifying features, TE2 is watermarked Waterlow Bros & Layton - TE15 and TE19 have a Bradbury, Wilkinson & Co. Ld. printer's imprint. So in most cases it is a matter of informed judgement as to which security firm has been allocated a design. The British Museum holds many hand-drawn and part-printed essays which need further research and do not form part of this listing.

I would like to give a huge vote of thanks to Mr L. Manzi without whom this section of the catalogue would not have been possible.

- * Essays to be found in Archives only
- (3) Approximate number of essays known to be in private hands

A remarkable group of Photographic Essays / Proofs came on the market in 2014 from the De La Rue archive day books, too numerous to list. TE15 and TE19c are examples of the group that were previously recorded.

£1 **Essay** prepared by Carlton Studios = De La Rue 1915

Mainly in blue with large St. George and the Dragon at left, oval vignette showing ¾ uniformed head and shoulders of King George V in garter. Central value tablet in old english cameo font with floral pattern in background. Uniface 156 x 105mm.

TE 1a * Essay: Part design without text or value.

© National Archive

TE 1b * Essay: £1 value added lower left, plus John Bradbury signature to right, above 'Secretary to the Treasury'. Wording included in italic lettering. 'United Kingdom of Great Britain and Ireland' 'Currency Notes are Legal Tender for the payment of any amount' 'Issued by the Lord's Commissioners of His Majesty's Treasury Under the Authority of Act of Parliament (4 & 5 Geo.V.ch.14.)'.

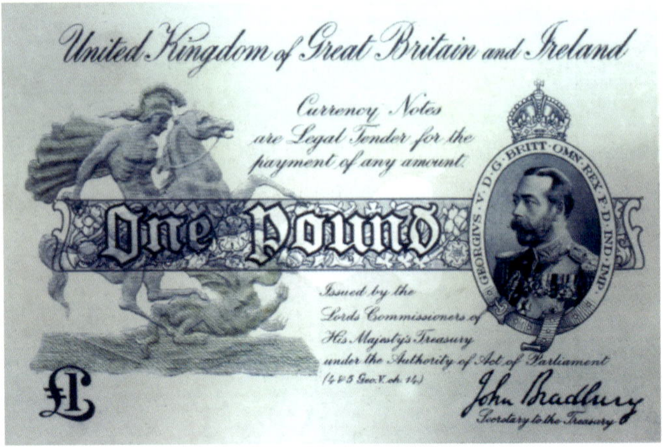

© National Archive

TE 1c * Essay: Text and layout changed, 'One Pound Currency Notes are Legal Tender for the payment of any amount….'. £1 value design bottom left changed, prefix V/65 №. 234567 incorporated twice.

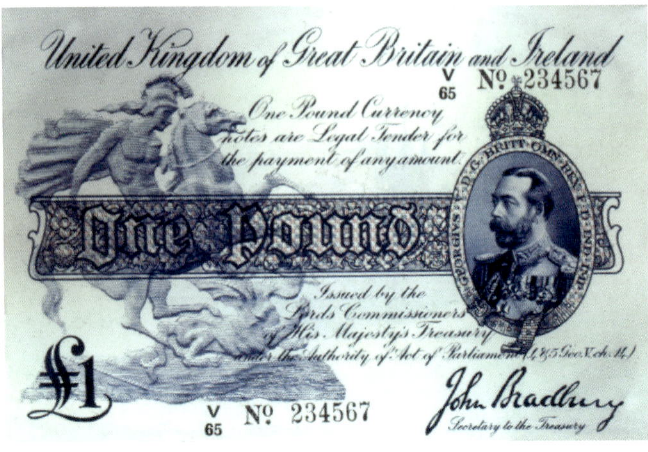

© National Archive

£1 **Essay** prepared by B. Mackennal / Waterlow Brothers & Layton

TE 2a (7) Essay: Basic design as TE 1c text layout changed, signature now central, no £1 value or prefixes, with and without squared mesh background. Uniface, shades, 156 x 100mm. From £4000 EF

No £1 sign

TE 2b (2) Essay: as TE 2a but with St. George and the Dragon facing in the opposite direction on a different base. Shaded £1 value re-introduced lower left. From £4000 EF

St. George and the Dragon facing in the opposite direction

TE 2c (2) Essay: as TE 2b but with font changed from italics to an upright font matching TE 3c, the D/O of kingdom intertwined, shading in denomination removed, job title moved down and to right. Found with and without squared mesh background. Both TE 2b/c exist in one and two head/garter format. From £4000 EF

Extra portrait £1 not shaded

TE 2d (1) Essay: as TE 2b but with one pound value tablet in an encased solid capital font, background now wavy lines. Job title as TE 2a/b. From £3000 AEF

£1 shaded

£1 **Trial/Proof** prepared by B. Mackennal / Waterlow Brothers & Layton

St. George and the Dragon in green, purple and brown with cameo head of the King in garter substituting the Mackennal ¾ head. Dimensions 155 x 100mm. The British Library has a holding of TE 3a in full sheets.

TE 3a (1) Plate Proof: Single colour working without wording, value etc. Uniface Small part design trials also exist (2). From £1800 GEF

Plate Proof

TE 3b (6+) Trial: Text added in italics, two prefixes W/87 № 000000. One pound value tablet in a thin solid capital font with scrollwork background. Signature moved back to bottom right. From £2400 EF £3000 UNC

Italicised text

TE 3c (12+) Trial: as TE 3b, text now in an upright capital font and one pound value tablet in a solid capital font. Prefix/serials W/87 Nº 191127. The D/O of kingdom intertwined, as T11 & T12. Dimensions 155 x 100mm.

From £2400 UNC

Large format

TE 3d (2) Proof: as TE 3c, D/O of kingdom not intertwined, with and without ink annotations. Issued dimensions and reverse as T16. W prefix used on Fisher T24 only.

From £1000 VF £1600 EF

As issued banknote

TE 1c, TE 2a, TE 3b & TE 3c can be found with four distinct reverses depicting the Houses of Parliament with the River Thames in the foreground. Proofs of the small rectangle reverse by Carlton Studios exist.

Reverses:

			seen on
•	Oval	*by* Mackennal	TE 1c & TE 2a
•	Large rectangle green shading	*by* Mackennal	TE 3b
•	Large rectangle brown clouds	*by* Mackennal	TE 3c
•	Small rectangle	*by* Carlton Studios	TE 3c

Green shading TE3b

Brown clouds TE3c

Waterlow & Sons also prepared several variations (boats on river) of the Houses of Parliament reverse. Proofs in both blue and black exist.

£1 Essay prepared by B. Mackennal / Waterlow Brothers & Layton

Standing Britannia with Union Jack shield to left. King George V head by Mackennal in ornate oval frame at right with sunburst behind. This design may have been modified and adopted for the ten-shilling notes. 1916/17.

TE 4a (1) Artwork: Complete design, two prefix/serials W/57 N°. 191128. Uniface 150 x 85mm on thick card. From £5000 UNC

Artwork

TE 4b (1) Progressive Proof: Part completed frame. 140 x 78mm design area. From £4000 GEF

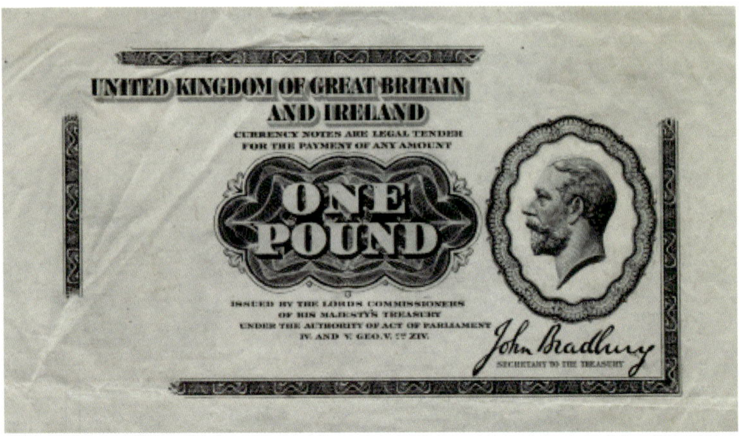

Incompleted borders (large margin not shown)

TE 4c (1) Essay: Blank value tablet and prefix area. Part completed borders.
From £1500 AVF

Corners incomplete

10s **Essay** prepared by B. Mackennal / Waterlow Brothers & Layton

TE 5 (1) Essay: Mackennal head of George V in central oval frame, flanked by 10/- value tablets within geometric patterns. Prefix areas blank. 1916/17.
From £4000 UNC

Ten shilling Essay

5s **Essay** prepared by B. Mackennal / Waterlow Brothers & Layton

TE 6 * Essay: Mackennal head in central garter frame, crown above, flanked by lion left and unicorn right. FIVE SHILLINGS top left and bottom right. 1916/17. Mounted in sunken card frame.

Fractional Essay © National Archive

5s **Essay** prepared by B. Mackennal / Waterlow Brothers & Layton

TE 7 * Essay: Mackennal Head in royal blue oval frame at right, crown above. Value in central tablet and at base. Dark blue background consists of large circle with St. George and the Dragon and horizontal chains of 'five shillings' in ovals.

Fractional Essay © British Library

£1 **Essay** prepared by De La Rue (believed to be)

TE 8a (4) Essay: Squared mesh background, incorporating large GR motif. Black, green (two shades) red and pink, King George V head at left in oval, Bradbury signature at centre. Uniface 151 x 87mm.

From £3500 UNC

Bradbury signature centre

TE 8b (1) Essay: as TE 8a but with Bradbury signature moved to the right. Lower two lines of text condensed and moved to base of design.

From £3000 AEF

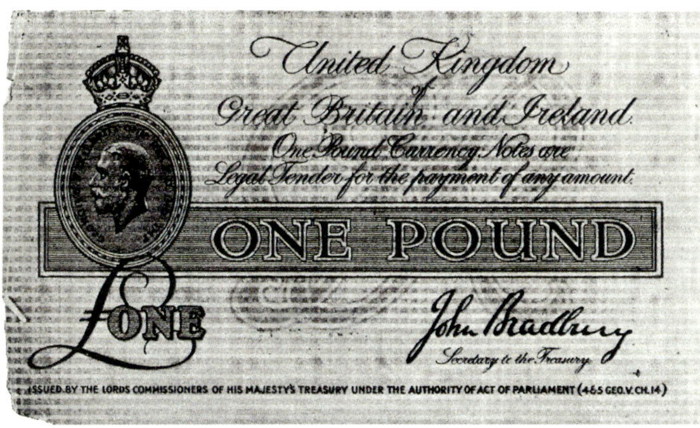

Bradbury signature to the right (B & W scan)

£1 **Essay** prepared by De La Rue (believed to be)

TE 9 (2+) Essay: King George V head in circle at left. Bradbury signature at bottom right, royal crest above. Ornate ovoid central panel one pound in old english font. Squared mesh background. Uniface 148 x 82mm.
From £2500 UNC

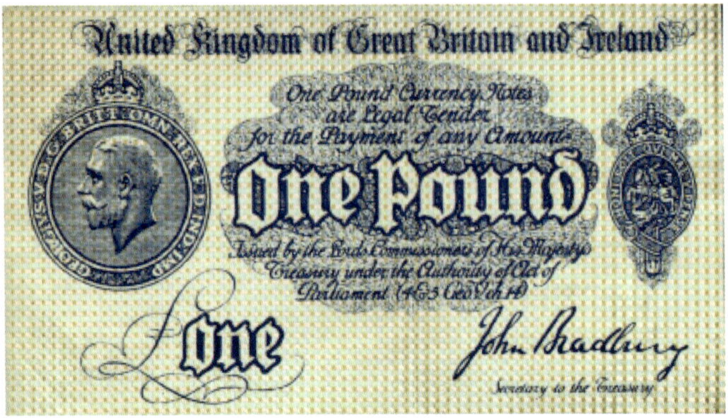

Basic design

£1 **Essay** prepared by De La Rue (believed to be)

TE 10 (1) Essay: King George V crude head top left in square. Central one pound value in upright capitals. Prefix printed once F/90 № 91062. Squared mesh background. Uniface 156 x 89mm. From £4500 UNC

Naive design

£1 **Essay** prepared by De La Rue 1915 (believed to be)

TE 11a (1) Photographic Plate Proof: Matt finish in pale tan and black. Set in wide frame, with King George V head to right, £1 to left both in ovals. Prefix/serial P/23 Nº 97603. Various annotations concerning colours on front. Uniface 147 x 96mm. From £3000 AUNC

Photographic Plate Proof

TE 11b (1) Essay: Colours as indicated on TE 11a and in blue, background added, laurel leaves re-engraved with ribbon added and prefix/serial changed to P/10 Nº 00000. Annotated 'A. A print as duplicate for sketch' 1915. From £2700 GVF £3500 UNC

Background added

TE 11c (1) Essay: Uniface with George V head centre right and value centre left. Heraldic shields in the four corners, Scotland, England, Wales and Ireland. Background design, two medium and one large oval, the latter engraved with flowers of the realm in peach. From £2500 EF

Heraldic shields in the four corners

10s **Essay** prepared by De La Rue ?

TE 12 (1) Essay: George V head top right in garter, crown above. Central ten shilling sum block in upright serif font. Vertical lined background, with central scroll pattern. St. George reverse. From £6000 GVF

Ten shilling Essay, basic design

£1 **Essay** prepared by De La Rue (Waterlow & Sons?)

Largest group of Essays. 'United Kingdom of Great Britain & Ireland.' in arc at top over a one pound value block. King George V in a military uniform profile or 7/8 head centre bottom. Background has the word ONE in an arc across the centre. All have a reverse with The Houses of Parliament with a tug pulling a barge on the River Thames in the foreground.

TE 13a (1) Artwork: Hand painted light blue central background, brown border with profile head of George V at lower centre. Zero serials at top left and lower right. Uniface (reverse separate artwork).

TE 13b (1) Artwork: Pink background brown border, with 7/8 head of George V at lower centre with two painted red serials 0000000 lower left and upper right. Uniface (reverse separate) 157 x 101mm on white card.

TE 13c (1) Essay: Green borders with blue background. Three red serials 0000000 printed at lower left, upper right and a smaller set at lower right. Watermark, five small stars surrounding a large five pointed star with '5' at its centre. From £4000 EF

Three serials

TE 13d (8+) Essay: as TE 13c but no serials, large borders (208 x 155mm) incorporating the large five pointed star watermark. Manuscript 'passed' bottom corner on one copy. Printed area 93 x 146mm. A group was bought in the 1980's, subsequently appearing in auction houses. From £1500 UNC

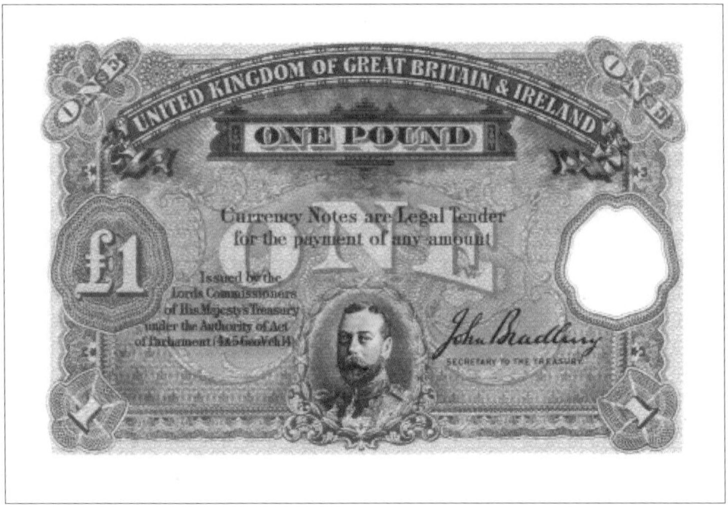

No serials, large border (not shown)

TE 13e (6) Essay: as TE 13c, but no serials, found in a variety of bi-colour combinations. Dimensions 156 x 99mm. From £3500 UNC

No serials

TE 13f (4) Essay: as TE 13e, crowns inserted either side of the central text. Found in a variety of bi-colour combinations. Dimensions 156 x 99mm. Some on waxy paper. From £3800 UNC

Crowns added

£1 **Essay** prepared by Waterlow & Sons

Uniface Essay in a wide variety of colours, vignette of King George V profile head centre left with vignette of St. George and the Dragon centre right, both photographs pasted on. Large thick £1 sign in the centre of the background behind legal tender text. Mounted in sunken card frame. Watermark two shields with monogrammed watermark C F & O 1867. From £2500 UNC

TE 14a (2) Essay: Prefix/serial №. 000000 with ONE POUND text background. Found in bi-colour combinations. Dimensions 150 x 85mm.

Horizontal signature

TE 14b (2) Essay: Bradbury signature at an angle lower right. Prefix №. only serials omitted with square pattern background. Found in bi-colour combinations. Dimensions 150 x 85mm.

Sloping signature

TE 14c (1) Essay: as TE 14b, but with a background of The Houses of Parliament. Dimensions 150 x 85mm.

Houses of Parliament background in EPM 1st edition (B & W scan)

£1 **Essay** prepared by Bradbury, Wilkinson & Co. Ld.

TE 15 * Essay: Vignette of King George V at centre right, shield depicting national emblems at left. The centre of the note with engine turning, £1 values at the four corners. Prefix 0/0 № 000000. From £1200 AUNC

Photographic essay 29/8/1918

£1 **Essay** prepared by Waterlow & Sons

TE 16 * Essay: Large portrait of King George V in military uniform at lower left. Prefix O/24 №. 000001 printed upper left and lower right. Large £1 sign in the centre of the background behind text. Mounted in sunken card frame.

King George V in military uniform

£1 **Essay** prepared by Waterlow & Sons

TE 17 * Essay: Brown and green with head and shoulders portrait of King George V in military uniform to right. Ornate £1 in oval to left. Two colour variations. Dimensions 154 x 84mm.

© British Museum

£1 **Essay** prepared by Bradbury, Wilkinson & Co. Ld.

TE 18 (1) Artwork: Green and orange with King George V head in a round vignette on the left and St. George and the Dragon in similar vignette on the right. Prefix 0/00 000000 lower left with sloping Bradbury signature to the right. Background is a large £ sign. Mounted in sunken card frame. Uniface (reverse separate artwork). From £7000 UNC

Border not shown

£1 **Essay** prepared by Bradbury, Wilkinson & Co. Ld.

TE 19a (1) Progressive Proof: Full face portrait of King George V in Admiral's uniform at left. Blue only, engine turned background omitted. On thick brown card. Bradbury W T Dunson & Co. Ld. London (on reverse). From £2500 EF

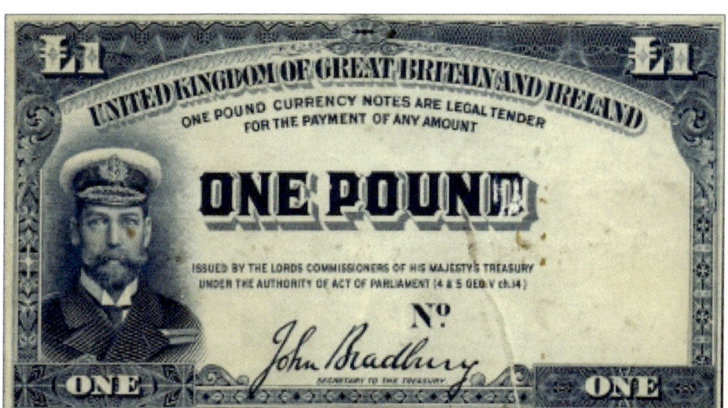

Progressive Proof in blue

TE 19b (2) Essay: as TE 18a but in magenta and orange, central circular sunburst design over pale green and blue background. The reverse shows the Houses of Parliament with barges in the foreground and a vignette of St. George and the Dragon to the right. Dimensions 149 x 85mm. The portrait was used on Rhodesian stamps of 1913. From £6500 AUNC

Central circular sunburst

TE 19c (1) Photographic Essay: as TE 19b but sepia high gloss photograph, prefix/serial O/OO Nº 000000. Annotated helmeted head watermark in design. Dimensions 150 x 85mm. From £1200 AUNC

Photographic Essay

10 **Essay** prepared by Printer Unknown

TE 20 (1) Essay: Art Deco style Britannia on throne to left. King George V in military uniform at right. Centre circular vignette. Background swirling design including bunches of grapes. Prefix №. 261023. No currency indicator, may have been prepared for military use? From £3500 UNC

Courtesy Croydon Coin Auctions 1984 (B & W scan)

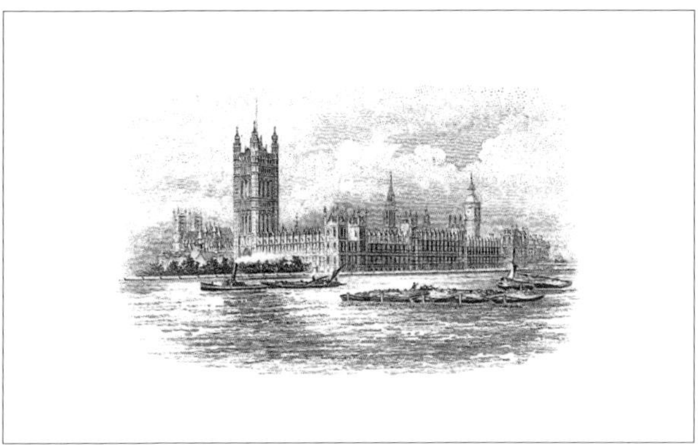

Die Proof reverse only

A number of Die Proof reverses have come on the market over the last six years, from various printers. Most depicting the Houses of Parliment as seen from the South Bank (boats/bridge in foreground). From £260 AUNC

JOHN
SWANWICK BRADBURY
1914-1919

John Bradbury was born in 1872 and entered the Civil Service in 1896, first in the Colonial Office and then the Treasury. After serving under Asquith and then Lloyd George (including help with the famous budget of 1909), Bradbury was appointed one of two permanent secretaries to the Treasury in 1913 along with Sir Thomas Heath.

At the outbreak of the First World War, Bradbury quickly realised the necessity of replacing gold with paper currency, the banknotes which were issued by the Treasury carried his signature; they were immediately nicknamed 'Bradburys'. He remained the government's chief financial adviser during the war and left the Treasury on 27th August 1919 to become principal British delegate to the Reparation Commission. He was knighted in 1913, created the first Baron Bradbury in January 1925 and died in 1950.

Collectors are warned to be aware that full stops may have been removed from T1 to create a T2. If in doubt seek a second expert opinion.

FIRST ISSUE

ONE POUND 7 August 1914

Emergency Issue designed at the Royal Mint from sketches by Sir Frederick Atterbury. Surface-printed in sheets of 36 (4 x 9) (plus sideways and sideways inverted watermark banknotes due to the practice of printing additional banknotes on the sheet margin) on one side only by Waterlow Bros. & Layton from plates by Eyre & Spottiswoode, on stamp paper with watermark showing the simple version of the Royal Cypher and the word POSTAGE. First Issue Treasury £1 banknotes measure 127 x 63·5mm and were legal tender until 12th June 1920. The first 2·5 million banknotes, which were among those delivered to the banks on Thursday 6th August for issue the following morning, can be identified by the large capital A, B or C prefix (see T1 and T2). Overall the issue totalled around 31·5 million, although records show a total of nearly 64 million banknotes were printed.

Because of the speed with which the Treasury banknotes were produced and the different numbering machines used, there may be differences between prefix/serial within a given T number. Some banknotes have inverted watermark where the paper was fed in the wrong way round. Varieties are likely to command a premium.

			F	VF	EF
T1	**£1**	Black			
		Quantity printed: 2·5 million	F	VF	EF
		Prefixes: **Full Stop** Six digit serial			
	A.	B. C.	850	1800	2600
T2	**£1**	Black			
		Quantity printed: Included in T1			
		Prefixes: **No full stop** Six digit serial			
	A	B C	1600	2800	4500

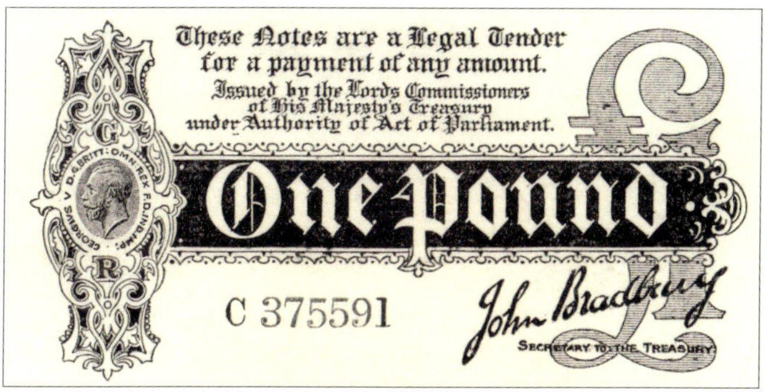

T2 C prefix (printed to 803000) no full stop

T3 **£1** Black

Quantity printed: Not known

Prefixes: **Dot**

A	B	C	D	E	F	G	H	
J	K	L	M	N	O	P	Q	
R	S	T	U	V	W	X	Y	Z

	F	VF	EF
Type 1: Four digit serial (G N)	1200	2000	-
Type 2: Five digit serial (A B D E I J L Q R T U V W)	500	1000	1500
Type 3: Six digit serial (A *to* Z / L Q V *not logged*)	400	800	1250
Type 4: Seven digit serial (B only)	1000	1650	-

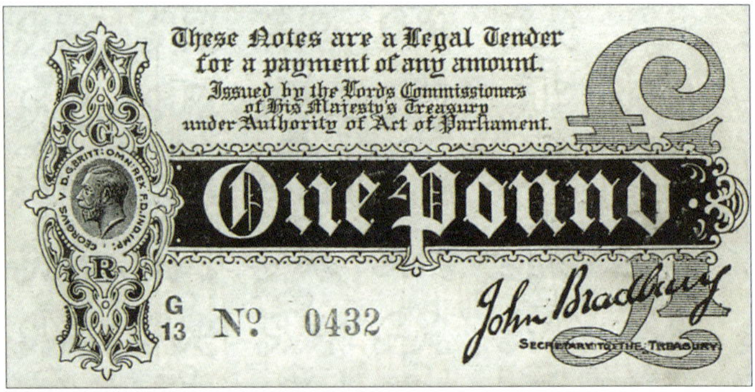

T3-1 four digit

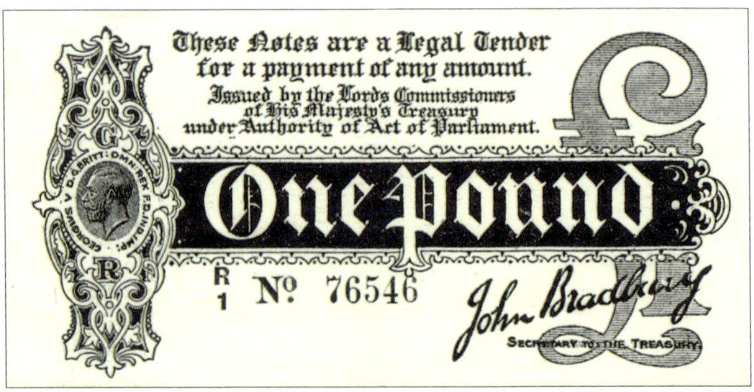

T3-2 five digit sideways watermark

I prefix not used for First Issue Bradbury.

T3-3 Variant

Variants of T3-3 exist on sideways watermark paper: flatter / squatter font in serial, particularly the noughts, the 2s have a flat base, prefix C/40 and K/38 recorded.

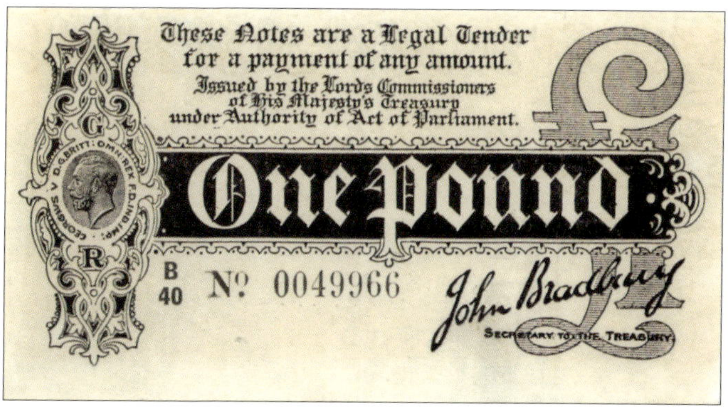

T3-4 seven digit

			EF	UNC
T3s	**£1**	Specimen *Prefix:* T/18 (*Type 2*)		
		Red capitals printed twice diagonally, two font sizes	-	4000
T3c	**£1**	Cancelled *Prefix:* T/37 (*Type 2*)		
		Black capital printed once horizontally	-	3000

T4 **£1** Black

Quantity printed: Not known

Prefixes: **Dash**

E J K L T

		F	VF	EF
Type 1:	Four digit serial (L only)	850	1500	3000
Type 2:	Five digit serial (E J K L T)	600	900	1750

T4-1 four digit

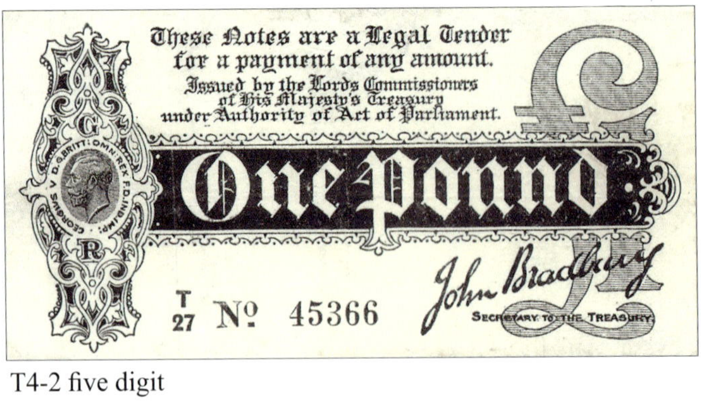

T4-2 five digit

T5	**£1**	Black			
		Prefixes: **Dash** № 3mm & 4mm or **Dot**	F	VF	EF
	B D K				
		Type 3a: Dash Six digit serial № 3mm (D only)	500	900	1600
		Type 3b: Dash Six digit serial № 4mm (D only)	500	900	1600
		Type 4a: Dot Six digit serial (B only one recorded)	-	4500	-
		Type 4b: Dot Seven digit serial Smaller font (B K)	750	1250	2400

T5-3a 0 rounded noughts

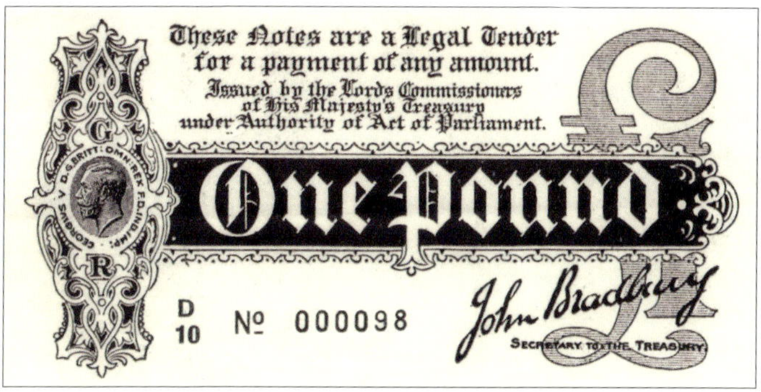

T5-3b 0 oval noughts

To help identification T5-3a has rounded noughts (0) and T5-3b oval noughts (0).

T6	**£1**	Black	F	VF	EF
		Prefixes: **Dot** Six digit serial			
	AA	(first series)	2200	-	-
	BB CC DD EE FF GG HH JJ KK		650	1100	1800
	LL	(last series)	1100	2400	-

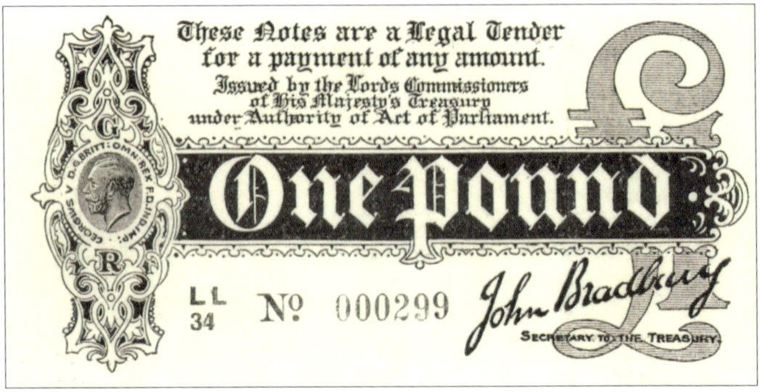

T6 LL last series

T7	**£1**	Black (Replacement?)			
		Prefixes: **Dot** Prefix NO. smaller Four digit serial in larger font			
	LL	(one recorded)	-	Rare	-

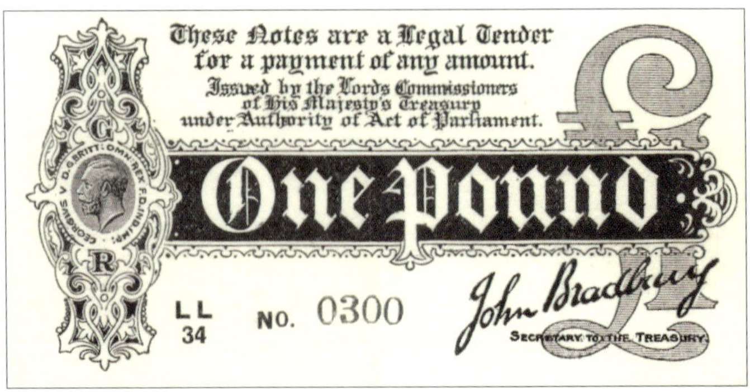

T7 Consecutive to T6 LL/34

The following illustrations of prefix/serial fonts, T1 to T7 have been reproduced from actual banknotes to facilitate identification:

A.193379 T1	L/8 No 20479 T4-2
C 375591 T2	D/27 No 015387 T5-3a
G/13 No 0432 T3-1	D/10 No 012689 T5-3b
U/18 No 06563 T3-2	B/5 No 036734 T5-4a
A/7 No 011907 T3-3	B/13 No 0034287 T5-4b
B/40 No 0049966 T3-4	EE/16 No 083385 T6
L/4 No 7808 T4-1	LL/34 NO. 0300 T7

K/38 No 020693

T3-3 Variant flatter / squatter font

TEN SHILLINGS 14 August 1914

Emergency Issue designed at the Royal Mint. Surface-printed in sheets of 36 (4 x 9) (plus sideways and sideways inverted watermark banknotes due to the practice of printing additional banknotes on the sheet margin) on one side only by Waterlow Bros. & Layton (banknotes with six digit serial) and by De La Rue & Co (banknotes with five digit serial) from plates by Eyre & Spottiswoode, on stamp paper with watermark of the Royal Cypher (simple) and the word POSTAGE. First Issue Treasury 10s banknotes measure 127 x 63·5mm and were legal tender until 12th June 1920.

It is now believed that the first (and by far the largest) production run T9 was by De La Rue. As with the £1 inverted watermarks are known and minor variations may be found. Varieties are likely to command a premium.

			F	VF	EF
T8	**10s**	Waterlow Red			
		Quantity printed: 4·482 million	F	VF	EF
		Prefixes: **Dot** Six digit serial			
	S	(first series, traced from 1)	400	700	1200
	T	(last series, traced to 36)			

T8 Last series

			EF	UNC
T8s	**10s**	Specimen		
		Prefix: T/33		
		Black capitals printed once diagonally	-	4000
T8c	**10s**	Cancelled		
		Prefix: T/29		
		Black capital printed once horizontally	-	3000

			F	VF	EF
T9	**10s**	De La Rue Red			
		Quantity printed: 22·5 million	F	VF	EF
		Prefixes: **Dash** № ornate font Six digit serial			
	A	(traced in 1 to 23)	260	520	820

T9 First 10s issued A/1 000001

Prefix/serial spacing variants on some banknotes.

			VF	EF	UNC
T9ct	**10s**	Colour Trial Black - Blue - Green - Deep Red	VF	EF	UNC
		Prefix: None			
		No prefix/serials	1200	3000	5000

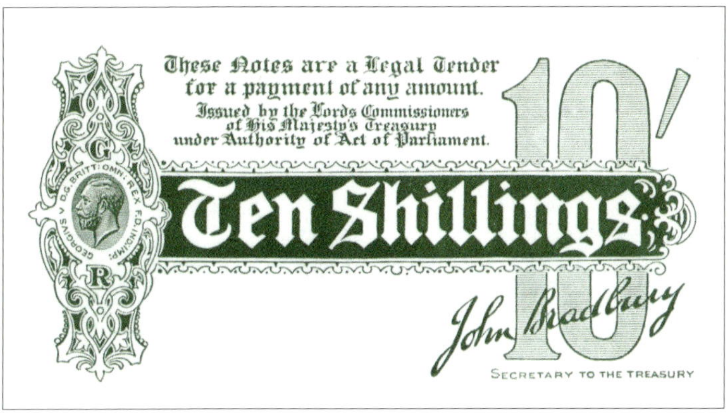

T9ct Colour Trial

Examples of proof status T9ct found in various colours including black, which was the chosen colour for the £1.

			F	VF	EF
T10	**10s**	De La Rue Red			
		Quantity printed: 3·024 million	F	VF	EF
		Prefixes: **Dot** Five digit serial			
	B	(first series, traced from 1 to 37)	450	950	1500
	C	(last series, traced to 18)	550	1050	1600

T10 C/18 Last

T10 was printed in December 1914 to ensure sufficient stock of 10s banknotes were available prior to the introduction of the Second issue.

The following illustrations of prefix/serial fonts, T8 to T10 have been reproduced from actual banknotes to facilitate identification:

T/34 No. 022554

T8

No. A/10 178244

T9

B/30 No. 06414

T10

SECOND ISSUE

ONE POUND 23 October 1914

Designed by George Eve. Surface-printed in sheets of 30 (5 x 6) on one side only by De La Rue on banknote paper manufactured by William Joynson & Co with watermark of wavy lines incorporating the Royal Cypher, the ONE POUND denomination and the four British emblems: rose, thistle, shamrock and daffodil. Second Issue Treasury £1 banknotes measure 149 x 85mm and were legal tender until 12th June 1920. Trials of T11-1 exist overprinted SPECIMEN in blue in archives. *Number in brackets after* 'traced to' *is the highest possible prefix.*

T11 **£1** De la Rue Black
Quantity printed: 333 million
Prefixes: Five digit serial

		F	VF	EF
	Type 1: Letter only			
A	(first series, traced from 1)	250	520	950
B C D E F G H J K L M N O P Q R S T U V W X Y		200	380	700
Z	(last series, traced to 76 [90])	220	400	750
	Type 2: Letter & 1			
A1	(first series, traced from 1)	250	520	950
B1 C1 D1 E1 F1 G1 H1 J1 K1		200	380	700
L1	(last series, traced to 57 [60])	220	400	750

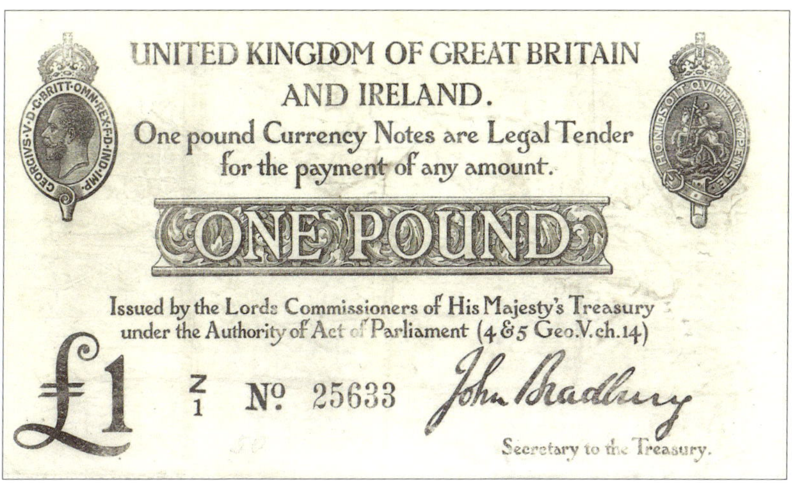

T11-1 Z/1 First of last

T11-2 Last

			EF	UNC
T11s	**£1**	Specimen *Prefix:* B/31 (*Type 1*) Red capitals printed once diagonally	-	3500
T11c	**£1**	Cancelled *Prefix:* B/35 (*Type 1*) Black capitals printed once horizontally	-	2500
T11ct	**£1**	Colour Trial Black - Red *Prefix:* None No prefix/serials (black £3500) red	-	5000

T11ct Colour Trial red

TEN SHILLINGS 21 January 1915

Designed by George Eve. Surface-printed in sheets of 30 (5 x 6) on one side only by De La Rue on banknote paper manufactured by William Joynson & Co. with watermark of wavy lines incorporating the Royal Cypher, the 10/- denomination and the four British emblems: rose, thistle, shamrock and daffodil. Second Issue Treasury 10s banknotes measure 136 x 76mm and were legal tender until 12th June 1920. The total number of banknotes issued is estimated to be 453 million, split roughly 50/50 between the two printers. A Trial of T13-1 exists in archives overprinted CANCELLED in blue once horizontally.

T12 **10s** De La Rue Red
Quantity printed: ~ 226 million
Prefixes: **Five digit serial**

	F	VF	EF
Type 1: Letter only (traced in A/1 to M/77 [90])			
A B C D E F G H J K L M	200	420	700
Type 2: Letter & 1 (traced in A1/1 to M1/61 [90])			
A1 B1 C1 D1 E1 F1 G1 H1 J1 K1 L1 M1	200	420	700
Type 3: Letter & 2 (traced in A2/1 to C2/88 [90])			
A2 B2 C2	270	600	950

T12-1 First A/1

It appears that De La Rue were allocated the first half of the alphabet A to M and Waterlow the second half N to Z.

T12-2 Last M1/22

T12-3 Last C2/88

T13 **10s** Waterlow Red

Quantity printed: ~ 226 million

Prefixes: **Six digit serial**

	F	VF	EF
Type 1: Letter only (traced in N/22 to Z/71 [90])			
N O P Q R S T U V W X Y Z	180	380	650
Type 2: Letter & 1 (traced in O1/1 to Z1/73 [90])			
O1 P1 Q1 R1 S1 T1 U1 V1 W1 X1 Y1 Z1	180	380	650

N1 has not been recorded and may not exist. Some of the Y and Z prefixes were used for the Dardanelles Overprints. Prefix W/45, has been reported to have the 'misshapen shamrock' watermark variety, similar to T33a, but not in the same sheet position.

T13-1 Y/30 Without overprint & T13-2 Z1 last

T13s **10s** Specimen

Prefix: V/24 (*Type 1*)

	EF	UNC
Black capitals printed once diagonally	-	3500

T13c **10s** Cancelled

Prefix: V/24 (*Type 1*)

Black capitals printed once horizontally	-	2500

DARDANELLES CAMPAIGN OVERPRINTS

The official Treasury minute in the Public Record Office states that the £1 and 10s currency banknotes were issued for use by the entire British Military Expeditionary Forces in the Mediterranean and the Naval Expeditionary Forces from May to June 1915. The banknotes we now know were overprinted from May to November 1915 (Inland Revenue records state 21st May 1915), being sent only to Alexandria, some arriving after the Gallipoli campaign had ended on 9th January 1916. 240,000 £1 were sent and 1,620,000 10s. S and T prefix £1's were also printed and later destroyed as were W and X 10s. Prefixes used for T14 overprinting were drawn from the print run of T11-1 and T15 from T13-1.

ONE POUND 1915-1916

			F	VF	EF
T14	**£1**	Black *with* Red Overprint			
		Quantity overprinted: 330,000	F	VF	EF
		Prefixes: Five digit serial (as T11-1)			
	F J M P (traced in tranches)		3000	4500	9000

The translation on the £1 in Arabic characters reads:

Piastres silver 120 / Piastres silver one hundred and twenty

Prefix	Lowest serial	Highest serial	
F/61 *to* F/70	39501	50000	
J/51 *to* J/60	58501	64000	J/51 not logged
M/31 *to* M/40	41001	60000	M/31 not logged
P/51 *to* P/60	88001	97500	
S/1 *to* S/10	501	15500	Not Inclusive not issued
T/31 *to* T/40	61501	95000	Not Inclusive not issued

Two distinct overprint types exist, study the tails to the left of the overprint:

Thin logged on F / Thick on J - M - P

Thin 2nd & 3rd tails on genuine T14 F prefix

Thick 2nd & 3rd tails on genuine T14 J - M - P prefixes

T14 Dardanelles Thin Overprint

T14 Dardanelles Thick Overprint

TEN SHILLINGS 1915-1916

T15	**10s**	Red *with* Black Overprint			
		Quantity overprinted: 2·08 million	F	VF	EF
		Prefixes: Six digit serial (as T13-1)			
	Y	Z (both traced in tranches 1 to 30)	480	820	1600

The translation on the 10s in Arabic characters reads:

Piastres silver 60 / Piastres silver sixty

Dardanelles Overprint Trial © British Museum

Prefix			Lowest serial	Highest serial	
W/1	*to*	W/30	087501	094500	not issued
W/61	*to*	W/90	093001	100000	not issued
X/1	*to*	X/30	087501	094500	not issued
X/61	*to*	X/90	093001	100000	not issued
Y/1	*to*	Y/30	018501	100000	Not Inclusive
Z/1	*to*	Z/30	010001	100000	Not Inclusive

T13-1 Y/1 Without overprint

T15 Z/22 Dardanelles Overprint

THIRD ISSUE

ONE POUND 22 January 1917

Designed by Bertram Mackennal. Vignette of St. George and the Dragon based on the work of Benedetto Pistrucci for the Royal Mint. Printed by photogravure in sheets of 21 (3 x 7) by Waterlow Bros & Layton on white/cream banknote paper manufactured by William Joynson & Co with multiple watermark of Vandyck lines (diagonal) incorporating the Royal Cypher, the denomination ONE POUND and the four British emblems. Third Issue Treasury £1 banknotes measure 151 x 84mm and were legal tender until 31st July 1933.

			F	VF	EF
T16	**£1**	Brown, Purple & Green (shades)			
		Quantity printed: 643 million	F	VF	EF
		Prefixes: **Dot**			
	A	(first series, traced from 1)	95	180	330
	B C D E F G		70	140	280
	H	(last series, traced to 20)	110	190	370
	Control Note:	(links Fisher T24)			
	Z	(traced in 1 to 32 [33])	140	280	500

T16 A/1 First

Bradbury and Fisher £1 banknotes with the prefix Z or Z1 are from the bottom right-hand corner of the sheet giving a ratio of 20 to 1. Highest prefix for T16 20 (not 21). It is thought that these Z / Z1 banknotes may have been used for control purposes. Z/32 links to Z/38 (T24), true link prefix not yet traced.

T16 Houses of Parliament by the Thames *reverse*

T16c	**£1**	Cancelled		EF	UNC
		Prefixes: G/51 G/52			
		Type 1: Black capitals printed twice horizontally	-	850	2000
		Type 2: As type 1, but prefix/serial omitted		-	2300

T16c Cancelled *Type 2*

ADMIRALTY ANCHOR BANKNOTE

In early 1918, Allied governments became aware of substantial buying of British and American currency in neutral European countries by various sources associated with the enemy powers. This caused great concern, as it was feared that the currency was to be used against the Allies for purposes connected with espionage or economic subversion. In order to detect where the currency was going, and how it was subsequently used, the British government decided to mark every Bank of England and Treasury banknote leaving the country in such a way that when it returned to the United Kingdom, it was possible to know when it left, who sent it, and to whom. As well as banknotes leaving in the post, or carried out by hand at ports, the Admiralty regularly sent large quantities of banknotes by official bag to naval bases abroad. The question of how these latter banknotes should be monitored was the subject of some debate in mid 1918 between the Treasury and the Postal Censorship (who had the task of monitoring the banknote traffic). It was impractical to handstamp each banknote destined for the Admiralty, but some way was needed of visually identifying re-imported banknotes at ports. Finally, it was decided in July 1918 to incorporate an identifying mark (Fouled Anchor under the clock tower) into the reverse design of the £1 banknotes for the Admiralty. It is not currently known to how many naval bases the Anchor banknotes were sent. However, one base was certainly Malta, which was receiving around 50,000 £1 banknotes a month in late 1918. The scheme for monitoring currency movements by marking banknotes was discontinued in December 1918 after the Armistice. A CANCELLED T16a banknote prefixed E/34 is held in the National Archive at Kew. *The A/1 and B/3 prefix confirmed not to have been issued.*

T16a	**£1**	Admiralty Anchor			
		Quantity printed: 1·26 million	F	VF	EF
		Prefixes:			
	B	(traced in B/1 B/2)	1500	2500	4000

B/1 200001 *to* 935000 July 1918 - B/2 136501 *to* 661500 November 1918.

T16a Anchor on reverse

TEN SHILLINGS 22 October1918

Designed by Bertram Mackennal. Printed by photogravure in sheets of 20 (4 x 5) by Waterlow Bros & Layton on white banknote paper manufactured by William Joynson & Co with composite watermark incorporating the Royal Cypher, the denomination TEN SHILLINGS at the top and the four British emblems. Third Issue 10s banknotes measure 138 x 78mm and were legal tender until 31st July 1933.

T17	**10s**	Brown, Purple & Green			
		Quantity printed: 31 million	F	VF	EF
		Prefixes: Black **Dot**			
	A	(traced in 1 to 40)	220	540	850
T17c	**10s**	Cancelled		EF	UNC
		Prefix: None			
		Type 1: Black capitals printed twice horizontally		-	2000
		Type 2: As type 1, but prefix/serial omitted		-	2300
T18	**10s**	Brown, Purple & Green			
		Quantity printed: Included in T17	F	VF	EF
		Prefixes: Black **Dash**			
	A	(traced in 1 to 40)	200	510	830

T17 Dot First A/1 & T18 Dash First A/1 low serial

T17 *reverse*

TEN SHILLINGS 16 December 1918

Production of the 10s banknotes with black prefix/serials was halted within two months because of widespread complaints that they were too easily confused with the £1 T16. The problem was addressed by printing the prefix/serials in red.

T19	**10s**	Brown, Purple & Green			
		Quantity printed: Included in T20	VG	F	VF
		Prefixes: Red **Dot**			
	B	(traced in 1 to 100) C (traced to 6)	700	1200	2000

T19 Dot B prefix

			F	VF	EF
T20	**10s**	Brown, Purple & Green *Quantity printed:* 105 million (Including T19) *Prefixes:* Red **Dash** or **Square Dot**	F	VF	EF
	B	(traced in 1 to 100)	160	370	650
	C	(traced to 15)	180	430	750

T20 Dash B/1 First

			EF	UNC
T20c	**10s**	Cancelled *Prefix:* B/75 **Square Dot**	EF	UNC
		Black capitals printed twice horizontally	-	2000

T20c Cancelled

FRACTIONALS

FIVE SHILLINGS 1 December 1917

Approved for distribution on 21st February 1918. Designed by Bertram Mackennal. Printed by photogravure in sheets of 35 (5 x 7) by Waterlow Bros & Layton on white banknote paper manufactured by William Joynson & Co, with composite watermark incorporating the Royal Cypher and FIVE SHILLINGS. Treasury 5s banknotes measure 127 x 76mm and were distributed to the clearing banks in Great Britain and Ireland. They were not issued and destroyed in November 1919.

T21 **5s** Unissued Deep Violet & Green
Quantity printed: 7·9 million
Prefix: (none or A?)

			EF	UNC
T21p	**5s**	Proof colour as T21		
		Prefix: Red №000000		
		No overprint (only one recorded)	Rare	-

T21p Proof

T21c	**5s**	Cancelled		
		Prefix: None		
		Black capital printed twice horizontally (only one recorded)	-	Rare

TWO SHILLINGS & SIX PENCE November 1918

Designed by C. Howard with vignette of King George V by T.S. Harrison. Proofs and Colour Trials were prepared by De La Rue but it appears that there was no production run of 2s6d (half-crown) banknotes signed by Bradbury. Banknotes measure 116 x 70/75mm, with composite watermark incorporating two Royal Cyphers, two 2/6 and HALF CROWN.

T22 **2s6d** Olive-Green & Chocolate
Quantity printed: None (not printed)
Prefix: (A?)

T22p **2s6d** Proof colour as T22 EF UNC
Prefix: A/T № 00000
No overprint - 7500

T22p Proof five noughts

T22ct **2s6d** Colour Trial various bi-colours browns - violets - greens
Prefix: A/T № 000000
No overprint No watermark - 8500

T22 / T23 Die Proofs of the head and crown in various engraved stages, found singly in blue or black and pairs in blue & black. From £220 UNC

ONE SHILLING November 1918

Designed by C. Howard with vignette of King George V by T.S. Harrison. Proofs and Colour Trials were prepared by De La Rue and it seems that there was no production run of 1s banknotes signed by Bradbury. Banknotes measure 105 x 67mm, with composite watermark incorporating two Royal Cyphers, and ONE SHILLING.

T23 **1s** Green & Brown
Quantity printed: None (not printed)
Prefix: (A?)

			VF	EF	UNC
T23p	**1s**	Proof colour as T23 *Prefix:* A/T Nº 00000 No overprint (tape on banknote)	4500	-	
T23ct	**1s**	Colour Trial various bi-colours blues - browns - greens *Prefix:* A/T Nº 00000 No overprint No watermark	-	6000	8500

T23ct Colour Trial gold & green

T22 & T28 *reverse*, depicting 1918 half-crown reverse

T23 & T29 *reverse*, depicting 1918 1 shilling reverse

© By courtesy of the
National Portrait Gallery, London

NORMAN FENWICK
WARREN FISHER
1919-1928

Warren Fisher was born in 1879 and entered the Civil Service in 1903. His first post was at the Inland Revenue and in 1907 he became private secretary to the Chairman of the Board, Robert Chalmers. In 1912 he moved for a short time to the National Health Insurance Commission for England but returned the following year to Somerset House as a Commissioner of Inland Revenue. In 1914 he was appointed Deputy Chairman of the Board, in August 1918 he became Chairman. Fisher was knighted in 1919 and on 1st October that year became Permanent Secretary to the Treasury where he stayed until his retirement in 1939. He died in 1948.

T24 First K/1

FIRST ISSUE

ONE POUND 30 September 1919

Design, watermark and dimensions as for *T16* Bradbury. Printed by photogravure in sheets of 21 (3 x 7) by Waterlow Bros & Layton on white/cream banknote paper manufactured by William Joynson & Co. *Number in brackets after* 'traced to' *is the highest possible prefix.*

T24	**£1**	Brown, Purple & Green (shades)			
		Quantity printed: 982 million	F	VF	EF
		Prefixes: **Dot** (overlaps Bradbury T16 Z)			
	K	(first series, traced from 1 to 100)	85	170	300
	L	M N P R T U W	45	80	170
	X	(last series, traced to 39 [40])	95	200	350
	Control Note:				
	Z	(traced in 38 to 84)	75	160	250

T24 Last Control Note Z/84

For information on banknotes carrying the Control Note prefix Z, see under T16.

TEN SHILLINGS 30 September 1919

Design, watermark and dimensions as for *T19* Bradbury. Printed by photogravure in sheets of 20 (4 x 5) by Waterlow Bros & Layton on white banknote paper manufactured by William Joynson & Co.

			F	VF	EF
T25	**10s**	Green, Purple & Brown			
		Quantity printed: 440 million	F	VF	EF
		Prefixes: Red **Dot**			
	D	(first series, traced in 1 to 100)	130	300	560
	E	F G	100	250	450
	H	(last series, traced to 41)	140	310	580
T26	**10s**	Green, Purple & Brown			
		Quantity printed: Included in T25			
		Prefixes: Red **Dash**			
	D	(first series, traced in 1 to 100)	110	280	520
	E	F G	90	220	400
	H	(last series, traced to 39 [40])	110	270	510

T25 Dot & T26 Dash

FRACTIONALS

FIVE SHILLINGS 28 November 1919

Design and watermark as for *T21* Bradbury. Printed by photogravure in sheets of 35 (5 x 7) by Waterlow Bros & Layton on white banknote paper manufactured by William Joynson & Co. 119 x 69mm with composite watermark incorporating at top FIVE SHILLINGS, striped box flanked by 5's below. Although Fisher 5s banknotes were not officially issued a few evidently found their way into circulation.

			F	VF	EF
T27	**5s**	Unissued Violet & Green *Quantity printed:* 10 million *Prefixes:* Red			
	B	approx twenty five examples in private hands Ten have water damage From £2000 Good	5500	8000	12000

T27 5s Fractional

T21 & T27 *reverse*

TWO SHILLINGS & SIX PENCE 19 November 1919

Design as for *T22* Bradbury. Surface-printed in sheets of 40 (4 x 10) by De La Rue & Co on white banknote paper manufactured by William Joynson & Co with composite watermark incorporating two Royal Cyphers, two 2/6 and HALF CROWN. Fisher 2s6d banknotes measure 119 x 72mm and were not officially issued, but a few evidently found their way into circulation.

T28	**2s6d**	Unissued Olive-Green & Chocolate			
		Quantity printed: 10 million	F	VF	EF
		Prefixes:			
	A		7000	9500	-

T28t	**2s6d**	Trial / Paste Up colour as T28	VF	EF	UNC
		Prefixes: A/9 №. 00000			
		As T22p, Fisher's signature pasted over Bradbury		-	8000

T28c	**2s6d**	Cancelled		
		Prefixes: B/18		
		Type 1: Black capitals printed twice horizontally	-	9000
		Type 2: As type 1, but prefix/serial omitted	-	9000

T28c Cancelled

ONE SHILLING 19 November 1919

Design as for *T23* Bradbury. Surface-printed in sheets of 49 (7 x 7) by De La Rue & Co on white banknote paper manufactured by William Joynson & Co with composite watermark incorporating two Royal Cyphers and ONE SHILLING. Fisher 1s banknotes measure 105 x 67mm and were not officially issued, but a few evidently found their way into circulation.

T29	**1s**	Unissued Green & Brown			
		Quantity printed: 10 million	F	VF	EF
		Prefixes:			
	A	B (approx twelve examples in private hands)	6500	9000	-

T29 1s Fractional

T29c	**1s**	Cancelled	VF	EF	UNC
		Prefixes: B/8			
		Type 1: Black capitals printed twice horizontally	-	5500	-
		Type 2: As type 1, but prefix/serial omitted	-	5500	-

The Bank of England Museum has examples of Warren Fisher Fractionals with SPECIMEN overprint, prefix B on the 5s, prefix C on the 2s6d and 1s.

SECOND ISSUE

TEN SHILLINGS 6 November 1922

Design, watermark and dimensions as for *T25* Fisher. The difference is in the red prefix standing by itself with the word N° omitted. Printed by photogravure in sheets of 20 (4 x 5) by Waterlow & Sons (who replaced Waterlow Bros & Layton in 1920) on white banknote paper manufactured by Portals, who had replaced William Joynson.

			F	VF	EF
T30	**10s**	Green, Purple & Brown			
		Quantity printed: 880 million	F	VF	EF
		Prefixes: Red N° omitted			
	J	(first series, traced from 1)	95	210	360
	K	L M N O P R	85	170	330
	S	(last series, traced to 78 [80])	95	210	360

T30 First J/1

			VF	EF	UNC
T30c	**10s**	Cancelled	VF	EF	UNC
		Prefixes: J/31			
		Black capitals printed twice horizontally	-	850	2000

ONE POUND 26 February 1923

Design and dimensions as for *T24* Fisher. The difference is in the watermark which is now composite so that the words ONE POUND appear at the top of each banknote and the addition of ^{1} to the prefix. Printed by photogravure in sheets of 21 (3 x 7) by Waterlow & Sons on white banknote paper manufactured by Portals Ltd.

								F	VF	EF
T31	**£1**	Brown, Purple & Green								
		Quantity printed: 1,533 million						F	VF	EF
		Prefixes: **Dot**								
	A^1	(first series, traced from 1)						60	100	220
	B^1	C^1	D^1	E^1	F^1	G^1	H^1	50	95	190
	J^1	K^1	L^1	M^1	N^1	P^1				
	R^1	(last series, traced to 59 [60])						65	110	230
	Control Note:									
	Z^1	(traced in 1 to 73)						70	140	240

For information on T31, T32, T34 and T35 banknotes carrying the Control Note prefix Z^1, see under T16.

T31 First Control Note Z^1/1

			VF	EF	UNC
T31s	**£1**	Specimen	VF	EF	UNC
		Prefixes: A^1/13			
		Black capitals printed twice horizontally		-	2000
T31c	**£1**	Cancelled			
		Prefixes: A^1/13			
		Black capitals printed twice horizontally	-	850	2000

T32	**£1**	Brown, Purple & Green							
		Quantity printed: Included in T31					F	VF	EF
		Prefixes: **Square Dot** or **Dash**							
	H^1	(first series, traced from 71)					90	210	420
	J^1	K^1	L^1	M^1	N^1	P^1	80	190	360
	R^1	(last series, traced to 60)					90	210	420
	Control Note:								
	Z^1	(traced in 42 to 71)					100	220	380

T32 Last R^1/60

T32 First Control Note Z^1/42

THIRD ISSUE NORTHERN IRELAND

TEN SHILLINGS 25 July 1927

Design, watermark and dimensions as for *T30* Fisher. The difference is that following the Royal and Parliamentary Titles Act of 1927, the wording reads: **UNITED KINGDOM OF GREAT BRITAIN AND NORTHERN IRELAND** Printed by photogravure in sheets of 20 (4 x 5) by Waterlow & Sons on white banknote paper manufactured by Portals Ltd.

			F	VF	EF
T33	**10s**	Green, Purple & Brown			
		Quantity printed: 275 million	F	VF	EF
		Prefixes: Red Nº omitted			
	T	(first series, traced from 1)	120	270	510
	U		90	210	480
	W	(last series, traced to 80)	120	270	510

T33 First T/1 & Last W/80

T33a	**10s**	Faulty Watermark	110	200	500

Some of the banknotes of this issue have a faulty watermark. A misshapen shamrock which is not properly indented on its right-hand side. When it occurs, it is on the fourth banknote of the third row, i.e. banknotes with prefix 12, 32, 52, 72 and 92.

ONE POUND 25 July 1927

Design and dimensions as for *T31* Fisher. Following the Royal and Parliamentary Titles Act of 1927, the wording on the banknotes had NORTHERN added reading: **UNITED KINGDOM OF GREAT BRITAIN AND NORTHERN IRELAND** Printed by photogravure in sheets of 21 (3 x 7) by Waterlow & Sons on white banknote paper manufactured by Portals Ltd.

			F	VF	EF
T34	**£1**	Brown, Purple & Green			
		Quantity printed: 470 million	F	VF	EF
		Prefixes: **Dot**			
	S1	(first series, traced from 1)	100	160	280
	T1	U1 W1	65	120	210
	X1	(last series, traced to 60)	90	140	240
	Control Note:				
	Z1	(traced in 76 to 98)	100	220	360

T34 First S1/3 & Control Note Z1/97

			F	VF	EF
T35	**£1**	Brown, Purple & Green			
		Quantity printed: Included in T34			
		Prefixes: **Square Dot**			
	S^1	(first series, traced from 7)	120	260	480
	T^1	U^1 W^1	85	210	420
	X^1	(last series, traced to 51)	120	260	490
	Control Note:				
	Z^1	(traced in 78 to 98)	140	260	490

T35 X^1/31 & Last Control Note Z^1/98

A memorandum dated 15th November 1928 states that the total production of Treasury Third Issue £1 banknotes was 3,624 million and 10s banknotes 1,739 million. This broadly tallies with the prefixes/serials used, but unfortunately the quantities cannot be allocated precisely between the various Bradbury and Fisher T numbers. From November 1928 the Bank of England took over production of the 10s and £1 banknotes. Treasury banknotes from the Bradbury Third Issue onwards remained legal tender until the end of the July 1933.

BANK OF ENGLAND BANKNOTES 1694 *to* 1928

HISTORICAL BACKGROUND

The Bank of England was founded under a Royal Charter granted on 27th July 1694. During the reign of William and Mary 1689-1702 more money was needed to finance the War of the Grand Alliance against France.

The idea for raising the money was put forward by a Scotsman, William Paterson, and a bill was drafted "for granting to their Majesties several rates and duties upon tunnage of ships and vessels and upon beer, ale and other liquors; for securing against certain recompenses and advantages in the said act mentioned, to such persons as shall voluntarily advance the sum of fifteen hundred thousand pounds towards carrying on the war against France". These recompenses and advantages were permission to set up "The Governor and Company of the Bank of England".

The first governor was Sir John Houblon, his deputy was Mr. Michael Godfrey and there were twenty-four directors. Temporary offices were set up at the Mercers' Hall in Cheapside. The first charter allowed the Bank to circulate notes up to the value of its capital of £1·2 million which was lent wholly to the government at 8% (yearly interest of £100,000). At this stage there was no guarantee of conversion of notes into gold, nor were the 'running cash notes', as they were called, given the status of legal tender.

The three cashiers were appointed on 30th July 1694. The head cashier was John Kendrick (at a salary of £200 a year) and his assistants were Robert Hedges and Thomas Madockes. Mr Kendrick's term was the shortest on record. He found the duties of the office "too onerous" and was allowed to step down on 11th August. Thomas Speed was appointed in his place, holding the post until 1699, he was succeeded by Thomas Madockes (1699-1739). By the end of 1694 the Bank's business had been transferred from the Mercers' Hall to the nearby Grocers' Hall where it remained until the move to Threadneedle Street, June 1734.

Within two years, however, the fledgling Bank was in trouble through no fault of its own. The problems arose from the passing of an Act in 1696 ordering re-coinage of the whole metallic currency. This had become hopelessly clipped and defaced, and given the choice people naturally wanted new sound money, although the poor were mostly unable to get it. Since the Bank's notes were not convertible they fell to a discount which at one stage was as high as 24%. Accounts submitted to Parliament on 4th December 1696 indicated that the £764,196 worth of notes outstanding were backed by only £35,664 in gold.

By March 1697 the position had greatly eased, the problems of the re-coinage had been overcome and on 1st April the Bank's charter was renewed until 1711 by Act of Parliament which provided that "no other bank or any corporation in the nature of a bank shall be established by Act of Parliament in this Kingdom". A new subscription list was opened and the Bank's capital was increased by just over one million pounds. The 1697 Act also contained a clause whereby the death penalty was to be imposed for forgery of the Bank's banknotes, though this was not to become a serious problem until the end of the 18th century.

In 1708 the Bank's monopoly was further strengthened by the veto of any banknotes payable on demand or at less than six months by joint stock banks with more than six partners. This was arguably the most important development in the early history of banking and was confirmed in the renewal of the Bank's charter in 1709 for twenty-one years and again when a thirty year renewal was enacted in 1713 following the Treaty of Utrecht.

The second major crisis for the Bank came in 1720 after the bursting of the 'South Sea Bubble'. Bankruptcy was rife, people naturally wished to get hold of their money and the queue of those wishing to withdraw gold from the Bank stretched down Ludgate Hill to Fleet Street. The situation was saved by the ingenious expedient of employing its own staff to withdraw money in large quantities and then take it round to the back of the Bank where it was re-deposited! Thus the tills were kept open until the public alarm subsided. A similar ploy was used with equal effect in 1745 when Bonnie Prince Charlie was marching on London.

The Bank's charter was renewed again in 1742, 1764 and 1781. The main development during these years was the rapid growth of small banknotes from the country banks (of fewer than six partners), since Bank of England banknotes did not circulate much outside London. An attempt to stem the tide of paper was made in 1765 when it became illegal to issue banknotes for less than £1 other than on demand in Scotland, and the same was applied in England from 1775. Two years later this provision was extended when all notes of £1 and above and less than £5 had to carry the names and places of abode of persons to whose order they were made, and the signature attested by at least one witness. The effect was to reduce the supply of £1 banknotes from the country banks very considerably (although this particular restriction did not apply to Scotland).

£15 Newland 1798

During this period the Bank enjoyed almost uninterrupted prosperity, but in February 1793 war was again declared between France and England and there followed a collapse of confidence. More than three quarters of the four hundred country banks were forced to close in the next two to three years despite the attempts by the Bank to alleviate the crisis. Napoleon was still relatively unknown but French activities were regularly reported and finally on Monday 27th February 1797 the Bank itself stopped payment in cash. The Bank Restriction Act became law on 3rd May 1797 under which the Bank was forbidden to pay cash for sums of 20 shillings or more to any creditor or use cash for any payment except to the Army or Navy, or Ordnance on a Privy Council order. It was, however, stated that payment in the Bank's banknotes might be "legal tender by consent" - that is if they were freely offered and accepted as such.

The act of 1797 was intended to be a temporary measure. In the event the Bank did not resume full cash payments until 1st May 1821, although they did sell captured Spanish Dollars (pieces of eight), held in their vaults as bullion. The coins were stamped with a small oval containing the head of George III and could be bought by the public at 4s 9d each. The famous £1 and £2 banknotes date from the Restriction. First they carried the name of Abraham Newland (they were nicknamed Newlands) and from 1807 that of Henry Hase. But confidence gradually returned and this was reflected in the fact that by 1810 the number of country banks had risen to more than seven hundred. From November 1816 the Bank began to ease its restrictions which it was entitled to do on due notice, and banknotes for less than £5 issued before 1812 were exchangeable for cash.

£10 Newland Proof 1806-7 *Heading:* Bank of England

By September 1817 soon after the gold sovereign had become legal tender, the Bank was paying out on all banknotes issued prior to January 1817. Unfortunately the position again deteriorated and restrictions had to be imposed until the end of January 1820. Meanwhile legislation had been passed which put a fixed time on permission to issue notes below £5 to bearer on demand. This was to be two years after the resumption of cash payments (1st May 1823). However, by an Act of 1822 permission was extended to 1833 for all banks. It was not a wise decision and a massive expansion of credit followed. By 1825 dozens of country banks were collapsing, the most serious failure being that of Pole Thornton and Co in September of that year.

The consequences were so severe that the Bank of England had to use all its resources to stem the panic - even to the extent of using an old stock of 600,000 £1 banknotes from the Restriction period, thus producing a banknote with two dates. In December 1825 the Bank's reserves fell to £1·25 million compared to £13·5 million in 1824. It was these events that lead to a series of Acts over the next eighteen years on which the modern banking system is based. The first of these in 1826 underlined the belief in the need for reliable joint stock banks. The Bank of England's monopoly was limited to a radius of sixty-five miles of London, thus making it possible for joint stock banks with more than six partners to operate outside the limit. These banks were able to issue their own banknotes for £5 and above. Existing banknotes of less than £5 payable to bearer on demand were to be redeemed not later than 5th April 1829. At the same time the Bank of England was allowed to open branches anywhere in the country and the first such branch opened in Gloucester on 19th July 1826.

In the 1833 Bank Charter Act, Bank of England banknotes were made legal tender for the first time on all sums above £5 except at the Bank itself so long as they were convertible into legal coin. This apparently strange proviso was to enable individual £5 banknotes to be changed into gold for the payment of wages. The Act also permitted the establishment of joint stock banks within sixty-five miles of the capital provided that they were for deposit only and did not issue their own banknotes. The first bank to take advantage of this was the London and Westminster, opened in London March 1834. The 1830s were times of boom and speculation, especially in railways, and credit was extended on a massive scale leading to inevitable collapses. The country banknote issue expanded by 50% in 1836 alone and it was against this background that Sir Robert Peel introduced the most far reaching Act of all, the Bank Charter Act 1844 (passed on 19th July). This finally put a stop to the free-for-all in banking and put strict controls on banknote issuing.

By this stage there were more than two hundred private banks and seventy-two joint stock banks in business. Under the Act new banks were forbidden to issue notes, limits were set on existing banks, and if a bank were taken over or wound up, the right of issue was forfeited. Two thirds of the lapsed banknote issuing limit passed to the Bank of England and just over seventy five years later the final country banknote issue ceased when Fox Fowler and Co of Wellington, Somerset, merged with Lloyds Bank in October 1921.

DESIGN & PRODUCTION

The first Bank of England notes were written by hand on ordinary paper purchased from stationers. Forgeries led the Bank at a very early stage to experiment with marbled paper, which could be matched exactly to a counterfoil. From 1697 watermarked paper was introduced with a watermark of looped border and scroll on the left, the words 'Bank of England' at the bottom. Produced by the Berkshire papermaker, Rice Watkins.

On 27th September 1724 the Bank signed a contract with Henry Portal of Whitchurch in Hampshire whose firm became the sole papermaker and remains so to this day. No one else is allowed to use the special Bank of England watermarked paper, although Portals (bought by De La Rue) themselves are suppliers to well over one hundred countries for security printing. The Bank held a stake of 25·5% in the company until 1989 when it was sold on the grounds that a substantial holding in a diversified public company was incompatible with its role as a central bank. The Bank gave an assurance that its relationship as a customer would not be affected by the sale.

For nearly one hundred years printing was in the hands of an outside contractor, James Cole until 1748, and then his son George Cole until 1791. Each month a supply of paper was sent in large iron bound chests by wagon to the printers in Great Kirby Street, Hatton Garden. Each morning the engraved copper plates would be drawn from the Bank in Threadneedle Street and taken to the printing works where a clerk counted the sheets of notes as they came off the press. In 1791 Cole's business was transferred to the Bank and from then until 1920 all Bank of England notes/ banknotes were printed on the premises.

Submission to the Bank of England

Although the design of the Bank of England white banknotes remained largely unchanged for some two hundred and fifty years there was a great deal of unobtrusive innovation. The over-riding concern at all times was to keep one jump ahead of the forgers, and to this end the Bank had a constant stream of designs and suggestions. Perhaps the best known efforts were by Applegath and Cowper. In December 1817 the Bank's attention was drawn to the work of a printer from Croydon called Augustus Applegath. He and his partner Edward Cowper were working on surface printing in several colours from blocks to be produced by stereotype from an original cut in wood or metal.

Applegath and Cowper engine turned design signed Rippon

The Committee advanced the sum of £1,200 to develop the system, followed by a further payment of £5,000. In February 1819 after receiving several specimens, the Bank's Court of Directors approved one of the designs. It was described thus: "The groundwork of each banknote will be black or coloured, or black or coloured line work, and the words 'Bank of England' will be replaced at the top of each banknote in white letters upon a black, sable or dark ground, such ground containing white lines intersecting each other, and the numerical amount or sum of each banknote in the body of the banknote will be printed in black and red register work, and the back of each banknote will distinctly show the whole contents thereof except the number and date in reversed impression".

The plan was to introduce the notes in 1820 and an Act of Parliament was passed to make it illegal to copy the banknote. Early proofs were monochrome, but later ones used as many as five colours. The master stroke was the reverse of the banknote bore a perfect mirror image of the front. This was made possible by the adaptation of his partner, Cowper's recent invention of a machine for printing wallpaper (1816), using stereotypes bent round a cylinder, able to print 1,200 banknotes per hour. Perfect registration was obtained by offset printing of the reverse of the banknote from a leather pad, which had already received the impression from the stereotype. The machine needed to revolve twice to print one sheet: on the first revolution the impression was made on the leather pad; on the second, paper was fed in, the front printed and the back set-off simultaneously.

Applegath and Cowper's association with the Bank of four years ended abruptly in September 1821 when the Bank's engraver Bawtree satisfied the Special Committee with his copy of the partners' latest five coloured banknote, imitating every aspect. The Bank had invested money and resources in the project. Secure accommodation for the printing process had been provided within the Threadneedle Street Bank building itself, and even a steam engine to drive the partners' machinery; also the Bank's papermakers, Portal and Bridges, had gone to the expense of installing special machinery to make paper to Applegath's specification. They were paid compensation and left the Bank's premises. By autumn 1821 the Bank had spent a total of £40,000 on developing the new banknotes. For further details see 'As Good As Gold - 300 Years of British Bank Note Design' by V. Hewitt and J. Keyworth.

In 1836 the Bank decided to adopt a new system of printing and engraving used in Ireland, which was the invention of John Oldham. He was appointed Mechanical Engineer and Principal of the Engraving, Plate Printing, Numbering and Dating Office and the system was introduced in 1838. The Bank continued to receive proposals for ambitious new designs, some of which have survived to this day, but the only significant change to the traditional white banknotes came in 1855 after the definitive version of Britannia, the work of Daniel Maclise R.A. was incorporated.

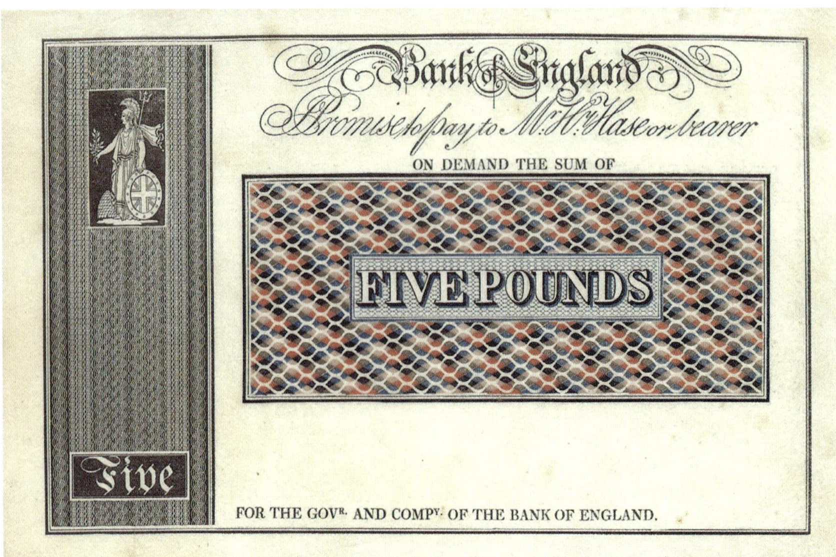

Applegath and Cowper honeycomb design

Trial overprint by B & W Lea on 1818 Hase banknote

In the 1880s a campaign was started by Randolph Churchill, the Chancellor of the Exchequer, to reintroduce the £1 note. It was taken up by his successor George Joachim Goschen, who had been a Director of the Bank of England at the age of twenty seven and who planned to double the supply of money by the issue of banknotes and the use of securities rather than gold as partial backing. The proposal was taken sufficiently seriously by the Bank of England for them to produce a trial £1 banknote, referred to as the Goschen pound, which is in the Bank's archives. It was hardly an inspired design and has none of the elegance of the 1914 'gold note' with its promise to "pay the bearer in standard gold coin".

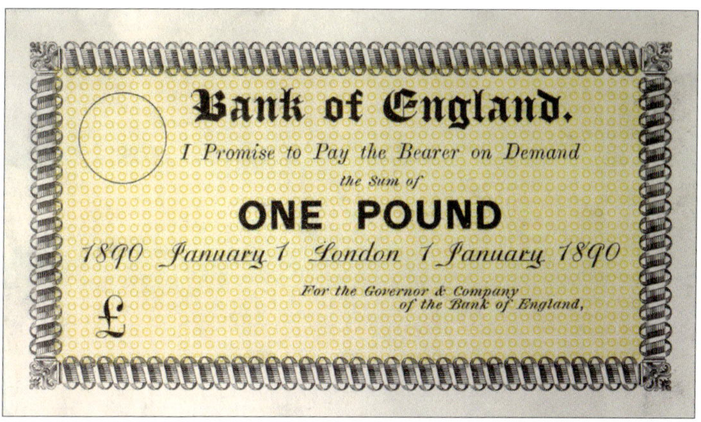

Goschen 1890 Trial © Bank of England

EARLY CHIEF CASHIERS

JOHN KENDRICK 1694 & THOMAS SPEED 1694 *to* 1699
1st & 2nd Chief Cashiers

The notes were at first written entirely by hand on ordinary paper purchased from stationers - a practice which soon ceased because of forgery. These notes could be part-paid. The holder could draw £5 from a note issued for £10 and have it duly recorded on the note, retaining the note as a receipt for the remaining £5 still on deposit with the Bank. The first meeting of the Bank's Court of Directors on 27th July 1694 was concerned with the 'method of giving receipts for running cash' and the first decision was that running cash notes should be issued.

RUNNING CASH NOTES

Running cash notes derive from the goldsmith notes which had been widely used by merchants from the reign of Charles I. The running cash note was a receipt for a deposit made out to bearer so that he could use it in a business transaction or present it to the Bank for gold or silver. The Bank's first running cash notes were issued for odd amounts but before long they were made out for regular amounts.

ACCOMPTABLE NOTES

Introduced four days after the running cash notes, these were certificates of deposit and were not intended to serve as banknotes. They gave the depositor the right to 'draw notes' on the Bank. Such withdrawals were then endorsed on the accomptable note. Later special forms were prepared by the Bank with a check pattern. The drawn notes were written by depositors on these forms which became early versions of the modern cheque.

SEALED BILLS

These were not banknotes in the strict sense; they were promissory notes, normally bearing interest issued against deposits or pledged assets. They were not a success and within twenty years went out of use altogether.

PRINTED & PART-PRINTED NOTES

In 1695 there was a short-lived issue of printed denominations of £5, £10, £20, £50 and £100. According to Mackenzie in 'The Bank of England Note', the order was placed on 5th June 1695 with the Bank's stationer, William Staresmore. No sooner had they been issued than a forgery appeared and they had to be withdrawn. The Bank then had the idea of using watermarked paper and in 1697 paper with a watermark of looped border and scroll on the left, the words Bank of England at the bottom was produced by the Berkshire papermaker, Rice Watkins. The first partially printed notes of the Bank were issued soon afterwards. They have a medallion of Britannia seated and holding a spear and olive branch, possibly the work of John Surt. For the most part these notes circulated within twenty miles of London.

THOMAS MADOCKES 1699 *to* 1739
3rd Chief Cashier

Notes continued to be issued for hand-written amounts, but in 1707 the design of the Britannia medallion was modified to show a foliate border surround and from 1725, fourteen denominations were printed by copper plate. In 1725 the Bank began using special paper produced by Henry Portal. Denominations were produced for: £20 - £30 - £40 - £50 - £60 - £70 - £80 - £90 - £100 - £200 - £300 - £400 - £500 - £1000. Dates of first issue vary.

A Madockes running cash note of 1705 for ninety-nine pounds, seven shillings and four pence exists in private hands, sold at Spink. (see page xii EPM ed 7)

JAMES COLLIER & DANIEL RACE 1739 *to* 1751
4th & 5th Chief Cashiers

Notes continued to be issued in the fourteen denominations as Madockes. By 1745 banknotes were all printed in round figures. However, the word pounds was not printed so that an odd amount could still be written by hand if required. The Bank has one such note for £28 10s on which the words ‘eight pounds ten shillings’ have been written after the printed ‘Twenty’.

DANIEL RACE & ELIAS SIMES 1751 *to* 1759
5th & 6th Chief Cashiers

From 1752 the hand-written name of the payee was usually that of the Chief Cashier. In 1759 two further denominations for £10 and £15 were issued and for the first time the word ‘pound/s’ was printed after the amount. Other denominations continued to have ‘pound/s’ hand-written until the end of the century.

DANIEL RACE 1759 *to* 1775
5th Chief Cashier

Banknotes continued to be issued for the sixteen denominations as above and in 1765 a note for £25 was added with the word ‘pounds’ printed on it.

CHARLES JEWSON 1775 *to* 1777
7th Chief Cashier

There were no significant developments during Charles Jewson’s short period in office.

Note: Since very few banknotes prior to the Newland period are known to have survived in private hands, a formal numbering system is not thought to be relevant.

WHITE BANKNOTE PREFIX HISTORY

The first Bank of England banknotes of 1694 were part printed with prefixes denoting the value of the banknotes: A £5 - B £10 - C £20 - D £30 - E £40 - F £50 - G £100. Later in 1695 a £15 banknote was introduced so letters for prefixes were A to H. This system soon stopped after forgeries were found. The banknotes were then numbered by hand, the clerk also entering the serials in a register. After a while it was found necessary to have more than one clerk. The second clerk prefixed his numbers with an A. When a third clerk was needed a prefix B was used, the highest prefix seen is C.

Printed numbering of the banknotes started in 1808. I do not believe these were numbered in sequence, but at random, that were subsequently recorded in ledgers to protect against forgery. But, it is probable that serials were not repeated. Once the numbering became rather large it was decided in 1838 to introduce a prefix. It is thought that prefix fonts (typeface) were not repeated, when a series is complete the font is changed or the design of the banknote. This chapter is based on original research by Michael Brill.

Prefix: Upright cameo letters - serif. Marshall £10 Hull 1856

When this series was complete in April 1844, a new series of prefixes was introduced the font now leaning to the right. The next series starts in 1849 with the prefix font bold upright sans serif (no serif). Then in 1853 upright cameo (hollow letters) font was introduced. In 1859 solid upright serif font prefixes introduced as had been used in 1838. This might have been a repeat, but, more likely it was utilising unused capacity from the first series such as A/H £10 London 12001 to 100000.

This was followed on 18th June 1864 by a repeat of the second series prefix font but letters are leaning to the right. In 1869 numbers were introduced to the prefix for the first time, letter over number. £5 London started at A/1 and finished in 1877 at F/86.

There are few recordings but it seems that:

1869 Prefix Letters

£5	London	A	B	C	D	E	F	(G not used)
£10	London	H	I					
£20	London	J	K					
£50	London	L						
£100	London	M	O					
£200	London	N						
£300	London	O						
£500	London	P						
£1000	London	R						
£5	Branch	S	T	M				
£10	Branch	U	M					

Numbers introduced: Letter, leaning to right, over number - serif. Forbes £5 1871

In 1877 number over letter sans serif starts with 1/A but this could be a different series as in 1878 we have £20, £50 and £100 London banknotes all C prefix only and 1885 £5 and £10 London both with T prefix. Maybe all values had same prefix? More research needs to be carried out for this early period.

1888 Prefix Letters

£5	London	A B C D E G (F not used)
£10	London	H I K
£20	London	J
£50	London	K
£100	London	L
£200	London	M
£500	London	N
£1000	London	O
£5	Branch	P R U V
£10	Branch	S T
£20	Branch	U
£50	Branch	V X
£100	Branch	W
£500	Branch	X
£1000	Branch	Y

Prefix: Letter over number - sans serif. May £5 Birmingham 1892

The Bank of England used F internally for Giants and Titans, banknotes of values higher than £1,000. The banknotes issued by the banks in Scotland and Northern Ireland are required to be backed pound for pound by Bank of England banknotes. Due to the large number of banknotes issued by these banks it would be cumbersome and wasteful to hold Bank of England banknotes in the standard denominations. High denomination banknotes, for up to £1,000,000 (Giants) and £100,000,000 (Titans), are used for this purpose. These are used only within the Bank and are never seen in circulation.

The Bank continues to use Giants and Titans to this day and their archive contains many signature and denomination varieties.

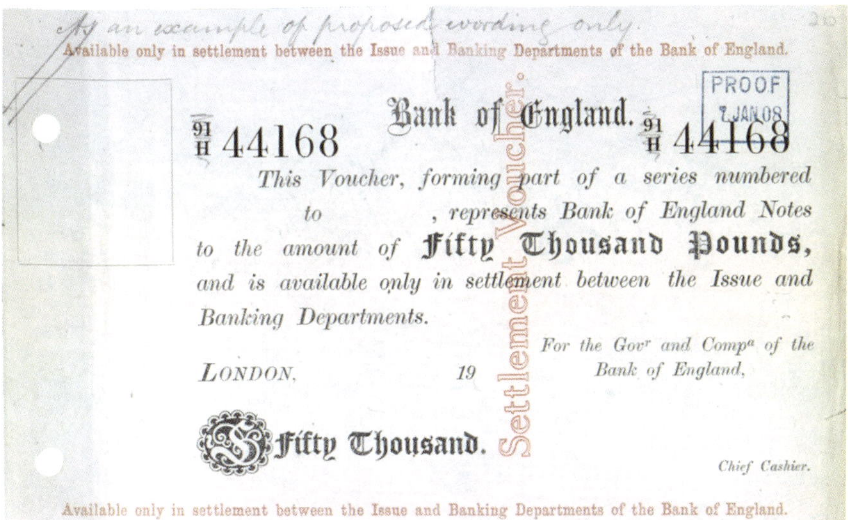

Giant 1908 £50,000 Trial for text, 91/H prefix crossed out © Bank of England

1894 Prefix Letters

£5	London	A B C D E G H J (F I not used)
£10	London	K L
£20	London	M
£50	London	N
£100	London	O
£200	London	M P
£500	London	N R
£1000	London	O S
£5	Branch	R T U
£10	Branch	V
£20	Branch	W
£50	Branch	X
£100	Branch	Y
£500	Branch	Z

Prefix: Letter over number - serif. Bowen £5 Hull 1900

PREFIX/SERIAL EVOLUTION (based in latter part on £5 London)

1694	Printed prefixes (A *to* G)
1695	Printed prefixes (A *to* H)
1696	Hand-written serials, clerk identification letters (A, B & C)
1808	Printed serials
1838	Letters introduced, upright - serif (A/A *to* A/Z)
1844	Prefix, leaning to right - serif
1849	Prefix, bold upright - sans serif
1853	Prefix, upright cameo letters - serif
1859	Prefix, solid upright - serif (as 1838 but, probably unused numbers)
1864	Prefix, leaning to right - serif (as 1844 but, probably unused number)
1869	Numbers introduced: letter, leaning to right, over number - serif
1877	Number over upright letter - sans serif (£5 starts 1/A)
1888	Upright letter over number - sans serif
1895	Letter over number - serif
1902	Number over letter - serif
1907	Letter over number - serif
1912	Number over letter - serif
1920	Letter over number - serif
1922	Third prefix/serial introduced, number over letter - sans serif
1934	Letter over three numbers - sans serif
1944	Letter over two numbers - serif
1955	Second letter introduced, letter number number letter - serif

Prefix: Number over letter - serif. Nairne £100 London 1913

£5 London

	1888	A/1	*to*	A/99		1889	sans serif	
	1889	B/1	*to*	B/99		1890	sans serif	
	1890	C/1	*to*	C/99		1891	sans serif	
	1891	D/1	*to*	D/99		1893	sans serif	
	1893	E/1	*to*	E/99		1893	sans serif	(F for internal use)
	1894	G/1	*to*	G/99	18 May	1895		
20 May	1895	A/1	*to*	A/99		1896	serif	
	1896	B/1	*to*	B/99		1897		
	1897	C/1	*to*	C/99		1898		
	1898	D/1	*to*	D/99		1899		
	1899	E/1	*to*	E/99		1900		
	1900	H/1	*to*	H/99	16 Mar	1901		
18 Mar	1901	J/1	*to*	J/99	18 Mar	1902		
19 Mar	1902	1/A	*to*	99/A		1902/3		
	1902/3	1/B	*to*	99/B		1903		
	1903	1/C	*to*	55/C	5 Mar	1904		

Third prefix printed on banknote from hereon. First 92/C 11 June 1904.

7 Mar 1904	56/C	*to*	99/C	7 Jul	1904	*continuing*

The third prefix/serial had been added to the bottom right corner to speed up accounting. The corner was cut off and filed in returns ledgers instead of being laboriously handwritten in the ledgers. Many banknotes were only used once, hence the rarity of early white banknotes. See under Nairne and subsequent Chief Cashiers for further listings of London £5. Last issued white London £5 banknote: O'Brien D99A 20 September 1956.

£10 London

	1888	H/1	*to*	H/99		1894	sans serif	
	1894	I/1	*to*	I/20	22 Mar	1894	sans serif	
23 Mar	1895	K/1	*to*	K/99		189?	serif	(not all used)
	189?	L/1	*to*	L/99		1900	serif	(not all used)
	1900	1/K	*to*	40/K	17 Jun	1903		

Third prefix printed on banknote from hereon.

16 Jul	1903	41/K	*to*	99/K	16 Mar	1907	
16 Apr	1907	1/L	*to*	7/L	17 Jul	1907	
16 Aug	1907	K/1	*to*	K/99	15 Apr	1912	
14 May	1912	L/1	*to*	L/13	14 Dec	1912	
17 Jan	1913	1/K	*to*	99/K	15 Feb	1921	
16 Feb	1921	001/L	*to*	199/L	18 Jan	1931	sans serif
19 Feb	1931	K/100	*to*	K/199	19 Jan	1938	sans serif
20 Jan	1938	L/100	*to*	L/141	18 Mar	1942	sans serif

£20 London

	1888	J/1	*to*	J/48	25 Mar	1895	sans serif	
24 Apr	1895	M/1	*to*	M/?		1900	serif	(not all used)
	1900	1/M	*to*	12/M	14 Aug	1902		

Third prefix printed on banknote from hereon.

	190?	13/M	*to*	?/M		1907		(not all used)
	1907	M/?	*to*	M/25		1912		
12 Feb	1913	1/M	*to*	59/M	19 Jan	1942		

Interestingly £20 and higher denominations changed to sans serif in 1921, but kept two number prefixes, £5 and £10 denominations changed to sans serif introducing three number prefixes.

£50 London

	1888	K/1	*to*	K/25	26 Feb	1895	sans serif	
26 Mar	1895	N/1	*to*	N/?		1???	serif	(not all used)
	1???	1/N	*to*	8/N	12 Jan	1903		
	1903	9/N	*to*	??/N		190?		(not all used)
	1908	N/1	*to*	N/19		1912		

Third prefix printed on banknote from hereon. First 5/N 17 April 1914.

13 Jan	1913	1/N	*to*	68/N	20 Jan	1941	sans serif starts 1921

£100 London

	1888	L/1	*to*	L/22	27 Feb	1895	sans serif
27 Mar	1895	O/1	*to*	O/?		1900	
	1900	1/O	*to*	7/O	17 Sep	1902	
	1903	8/O	*to*	?/O		1908	

Third prefix printed on banknote from hereon. First O/5 14 January 1909.

	1908	O/1	*to*	O/16		1912	
14 Jan	1913	1/O	*to*	63/O	21 Jan	1942	sans serif starts 1921

£200 London

	1888	M/1	*to*	M/8	28 Jan	1895	sans serif	
	1896	P/1	*to*	P/?		1900		
	1900	1/P	*to*	2/P	1 Mar	1902		(possibly continuing)

Third prefix printed on banknote from hereon. First 5/P 20 June 1918.

15 Feb	1913	1/P	*to*	5/P	20 Jun	1918	(out of sequence prefix)

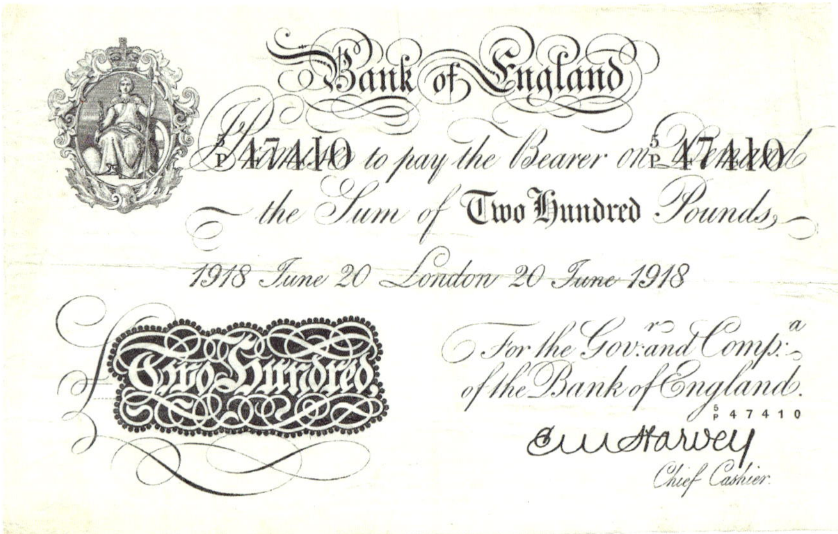

Prefix: Bold upright - serif. Harvey £200 London 1918, first date with third prefix

£500 London

	1888	N/1	*to*	N/?		1894	sans serif	(not full series)
	1896	R/1	*to*	R/?		1902	serif	(not full series)
	1903	1/R	only					

Third prefix printed on banknote from hereon. Earliest noted 4/R 15 February 1923.

	190?	2/R	*to*	?/R		190?		(not full series)
	190?	R/1	*to*	R/?		191?		(not full series)
19 Feb	1914	1/R	*to*	13/R	9 Jan	1941	sans serif from 1921	

£1000 London

	1888	O/1	*to*	O/?		1894	sans serif	(not full series)
	1896	S/1	*to*	S/?		1???	serif	(not full series)
	1???	1/S	*to*	2/S	20 Jan	1904		

Third prefix printed on banknote from hereon. Earliest noted 3/S 20 May 1918.

	190?	3/S	*to*	?/S		19??		(not full series)
	19??	S/1	*to*	S/?		1914		(not full series)
14 Feb	1915	1/S	*to*	14/S	18 Jan	1938	sans serif from 1921	

£5 Branch

	1888	P/1	*to*	P/99	5 May	1892	sans serif	
	1892	R/1	*to*	R/55	2 Jan	1895	sans serif	
3 Jan	1895	T/1	*to*	T/99		1898		
	1898	U/1	*to*	U/99		1901		
	1901	1/T	*to*	57/T		1904		

Third prefix printed on banknote from hereon. First 99/T 24 October 1904 Liverpool.

	1904	58/T	*to*	99/T	24 Oct	1904	
	1904	1/U	*to*	99/U		1907	
	1907	T/1	*to*	T/99		1910	
	1910	U/1	*to*	U/95	24 Oct	1912	
7 Jan	1913	1/T	*to*	99/T	8 Jan	1917	
9 Jan	1917	01/U	*to*	99/U	6 Mar	1919	
7 Mar	1919	T/1	*to*	T/99	22 Nov	1920	
27 Sep	1920	U/1	*to*	U/97	12 Jan	1921	(out of sequence date)
8 Aug	1921	101/U	*to*	499/U	26 May	1932	
24 May	1932	T/100	*to*	T/312	22 Feb	1938	

Last prefix T/312 22 February 1938 Birmingham. Last date T/310 25 July 1938 Liverpool. Banknotes were not always printed in date or prefix order.

£10 Branch

	1888	S/1	*to*	S/?		18??	sans serif	(not all used)
	18??	T/1	*to*	T/?		1894	sans serif	(not all used)
5 Jan	1895	V/1	*to*	V/99		1901	serif	(not all used)
	1902	1/V	*to*	15/V		1903		

Third prefix printed on banknote from hereon.

	190?	16/V	*to*	??/V		1908		(not all used)
	1908	V/1	*to*	V/46		1913		
5 Feb	1913	1/V	*to*	179/V	28 Nov	1938	sans serif starts 101/V	

Last prefix/date 179/V 28 November 1938 Plymouth.

£20 Branch

	1888	U/1	*to*	U/?		1894?	
	1894?	W/1	*to*	W/?		1901	
	1902	1/W	*to*	6/W		1903	

Third prefix printed on banknote from hereon.

	190?	7/W	*to*	?/W		1907	
	1908	W/1	*to*	W/16	1 Jul	1913	
1 Jan	1913	1/W	*to*	65/W	12 Apr	1937	sans serif starts 1921

Last prefix 65/W 12 April 1937 Newcastle. Last Date 64/W 13 December 1937 Manchester.

£50 Branch

	1888	V/1	*to*	V/?		1894	sans serif
	1894	X/1	*to*	X/?		1901	serif
	1902	1/X	*to*	10/X		1903	

Third prefix printed on banknote from hereon.

	190?	11/X	*to*	??/X		1908	
	1908	X/1	*to*	X/28		1912	
2 Sep	1913	1/X	*to*	94/X	31 Jan	1938	sans serif starts 1921

Last prefix 94/X 31 January 1938 Manchester. Last Date 92/X 29 March 1938 Liverpool.

Prefix: Number over letter - serif. Nairne £50 Manchester 1913

£100 Branch

	1888	W/1	*to*	W/24	May	1894	sans serif	(possibly continuing)
	1894	Y/1	*to*	Y/23		1900	serif	(possibly continuing)
	1901	1/Y	*to*	10/Y		1903		

Third prefix printed on banknote from hereon.

	1904	11/Y	*to*	??/Y		1908	
	1908	Y/1	*to*	Y/32		1913	
1 Nov	1913	1/Y	*to*	99/Y	13 May	1937	sans serif starts 1921
12 Mar	1937	Y/1	*to*	Y/09	29 Jun	1938	

Last prefix/date Y/09 29 June 1938 Leeds.

£200 No branch banknotes issued.

£500 Branch

	1888	X/1	*to*	X/?		1894?	sans serif
	1894/6	Z/1	*to*	Z/?		1901	serif
	1902	1/Z	*to*	5/Z		1903	

Third prefix printed on banknote from hereon.

	1904	6/Z	*to*	?/Z		190?	
	190?	Z/1	*to*	Z/?		1912	
4 Jul	1913	1/Z	*to*	47/Z	13 Nov	1937	sans serif starts 1921

Last prefix/date 47/Z 13 November 1937 Liverpool.

Prefix: Third prefix/serial introduced, number over letter - sans serif. £1000

£1000 Branch

1889 Y/1 Hull. The only issued branch £1000.

© P. West

ABRAHAM NEWLAND
1778-1807

Abraham Newland, the son of a miller and baker of Southwark, was born on 23rd April 1730, and entered service on 25th February 1748. He succeeded Charles Jewson as the 8th Chief Cashier on 8th January 1778 and held office until 17th September 1807. His name became a household word during the restriction period from 1797, £1 notes were often referred to as Newlands. History relates that his commitment to business was such that he never slept away from the Bank. A confirmed bachelor, he amassed a fortune of £200,000, declined a pension and was instead given a piece of silver plate to the value of 1,000 guineas. He died on 21st November 1807. There is a tablet in his memory in Southwark Cathedral where he is buried.

There are several varieties of Newland banknotes. From 1752 until 1781 the handwritten name of the payee was usually, but not invariably, that of the Chief Cashier. In fact, the oldest Newland banknote so far recorded in private hands, a £50 dated 13 April 1780, is not payable to Newland. From 1782 the Chief Cashier's name was used exclusively until 1855 when banknotes were made payable simply to bearer. In 1793 the economic difficulties caused by the Napoleonic War with France made small denominations necessary, starting with a £5 banknote. This was followed in 1797 by the £1 and £2 banknotes, which were issued on 2nd March.

Printed by copper plate in black on paper produced by Henry Portal. Denominations of: £1 - £2 - £5 - £10 - £15 - £20 - £25 - £30 - £40 - £50 - £60 - £70 - £80 - £90 - £100 - £200 - £300 - £400 - £500 - £1000 were produced. The £60 - £70 - £80 - £90 - £400 banknotes were no longer issued after 1803.

WHITE BANKNOTES

		Dates		VG	F	VF
B200a	**£1**	1797	sum block two ovals	5000	8500	-
B200b	**£1**	1798/1801	sum block three circles, rectangular frame	4500	8000	-
B200c	**£1**	1801-03	sum block circle + square	3600	5500	8000
B200d	**£1**	1803-07	sum block circle + square, value in watermark, printed Newland signature	2200	4200	7500
B200e	**£2**	1797	sum block irregular	-	8500	-
B200f	**£2**	1798/1801	sum block level, indented frame	-	8500	16000
B200g	**£2**	1801-03	sum block tilted, printed signature	-	7500	12000
B200h	**£2**	1803-05	sum block tilted, value in watermark	-	7000	9500
B200i	**£2**	1805-07	sum block tilted, Bank of England 2nd line	-	7000	9500
B200j	**£5**	1793	from 15th April	-	16000	-
B200k	**£5**	1804	hand-written signature, date/serial, countersigned	-	16000	-
B200l	**£10**	1790/1801		G 4500	22000	-
B200m	**£10**	1806/07	Proof - Bank of England heading		-	14000
B200n	**£15**	1798			-	30000
B200o	**£20**	1790			-	30000
B200p	**£50**	1780	hand-written signature, date/serial, countersigned		-	Rare
B200q	**£70**	1783	unissued (2)	-	35000	-
B200r	**£100**	1790			-	Rare

All have hand-written: date, serial, signature and countersignature, unless stated.

B200e £2 1797 unissued, sum block irregular

Very few denominations above £2 are in private hands, other varieties may exist.

B200f £2 1798 sum block level, indented frame

B200h £2 1803 sum block tilted

Proof banknotes in the following denominations existed from a Sample Book, now split up, prepared at the time: £1 1807 and £10 1788. Many other essay and trial banknotes exist.

B200k £5 1804 handwritten signature, date/serial and countersigned

B200p £50 1780 hand-written signature, date/serial and countersigned

© Bank of England

HENRY HASE
1807-1829

Henry Hase was known as the reluctant Chief Cashier. He entered service on 28th March 1793 and was appointed the 9th Chief Cashier on 17th September 1807 following the disgrace of the second cashier, Robert Aslett, who was found guilty of embezzling £500,000. Aslett had taken Exchequer Bills amounting to £200,000 in 1803 and had lodged these as security for advances with a lottery office keeper in Cornhill. He escaped the death penalty and was imprisoned in Newgate until 1820 when he was pardoned on condition he left the country. Hase died on 26th March 1829, aged 65.

WHITE BANKNOTES

Printed by copper plate on paper produced by Henry Portal. From 1807 the name of the Chief Cashier is printed as payee, dates and serials handwritten. From 1809 the dates and serials were printed, so the only part of the banknote not printed was the signature(s). This remained the case until 1853. No banknotes issued in 1807. Hase banknotes were also issued in the following eleven denominations: £15 - £20 - £25 - £30 - £40 - £50 - £100 - £200 - £300 - £500 - £1000. The £15 & £25 banknotes were withdrawn from 1822. Very few denominations above £2 are in private hands. Proof banknotes in the following denominations existed from a Sample Book prepared at the time: £1 1807 & 1810, undated £10, £100 & £1000. From £1600 VF

WHITE BANKNOTES

		Dates		VG	F	VF
B201a	**£1**	1808-09	hand-written date/serial, countersigned	2600	3800	5400
B201b	**£1**	1809-21	printed date/serial	900	1700	2800
B201c	**£1**	1825-26	Emergency issue, 2nd date 1821	900	1700	2800
B201d	**£2**	1808-09	sum block tilted, hd-wn date/serial, countersigned	2500	4500	7500
B201e	**£2**	1809-21	sum block level, printed date/serial	2000	4300	7200
B201f	**£5**	1808-09	hand-written date/serial, countersigned	-	8000	-
B201g	**£5**	1809-21	printed date/serial	3000	8000	18000
B201h	**£10**				-	Rare

The Emergency issue B201c can be identified by the date at the top reading 1821, although the actual date of issue is four or five years later, 17th December 1825 to 17th February 1826.

The London Gazette entry at the time makes it clear that the removing of entering clerk's signatures occurs at the same time as the introduction of printed date/serial.

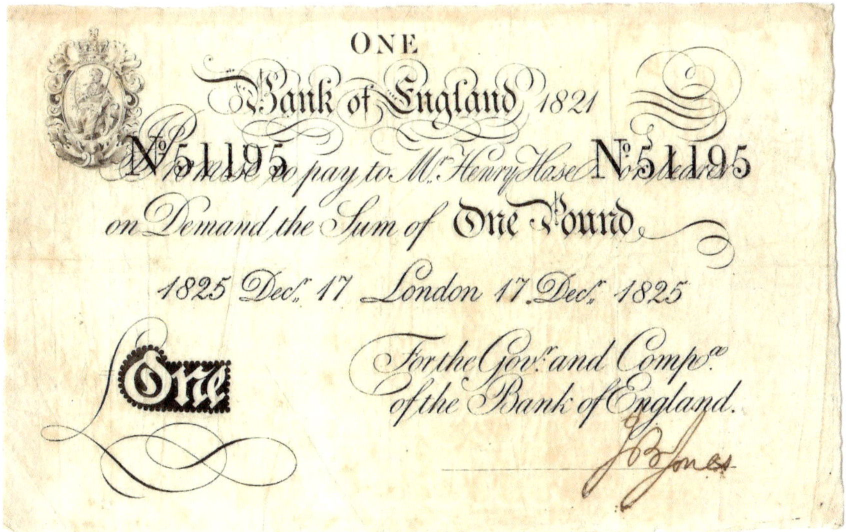

B201a £1 1809

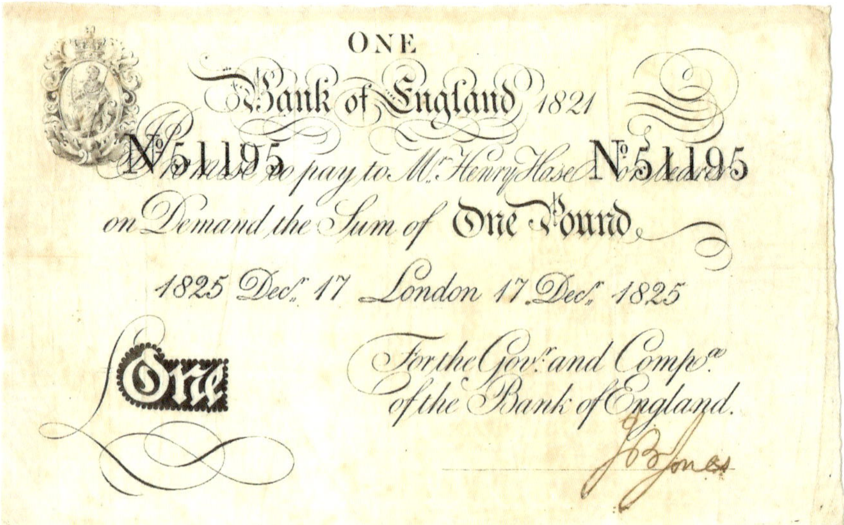

B201c £1 1825 Emergency Issue, also dated 1821

B201e £2 1817 sum block level, printed date/serial

B201g £5 1814 printed date/serial

BRANCH BANKNOTES

Following the Bank Act of 1826 when the joint stock banks were permitted to operate outside a sixty-five mile radius of London and the Bank of England was able to open branches in other towns and cities. Nine of them were opened during Mr Hase's period in office but there are no branch banknotes known to be in private hands. Branch opening dates shown.

BIRMINGHAM 1st Jan 1827
BRISTOL 12th Jul 1827
EXETER 17th Dec 1827
GLOUCESTER 19th Jul 1826
LEEDS 23rd Aug 1827
LIVERPOOL 2nd Jul 1827
MANCHESTER 21st Sep 1826
NEWCASTLE 21st Apr 1828
SWANSEA 23rd Oct 1826

© Bank of England

THOMAS RIPPON
1829-1835

Thomas Rippon was born at Tiverton, Devon, in 1760, the son of a Baptist Minister. He entered service with the Bank on 23rd May 1782. Following the dismissal of Robert Aslett in 1803, Rippon was promoted from third clerk in the drawing office to second cashier. When Henry Hase became Chief Cashier, Rippon was appointed as his chief assistant in 1807. He succeeded to the 10th Chief Cashier at the age of seventy in 1829 and remained in office until his death on 13th August 1835. He declared himself "nowhere so happy as in his business" and supposedly took only one holiday during his entire career with the Bank. Two of his sons were also elected into service with the Bank.

WHITE BANKNOTES

Plate-printed on paper manufactured by Henry Portal.

LONDON BANKNOTES		VG	F	VF
B202a	**£5**	11000	15000	20000
B202b	**£10**	16000	22000	32000

Rippon banknotes were also issued in the following nine denominations: £20 - £30 - £40 - £50 - £100 - £200 - £300 - £500 - £1000. The £40 banknote was withdrawn in 1851 and the £30 in 1852. Very few denominations above £5 are in private hands.

BRANCH BANKNOTES

Apart from four Manchester £50 of May and June 1832 and a Manchester £100 July 1832. There are no other branch banknotes known to be in private hands from the thirteen branches open during Mr Rippon's period of office. Branch opening/closing dates shown.

£50 From £35,000 AVF

BIRMINGHAM
BRISTOL
EXETER closed 30th Apr 1834
GLOUCESTER
HULL 2nd Jan 1829
LEEDS
LIVERPOOL
MANCHESTER
NEWCASTLE
NORWICH 19th Nov 1829
PLYMOUTH 1st May 1834
PORTSMOUTH 16th May 1834
SWANSEA

B202b £10 London 1835

© Bank of England

MATTHEW MARSHALL
1835-1864

Matthew Marshall was born in 1791 and was elected to the Bank on 19th July 1810 at the age of nineteen. He was appointed First Assistant to the Chief Cashier on 5th November 1829 and the 11th Chief Cashier on 17th September 1835. A critical period of his tenure was during the major commercial crisis of 1857 during which two banks in Liverpool failed. By November of that year the Bank of England was virtually the only bank prepared to discount bills of exchange. Marshall retired on 16th June 1864 and died on 30th June 1873.

WHITE BANKNOTES

There are three different Series of Marshall banknotes. The first series from 1835 to 1853 is the same as Thomas Rippon with various handwritten signatures. From 1853 to 1855 banknotes were printed bearing signatures of bank officials: **J. Vautin**, **H. Bock**, **J. Ferraby**, **J. Williams** and **J. Luson**. The second series from 1855 several important changes were made: The larger re-designed vignette of Britannia was by Daniel Maclise R.A.; the banknotes were made payable 'to the Bearer on demand' and not to the Chief Cashier by name, Marshall's name dropped from the text; a shaded watermark (the invention of the Bank's watermark mould-maker, William Brewer) was introduced, incorporating a reproduction of the Chief Cashier's signature; the quality of printing was improved by switching intaglio to letterpress, produced for the first time from electrotypes. The Times commented that "its superiority is very striking both as regards clearness of execution of the design and the watermark of the paper". Series three 1860 saw the introduction of printed signatures of bank officials, **W.P. Gattie**, **T. Kent** and **C.T. Whitmel**. Plate-printed on paper manufactured by Henry Portal.

LONDON BANKNOTES

		Dates of issue		VG	F	VF
B203a	**£5**	1835-55	hand-written signature, small vignette	7500	11000	15000
B203b	**£5**	1855-59	hand-written signature, large vignette	8000	14000	-
B203c	**£5**	1860-64	printed signature, large vignette	6500	8500	12000
B203d	**£10**	1835	hand-written signature, small vignette		-	20000
B203e	**£10**	1858	printed signature, large vignette		-	20000
B203f	**£20**	1850	hand-written signature, small vignette	-	23000	-
B203g	**£50**	1845	hand-written signature, small vignette		-	26000
B203h	**£50**	1858	hand-written signature, large vignette	-	26000	-
B203i	**£100**	1850	hand-written signature, small vignette		-	28000
B203j	**£200**	1858			-	Rare

Marshall banknotes were also issued in the following five denominations: £30 - £40 - £300 - £500 - £1000. The £40 banknote was withdrawn in 1851 and the £30 in 1852. Very few denominations above £5 are known to be in private hands.

All eleven denominations (originally sent to the Swedish government) exist, with manuscript text 'Specimen Delivered to…..Matthew Marshall Chief Cashier'. They are dated 1 to 13 May 1851 with various prefix/serials. £5: From £16,000 EF

A £1000 banknote on pink unwatermarked paper dated 13 May 1858, prefix U/W, was presented to Marshall on his retirement as a souvenir. The banknote which bears the signature of C.T. Whitmel was struck from a genuine plate and was overprinted twice 'NOT GENIUINE' to avoid it being redeemed. £3000 GF

B203g Small vignette £50 London 1845, cut and rejoined

BRANCH BANKNOTES

A surprising number of Marshall branch have appeared on the market. £5 branch banknotes with an asterisk/date (∗) in the table are known to exist in private hands, issue dates shown. *All are cut and rejoined* From £12,000 F £20,000 VF

BIRMINGHAM ∗ 1856	LIVERPOOL
BRISTOL ∗ 1850	MANCHESTER ∗ 1854
HULL	NEWCASTLE ∗ 1849
LEEDS ∗ 1862	PLYMOUTH ∗ 1848 & 1860
LEICESTER opened 1st Jan 1844	PORTSMOUTH ∗ 1849

Three higher denominations branch banknotes have been recorded: Hull £10 1856 - Liverpool £50 1862 - Liverpool £100 1855.

Three branches closed: GLOUCESTER 28th Feb 1849
NORWICH 31st Mar 1852
SWANSEA 28th Feb 1859

B203a £5 Manchester small vignette, cut and rejoined

B203b £5 Birmingham large vignette, cut and rejoined

B203c £5 Leeds large vignette, cut and rejoined

The editor would be grateful to hear from anyone who has a likeness of Mr Miller or knows if one exists.

WILLIAM MILLER
1864-1866

William Miller was born in 1810 and like his predecessor joined the Bank at the age of nineteen, in 1829. Apart from six years spent in Bristol from 1831-38, Miller spent virtually his entire career in cash offices. He died in service on 29th November 1866 two years after becoming the 12th Chief Cashier, on 23rd June 1864. Whereupon his widow received £1000 for his 'special and important services' to the Bank.

WHITE BANKNOTES

When Marshall's signature was removed from the watermark, for unknown reasons Miller's signature was not substituted. Instead it was replaced by the paper-making vat mark and only the date determines the Chief Cashier together with the printed signatures of bank officials **W.P. Gattie**, **T. Kent** or **C.T. Whitmel**. Plate-printed on paper manufactured by Henry Portal.

LONDON BANKNOTES

			VG	F	VF
B204a	**£5**	printed signature bank staff	9000	12500	17000
B204b	**£10**	printed signature bank staff	16000	20000	26000

Miller banknotes were also issued in the following seven denominations: £20 - £50 - £100 - £200 - £300 - £500 - £1000. No examples are known to be in private hands.

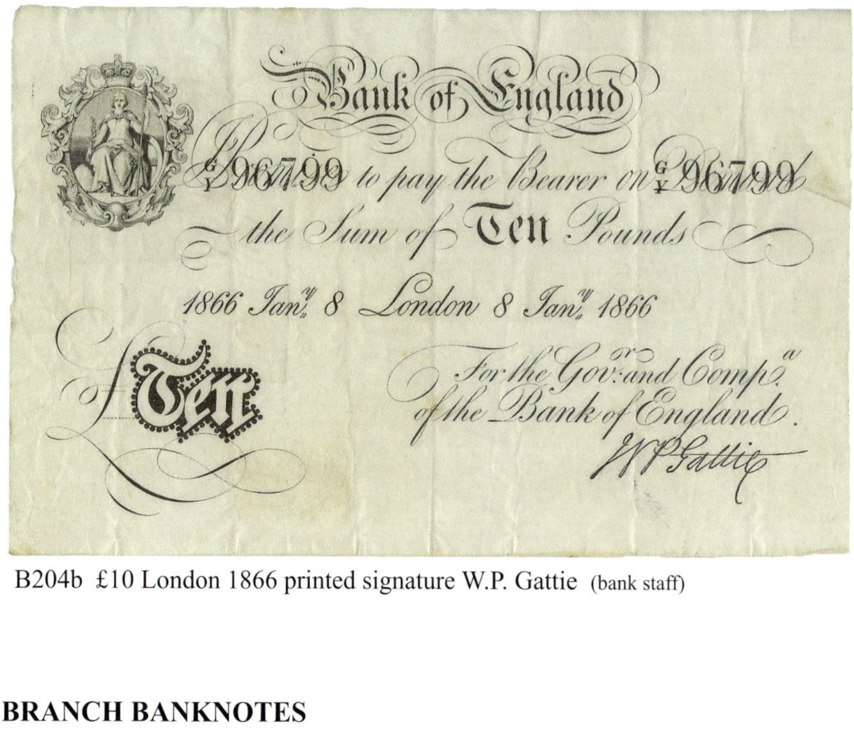

B204b £10 London 1866 printed signature W.P. Gattie (bank staff)

BRANCH BANKNOTES

Miller branch banknotes were issued from the following ten branch offices, no examples in private hands have come to light.

BIRMINGHAM	LIVERPOOL
BRISTOL	MANCHESTER
HULL	NEWCASTLE
LEEDS	PLYMOUTH
LEICESTER	PORTSMOUTH

The editor would be grateful to hear from anyone who has a likeness of Mr Forbes or knows if one exists.

GEORGE FORBES
1866-1873

George Forbes was born in 1825 and moved to London from Aberdeen to join the Bank in 1844 at the age of nineteen, as did his two predecesors. A copybook of his memoranda and letters survives in the Bank's archives, evidence of a wide ranging knowledge of its operations, he was the author of 'The Bullion Business of the Bank of England' privately published in 1869. Forbes the 13th Chief Cashier from 6th December 1866, suffered from ill health and resigned his office on 30th June 1873 at the age of forty-eight. Less than a year later he died of a spleen disorder.

WHITE BANKNOTES

There are two types of Forbes banknotes. The first type can only be identified (as with William Miller banknotes) by the date and the lack of reference to the Chief Cashier. The printed signatures are those of other bank staff: **Henry Dixon** (abbreviated to Hy Dixon), **T. Puzey** or **W.O. Wheeler**. The second type from 1st November 1870 with the printed signature of Geo Forbes has his title Chief Cashier below, earlier dates from October 1868 are known with his name to the left of his office. Illustrated in 'Promises to Pay' page103. Plate-printed on paper manufactured by Henry Portal. Banknotes printed two to a sheet, side by side and cut to give one straight edge and three deckled edges.

B205b £5 signed Geo Forbes

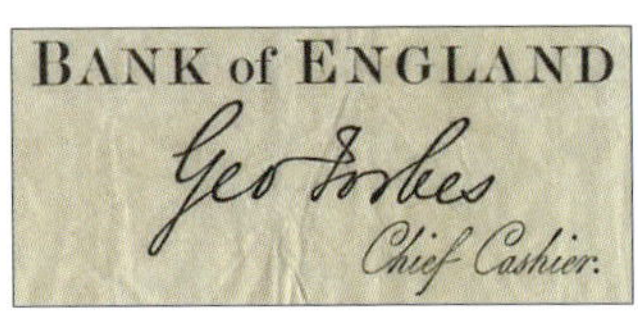

LONDON BANKNOTES

			VG	F	VF
B205a	**£5**	printed signature bank staff	9500	13500	19000
B205b	**£5**	signed Geo Forbes	9500	13500	19000
B205c	**£10**	printed signature bank staff	14000	18500	24000
B205d	**£10**	signed Geo Forbes	-	Rare	-

Forbes banknotes were also issued in the following seven denominations: £20 - £50 - £100 - £200 - £300 - £500 - £1000. No examples are known to be in private hands.

B205a £5 London 1869 printed signature Hy Dixon (bank staff)

BRANCH BANKNOTES

Ten offices were open during Mr Forbe's period of office, but only one branch banknote, a £5 from PORTSMOUTH 3 October 1868, is known to be in private hands.

BIRMINGHAM	LIVERPOOL
BRISTOL	MANCHESTER
HULL	NEWCASTLE
LEEDS	PLYMOUTH
LEICESTER closed 29th Feb 1872	PORTSMOUTH * 1868

© A. Georgiou

FRANK MAY
1873-1893

Frank May was born in Hull on 21st August 1832 and entered service with the Bank on 2nd September 1852, following in the steps of his father, Henry May. He rose to become the 14th Chief Cashier on 1st July 1873. He resigned from office on 9th November 1893, having "totally misconceived the nature of his trust" by favouring certain customers without the permission of the Governor. Some of them were introduced to his son's firm of stockbrokers, Colman and May. May had apparently allowed unauthorised overdrafts and had waived interest payments on other accounts. He ended his days in obscurity and died at Batcombe in Somerset on 9th February 1897. He left £2,620 15s 1d. The Reeves committee of enquiry which investigated the affair concluded that the Chief Cashier should become the highest paid official of the Bank thereafter.

WHITE BANKNOTES

Plate-printed on paper manufactured by Henry Portal. Banknotes printed two to a sheet and cut to give one straight edge and three deckled edges. May banknotes were also issued in the following five denominations: £50 - £200 - £300 - £500 - £1000. Very few examples above £5 are known to be in private hands.

All nine denominations (originally in the Portals archive) exist with SPECIMEN and CANCELLED overprints in red and punch hole cancellations. They are dated 24 Feb 1880, prefix/serial 14/H 00000. £5: £16,000 AEF

LONDON BANKNOTES		VG	F	VF
B206a	**£5**	4000	7000	10000
B206b	**£10**	9000	15000	25000
B206c	**£20**	12000	-	
B206d	**£100**	Rare	-	

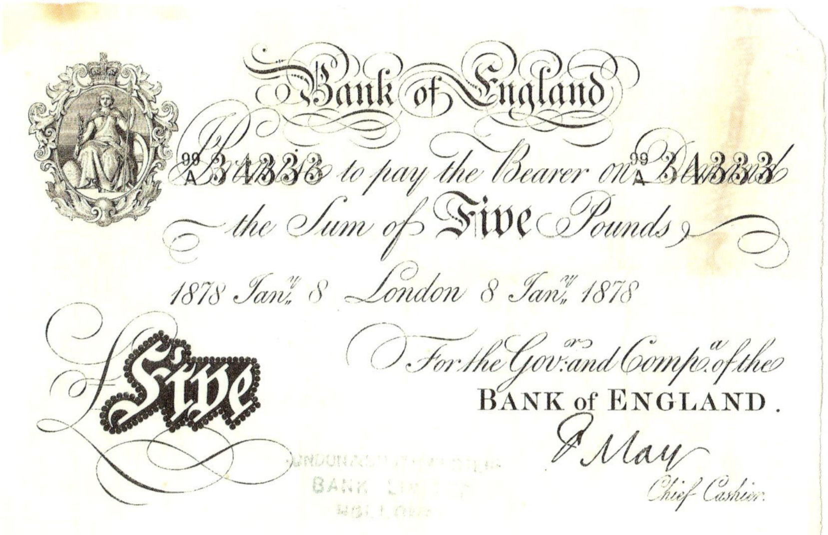

B206a £5 London 1878 prefix 99/A, paper maker's notch (top right corner)

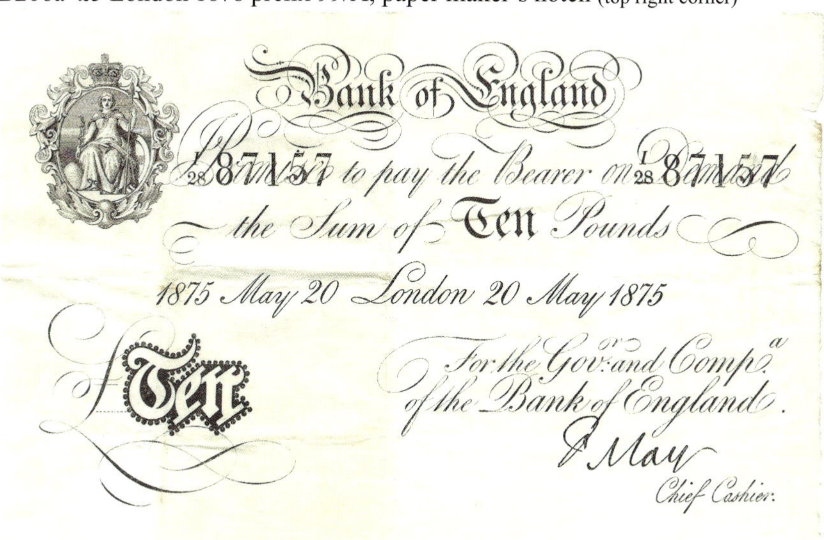

B206b £10 London 1875, paper maker's notch

BRANCH BANKNOTES

Several branch banknotes have appeared on the market from eight of the nine branches open during Mr May's period in office. £5 branch banknotes with an asterisk/date (∗) in the table are known to exist in private hands. Known banknotes shown, number in brackets after date quantity recorded.

£5: From £14,000 F £20,000 VF

BIRMINGHAM ∗ 1892	MANCHESTER ∗ 1891 (2)
BRISTOL ∗ 1891 & 1892 (3)	NEWCASTLE ∗ 1889 (2)
HULL	PLYMOUTH ∗ 18??
LEEDS ∗ 1875 & 1885	PORTSMOUTH ∗ 1882
LIVERPOOL ∗ 1888	

Branch banknotes are also recorded for: Leeds £10 1883 - Liverpool £10 1882 - Manchester £10 18?? - Birmingham £50 18??

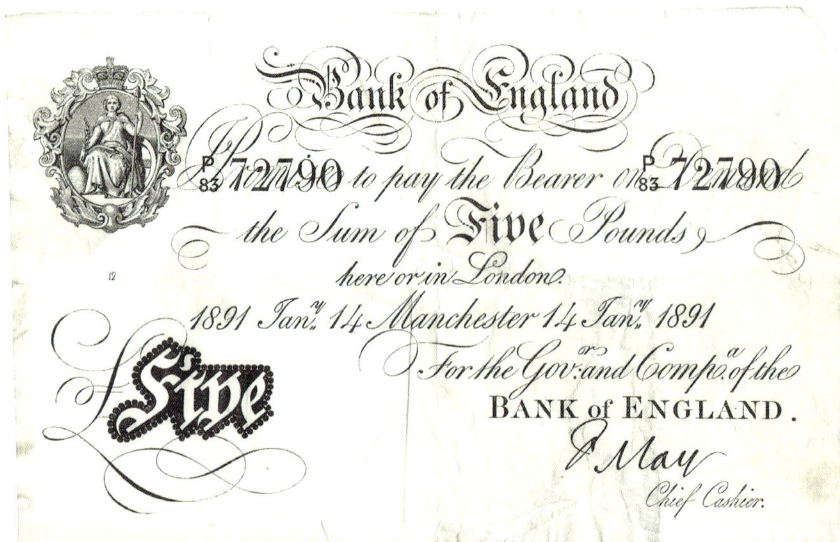

B206a £5 Manchester 1891, paper maker's notch (top right corner)

B206a £5 Newcastle on Tyne 1889

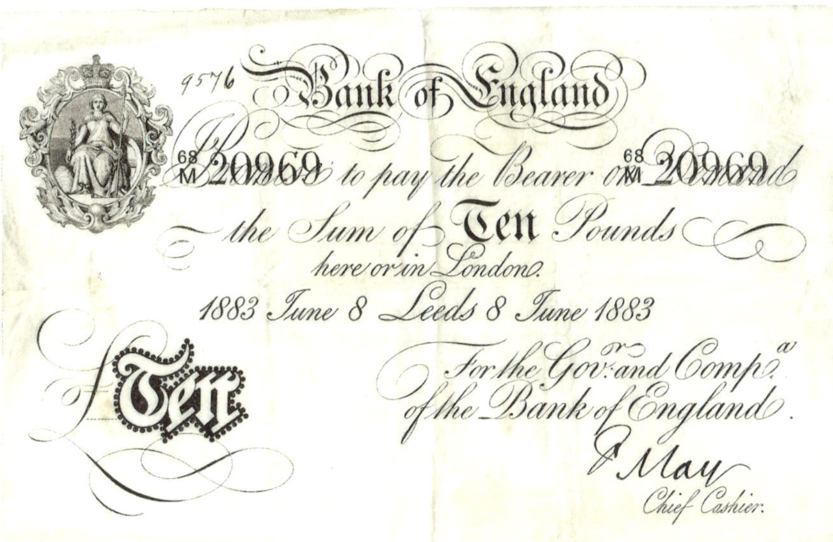

B206b £10 Leeds 1883

The editor would be grateful to hear from anyone who has a likeness of Mr Bowen or knows if one exists.

HORACE GEORGE BOWEN
1893-1902

Horace George Bowen was born in 1840. He served as Chief Accountant from 1888 and succeeded Frank May as the 15th Chief Cashier on 9th November 1893. The immediate consequence of May's disgrace was the setting up of a committee to report on 'Officers emoluments and safeguards for due control of advances and overdrafts and accounts generally, and the manner in which the services of the committee in daily waiting may be best employed.' In 1901 Bowen fell ill, had a leg amputated, resigned in January 1902 and died aged sixty-one, four months later on 6th May.

WHITE BANKNOTES

Plate printed on paper manufactured by Henry Portal. Banknotes printed two to a sheet and cut to give one straight edge and three deckled edges.

Bowen branch banknotes were also issued in the following six denominations: £20 - £50 - £100 - £200 - £500 - £1000. Very few denominations above £5 are in private hands.

LONDON BANKNOTES

		VG	F	VF
B207a	**£5**	5000	9000	12000
B207b	**£10**	11000	17000	27000

B207a £5 London 1901, paper maker's notch (top right corner)

B207b £10 London 1895, paper maker's notch

BRANCH BANKNOTES

Branch banknotes have appeared on the market from five of the nine branches open during Mr Bowen's period in office. £5 branch banknotes with an asterisk/date (∗) in the table are known to exist in private hands. Known banknotes shown, number in brackets after date quantity recorded. £5: From £14,000 F £22,000 VF

BIRMINGHAM	MANCHESTER
BRISTOL ∗ 1894	NEWCASTLE
HULL ∗ 1900 (3)	PLYMOUTH
LEEDS ∗ 1900	PORTSMOUTH
LIVERPOOL ∗ 1900	

Birmingham £100, two dated 19 May 1894 have been recorded.

B207a £5 Leeds 1900

B207a £5 Liverpool 1900

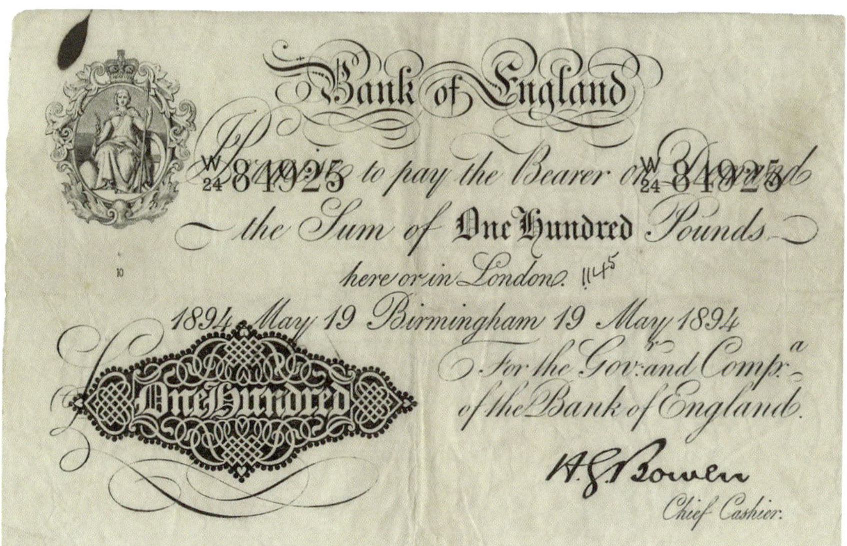

£100 Birmingham 1894

JOHN
GORDON NAIRNE
1902-1918

John Gordon Nairne was born on 4th January 1861 and entered Bank service in 1880. He was appointed the 16th Chief Cashier in 1902 and became Comptroller in 1918. Nairne was knighted in 1914 and created a Baronet in 1917. He was a Director of the Bank from 1925 to 1931 and died on 9th February 1945.

			EF	UNC
B208a	**£1**	Gold Banknote Proof *Prefix/Serial:* † 000000 Black on white Unissued Undated	-	8400

During the summer of 1914 it became increasingly clear that some form of paper money of a lower denomination than £5 would have to be substituted for the gold sovereign. The question was who would issue it? The Bank had no doubts about its claim and made preparations accordingly. The £1 Gold banknote proof (Gold Note), 162 x 97mm, in its unissued proof form is a sought after rarity in the English series, approximately fifteen examples are in private hands. Paste up essays (CB/77 74014) and trials also exist.

For details of white banknote prefixes, see page 100.

WHITE BANKNOTES

Plate-printed on paper manufactured by Henry Portal. Banknotes printed two to a sheet (2 x 1 *horizontal pair*) and cut to give one straight edge and three deckled edges. A third prefix, for filing purposes, was introduced above the signature between 1904 and 1914 depending on denomination.

LONDON BANKNOTES

		F	VF	EF
B208b	**£5**	500	900	1600
B208c	**£10**	800	1400	1900
B208d	**£20**	1900	2800	4200
B208e	**£50**	1900	2800	4200
B208f	**£100**	2800	4200	7000
B208g	**£200**		-	Rare
B208h	**£500**		-	Rare
B208i	**£1000**		-	Rare

Prices are for 1914 to 1916 banknotes. 1902 to 1913 banknotes add up to 50%

Prior to the First World War most white banknotes were only used once. Withdrawn from the bank, transaction completed and deposited back into a bank. Hence pre-war banknotes are rarely seen.

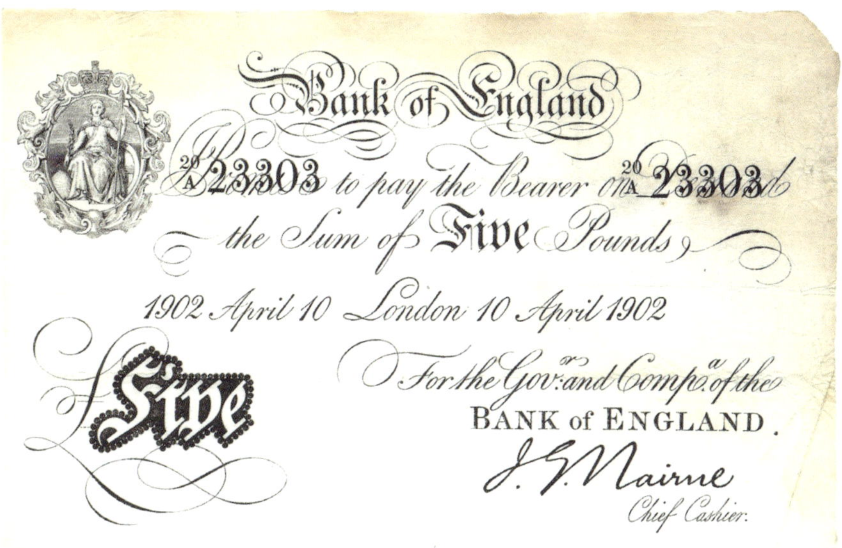

B208b £5 London 1902 first prefix, earliest Nairne known

LONDON FIVE POUNDS Prefixes/Serials/Dates

Printed/Dated from the 1st to 13th in even years & 18th to 30th/30th in odd years (not 1st year).

Number over letter

1/A	4 Apr 1902	to	7/B	Dec 1902	
8/B	1902	to	99/B	1902	
1/C	30 Sep 1903	to	27/C	Dec 1903	
28/C	1 Jan 1904	to	99/C	7 Jul 1904	*
1/D	8 Jul 1904	to	61/D	13 Dec 1904	
62/D	18 Jan 1905	to	99/D	26 Apr 1905	
1/E	27 Apr 1905	to	92/E	30 Dec 1905	
93/E	1 Jan 1906	to	99/E	8 Jan 1906	
1/H	9 Jan 1906	to	99/H	8 Oct 1906	
1/J	9 Oct 1906	to	27/J	13 Dec 1906	
28/J	18 Jan 1907	to	99/J	25 Jul 1907	

* From 56/C 7 March 1904, a third prefix was printed in the lower right hand corner, above the signature, to speed up accounting. Instead of having to write the prefix/serial in the ledger, this corner would be cut off and stuck in the ledger.

Letter over number

A/1	26 Jul 1907	to	A/58	30 Dec 1907
A/59	1 Jan 1908	to	A/99	9 Apr 1908
B/1	10 Apr 1908	to	B/70	13 Oct 1908
B/1	18 Jan 1909	to	B/99	24 Mar 1909
C/1	27 Mar 1909	to	C/99	27 Dec 1909
D/1	28 Dec 1909	to	D/4	31 Dec 1909
D/5	1 Jan 1910	to	D/99	7 Sep 1910
E/1	8 Sep 1910	to	E/38	13 Dec 1910
E/39	18 Jan 1911	to	E/99	27 Jun 1911
H/1	28 Jun 1911	to	H/70	30 Dec 1911
H/71	1 Jan 1912	to	H/99	7 Mar 1912
J/1	8 Mar 1912	to	J/99	6 Dec 1912

Number over letter

1/A	7 Dec 1912	to	6/A	13 Dec 1912
7/A	18 Jan 1913	to	99/A	24 Sep 1913
1/B	25 Sep 1913	to	37/B	30 Dec 1913
38/B	1 Jan 1914	to	99/B	9 Jun 1914
1/C	10 Jun 1914	to	70/C	12 Dec 1914
71/C	18 Jan 1915	to	99/C	26 Mar 1915
1/D	27 Mar 1915	to	77/D	26 Oct 1915
78/D	1 Jan 1916	to	99/D	12 Feb 1916
1/E	1 Mar 1916	to	11/E	13 Mar 1916

BRANCH BANKNOTES

As a rule, branch banknotes are scarce relative to those issued in London. However, in the case of Nairne a hoard of one hundred and thirty six banknotes was discovered by a Derbyshire gentleman and sold at an auction by A.F. Brock in 1989. These included £5, £10, £20, £50 and £100 banknotes, mostly Manchester. Consequently collectors will probably find it easier to acquire a Nairne Manchester £20, £50 and £100 (most are pre 1914) rather than London. The following VF price chart should be taken as general guidance as there could be pricing anomolies.
A dash (–) indicates examples of banknotes not currently known to be in private hands. NI indicates: None Issued.

	VF	B208b £5	B208c £10	B208d £20	B208e £50	B208f £100	B208h £500
a	BIRMINGHAM	2600	–	–	–	–	–
b	BRISTOL	?	–	–	NI	–	–
c	HULL	4000	–	–	–	–	–
d	LEEDS	1200	–	8000	8000	–	–
e	LIVERPOOL	2200	4500	7000	–	–	–
f	MANCHESTER	1200	3500	2800	2500	2700	?
g	NEWCASTLE	3500	–	NI	–	9500	NI
h	PLYMOUTH	4500	–	NI	–	–	NI
i	PORTSMOUTH	– *	–	NI	–	– *	NI

B208ba £5 Birmingham 1917

B208bc £5 Hull 1916

B208ce £10 Liverpool 1917

B208de £20 Liverpool 1917

B208ed £50 Leeds 1915

ERNEST MUSGRAVE HARVEY
1918-1925

Ernest Musgrave Harvey was born on 27th July 1867 and entered Bank service in 1885. He became Deputy Chief Cashier in 1902 and was the 17th Chief Cashier from 6th May 1918 to 30th March 1925. He was then appointed Comptroller, a Director from 1928-29 and Deputy Governor from 1929-36. Sir Ernest Harvey was knighted in 1920 and created a Baronet in 1933. Among his other honours were the CBE, Chevalier of the Legion of Honour 1918 and Chevalier of the Order of Leopold of Belgium 1919. He died on 17th December 1955.

WHITE BANKNOTES

Plate-printed on paper manufactured by Henry Portal. Banknotes printed on unitary watermarked paper, two to a sheet side by side, and cut to give one straight edge and three deckled (ragged/undulating) edges.

PAPER MAKER'S NOTCH

To aid the Printer in selecting the correct denomination watermarked paper, Portals created a notch in the right hand edge of the sheet (angled top corner on £5), placed at a specific height to indicate the denomination. This enables the printers to select the correctly watermarked paper for the value to be printed. Therefore 50% of banknotes up to 1944 have a paper maker's notch.

LONDON BANKNOTES 10 May 1918		F	VF	EF
B209a	**£5**	280	450	800
B209b	**£10**	360	600	900
B209c	**£20**	1250	1900	3200
B209d	**£50**	1200	1800	3000
B209e	**£100**	1400	2400	3400
B209f	**£200** discontinued 20th June 1918	-	28000	
B209g	**£500**		-	30000
B209h	**£1000**	-	Rare	

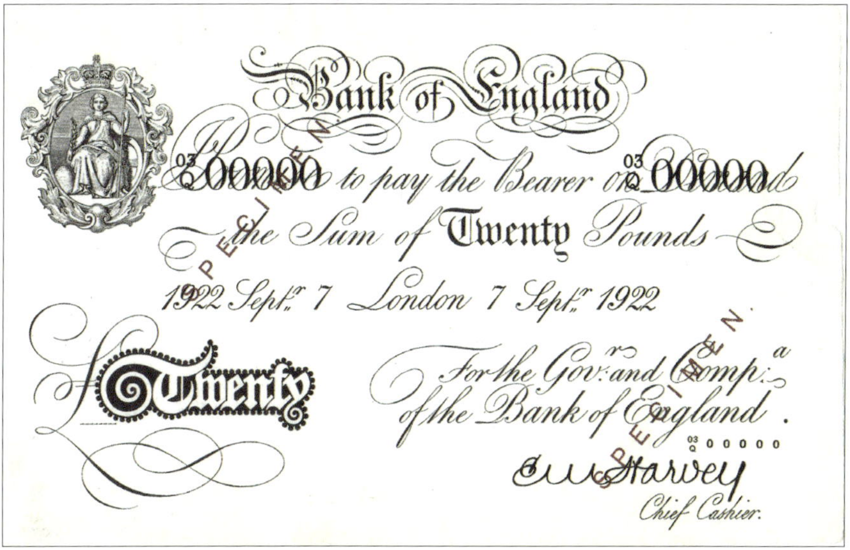

B209cs £20 London Specimen

In 1922 Harvey white banknotes overprinted SPECIMEN in all denominations were produced for the benefit of foreign central banks. The first five sets (one of which was sent to the German Reichsbank) were dated 4 Feby 1922, others were dated 7 Septr 1922. They should have been returned when no longer needed, but this was not always the case and a few examples have come on to the market. They are rare and to avoid repetition in the numbering only the £5 has been listed. The higher values are prefixed from 02/Q 00000 to 08/Q 00000.

			VF	EF	UNC
B209as	**£5**	Specimen *Prefix/Serial/Date:* 01/Q 00000 7 Septr 1922 Red solid capitals printed twice diagonally	-	5000	-

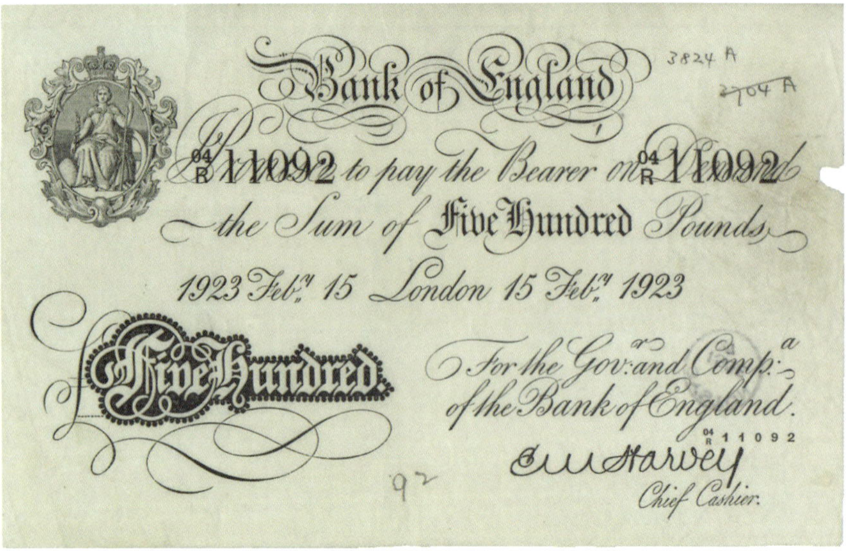

B209g £500 London 1923, paper maker's notch

LONDON FIVE POUNDS Prefixes/Serials/Dates

Printed/Dated from the 1st to 14th in even years and 18th to 30th/31st in odd years.
Number (one or two) over letter

12/E	10 May 1918	*to*	99/E	14 Dec 1918
1/H	18 Jan 1919	*to*	99/H	26 Sep 1919
1/J	27 Sep 1919	*to*	37/J	31 Dec 1919
38/J	1 Jan 1920	*to*	99/J	5 May 1920

Printed/Dated from the 1st to 17th in even years and 18th to 30th/31st in odd years.
Letter over number (one or two)

A/1	6 May 1920	*to*	A/99	1 Dec 1920
B/1	2 Dec 1920	*to*	B/14	17 Dec 1920
B/15	18 Jan 1921	*to*	B/99	24 Aug 1921
C/1	25 Aug 1921	*to*	C/52	31 Dec 1921
C/53	2 Jan 1922	*to*	C/99	5 Apr 1922
D/1	6 Apr 1922	*to*	D/73	6 Sep 1922

Number (three) over letter

101/D	7 Sep 1922	*to*	152/D	16 Dec 1922
153/D	18 Jan 1923	*to*	288/D	31 Dec 1923
289/D	1 Jan 1924	*to*	399/D	11 Aug 1924
001/E	12 Aug 1924	*to*	064/E	17 Dec 1924
065/E	19 Jan 1925	*to*	098/E	31 Mar 1925

BRANCH BANKNOTES

Inflation during the First World War meant that demand for banknotes increased during Mr Harvey's period in office. Harvey £5 London and £5 Branch banknotes (not Bristol) seem to be readily available. The following VF price chart should be taken as general guidance as there could be pricing anomolies.
A dash (–) indicates examples of banknotes not currently known to be in private hands. NI indicates: None Issued.

		B209a	B209b	B209c	B209d	B209e	B209g
	VF	**£5**	**£10**	**£20**	**£50**	**£100**	**£500**
a	BIRMINGHAM	1600	5000	6000	8000	8500	–
b	BRISTOL	7000	8000	NI	8000	–	–
c	HULL	1200	–	–	–	–	–
d	LEEDS	650	2000	4500	4000	8500	–
e	LIVERPOOL	800	1800	7000	–	7500	–
f	MANCHESTER	800	1600	5000	3000	7000	35000
g	NEWCASTLE	2200	–	–	–	–	NI
h	PLYMOUTH	3000	–	NI	–	–	NI

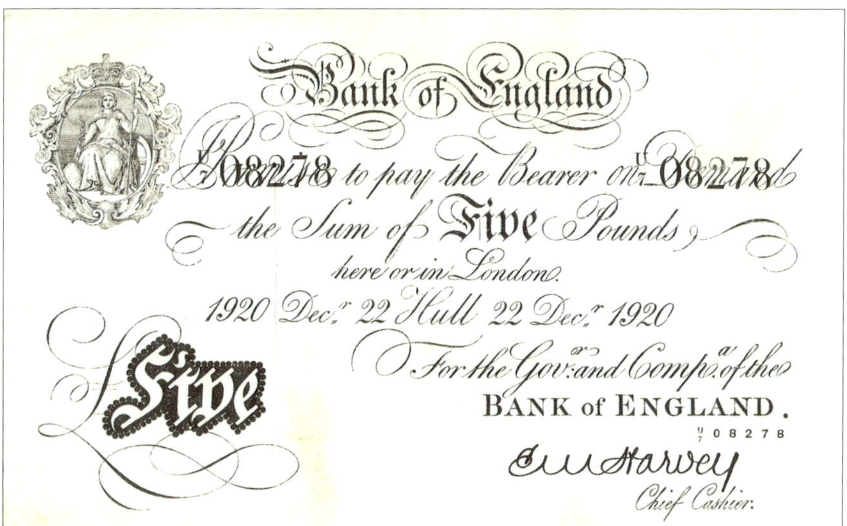

B209ac £5 Hull 1920

B209cf £20 Manchester

B209da £50 Birmingham

B209ea £100 Birmingham

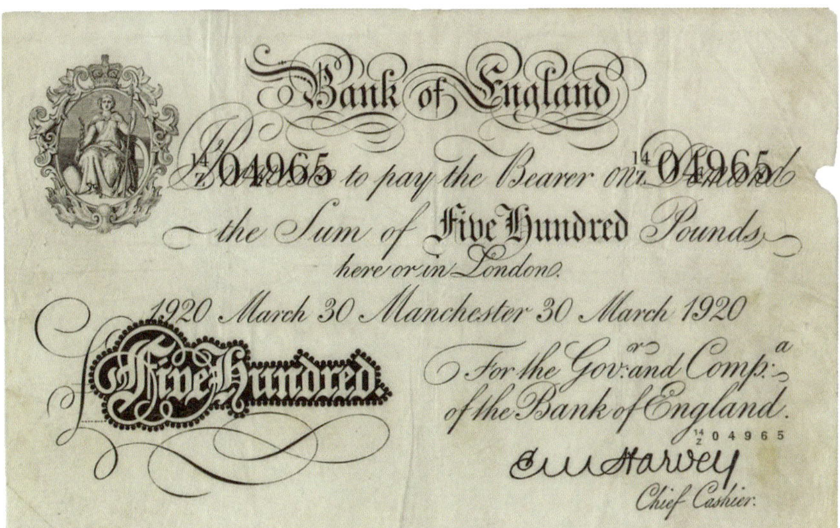

B209gf £500 Manchester, paper maker's notch

BANK OF ENGLAND NOTES 1928 *to* 1962

SERIES A BRITANNIA

The demands on the Bank during the First World War, not just in producing banknotes but also the numerous bonds and monetary instruments required by the government meant that it was no longer practical for everything to be done in Threadneedle Street. So in 1916 St. Luke's Hospital in nearby Old Street, was purchased, some work was transferred immediately, although reconstruction did not begin until 1919. The move was finally completed in April 1922 and, apart from the Second World War all banknotes were printed there until 1956.

The Bank was at last in a position to take back its role as the main banknote issuer. In May 1924 work began on a new design and various colourful essays have survived in the archives. By 1927 what can only be described as a composite design was approved. According to Derrick Byatt in 'Promises to Pay' at least seven people seem to have been involved in one aspect or another, although the main credit has gone to W.M. Keesey, Inspector of Art Schools at the Board of Education.

On 22nd November 1928, the Bank assumed responsibility for the banknote issue under the Currency and Banknotes Act 1928 and the Series A green £1 banknotes and red-brown 10s banknotes duly appeared on that day. They were signed by the Chief Cashier C.P. Mahon and joined the existing range of white fivers and higher denominations up to £1000. Treasury banknotes were withdrawn from circulation July 1933.

The Bank had anticipated that Series A might last for about five years. In fact they remained in circulation for thirty-four years until October 1962, by which time (Vincent Duggleby was officially told) a total of 20,000 million £1 and 10,500 million 10s banknotes had been issued. The quantities printed for individual prefixes are unofficial estimates. Back in June 1931, after consulting the Royal Mint Advisory Committee, three artists were invited to compete for the privilege of designing a new series: Stephen Gooden, Frederick Landseer Griggs and Kruger Gray. Griggs and Gray soon dropped out and Gooden was appointed as the Bank's designer. However, the various essays he produced during the 1930s, including some featuring Sir John Houblon the Bank's first governor, were not taken up, although they have been preserved in the Bank's archives.

The change that did take place in 1940, following the outbreak of war, was to the colour of the banknotes, blue/pink for the £1 and mauve for the 10s. At the same time a metal thread, the invention of S.B. Chamberlain, General Manager of the Bank's Printing Works, was inserted. In 1943, following the appearance of German forgeries (Bernhards), it was decided to withdraw the denominations above £5. It was twenty years before the £10 was to reappear, nearly thirty years before the country again had a £20 banknote and nearly forty years till the return of the £50. Following problems at the Royal Mint in 1940, the Bank was also asked as a matter of extreme urgency to produce small denomination banknotes of 2s6d and 5s. In the event the banknotes were not needed and were supposedly all destroyed after the Second World War, but a few examples survived and found their way into the hands of collectors.

In 1948 £1 and 10s banknotes of the pre-war colours, green and red-brown, were again issued and for a short time were unthreaded to use up the old stocks of paper. Subsequently all Bank of England banknotes incorporated the now familiar metal thread as a security precaution. In 1949 Stephen Gooden was asked to design a £2 in the Houblon series, Peppiatt signature, picking up his work from the 1930s, there was a trial run of the 10s, £1 and £5 with the signature of P.S. Beale. In 1950 he set to work on yet another series, this time featuring a helmeted figure of Britannia with Lion and Key reverse (Series B). The £5 was the only one issued in 1957, after Gooden's death, with the signature of L.K. O'Brien.

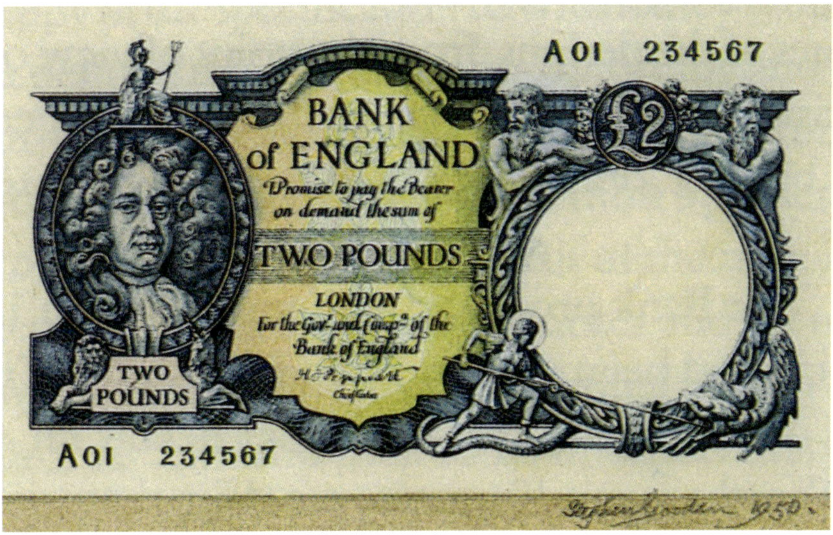

Gooden £2 Houblon Essay 1950 signed by Peppiatt © Bank of England

The listings that follow are arranged under the names of each Chief Cashier, beginning with C.P. Mahon. Prices are quoted in VF, EF and UNC throughout this section, with the exception of rarities. Specimen banknotes are also priced in one or more grades where applicable. In the forty-two years since the first edition, nearly all first prefixes (usually 1 million banknotes, 960000 from 1957 to around 1970) have been clearly established, and separate status has now been given to all these, first run/series have also been priced if warranted. The last prefixes are far more difficult to establish with certainty and in Series C many overlaps occur to complicate matters still further. Whenever possible lasts have now been priced. Modern first and last prefixes together with column sorts and replacements may prove dificult to obtain, even in low grades.

© Bank of England

CYRIL PATRICK MAHON
1925-1929

Cyril Mahon was born on 9th September 1882, the son of the Rev G.A. Mahon vicar of Leigh-on-Mendip in Somerset. He was educated at All Saints School, Clifton, and All Saints Bloxham, in Oxfordshire. His first job was in the Lincoln Bank at Grimsby where he spent a year before being elected to the Bank of England on 14th March 1901. According to his obituary in the Times Mahon was a man of outstanding character and his technical ability and clarity of judgement were of great service during the 1914-18 First World War. In 1916 he was appointed assistant principal of the Discount Office. He became Assistant Chief Cashier in 1918, Deputy Chief Cashier in 1923 and held the post of the 18th Chief Cashier from 1st April 1925 to 26th March 1929. His final job at the bank was as Comptroller from 1929-32 when he was forced to retire due to ill health. He returned to Somerset in retirement where he lived at Bishops Hull, just outside Taunton. He died on 14th July 1945.

SERIES A BRITANNIA 1928 *to* 1962

Designed by William Keesey (responsible for the reverse of both denominations) and other experts inside and outside the Bank. The front features the medallion of Britannia by Daniel Maclise originally used for the high denominations from 1855. The reverse of the 10s has two 10/- value tablets set among swirls of acanthus leaves in shades of red-brown. The reverse of the £1 shows the south front of the Bank prior to rebuilding together with vignettes of St. George and the dragon used by Benedetto Pistrucci in his design for the sovereign. These are contained in swirls of acanthus leaves of pale green, blue and mauve.

TEN SHILLINGS 22 November 1928

Designed collectively by William Keesey and other experts inside and outside the Bank. The front features the medallion of Britannia while the reverse has two 10/- value tablets set among swirls of acanthus leaves in shades of red-brown. Printed in sheets of 21 (3 x 7) at St. Luke's Works, Old Street, London, on banknote paper manufactured by Portals Ltd with a watermark of wavy lines and the helmeted head of Britannia facing right. The banknotes measure 138 x 78mm, the highest serial is 1000000 and ceased to be legal tender after 29th October 1962.

			VF	EF	UNC
B210	**10s**	Red-Brown			
		Quantity printed: 410 million	VF	EF	UNC
		Prefixes: (links Catterns B223 V)			
	A01	(inaugural run, one million banknotes)	500	900	1600
	Z01	(first production run)	400	680	1000
	Z--	(first series)	170	340	500
	Y--	X-- W--	130	270	450
	V--	(last series)	550	1000	-
	V13	(last run)	1600	-	

B210 First production run Z01

			VF	EF	UNC
B210s	**10s**	Specimen			
		Prefix/Serial: A00 000000			
		Type 1: Black small solid capitals printed diagonally	700	1550	2200
		Type 2: Perforated capitals horizontally (in Bank's archive)			

B211 **10s** Replacement (none logged)

ONE POUND 22 November 1928

Designed by William Keesey (responsible for the reverse of both the 10s and the £1) and other experts inside and outside the Bank. The front features the medallion of Britannia by Daniel Maclise originally used for the high denominations from 1855. The reverse shows the south front of the Bank prior to rebuilding together with vignettes of St. George and the dragon used by Benedetto Pistrucci in his design for the sovereign. These are contained in swirls of acanthus leaves of pale green, blue and mauve. Printed in sheets of 21 (3 x 7) at St. Luke's Works, Old Street, London, on banknote paper manufactured by Portals Ltd, with a watermark of wavy lines and the helmeted head of Britannia facing right. The banknotes measure 150 x 84mm, the highest serial is 1000000 and ceased to be legal tender after 28th May 1962.

			VF	EF	UNC
B212	**£1**	Green			
		Quantity printed: 725 million	VF	EF	UNC
		Prefixes: (links Catterns B225 H)			
	A01	(inaugural run one million banknotes)	500	980	1600
	A02	(first series, starts 02)	175	340	500
	A--	(first series)	75	160	300
	B--	C-- D-- E-- F-- G--	70	130	250
	H--	(last series)	110	190	350
	H32	(last run)		-	Rare

B212 Last H32

B212s	**£1**	Specimen			
		Prefix/Serial: A00 000000	VF	EF	UNC
		Red small solid capitals printed once diagonally	700	1550	2200
		as above but Lithography by ABNC		-	1100
		as above but no overprint no prefix/serials		-	1000

B213 **£1** Replacement (none logged)

No verifiable examples of replacements have come to light, they may have been handset? An invention for numbering single banknotes to replace spoils in production was patented by the Bank on 20th January 1928.

B210 Acanthus leaves & two 10/- *reverse*

B212 South front of the Bank and two St. George & dragon *reverse*

			VF	EF	UNC
B214	**10s £1**	Parchment Pair			
		Pair with matched prefix/serial + wallets + envelope	-	7000	8500

Matched pairs Mahon 10s & £1 A01 000001 to A01 000125 each banknote in a celluloid edged wallet within a parchment presentation envelope inscribed in black:

Bank of England 22 November 1928

King George V received A01 000001 (envelope inscribed in gold), followed by important members of: Royalty, Government, Civil Service and Chairmen of major banks. Each received pairs in order of hierarchy, remainders were then sold to the Bank's staff and the general public. Twenty five pairs are known to be in collectors' hands.

B214 Mahon Parchment Pair

WHITE BANKNOTES 18 April 1925

White banknotes from £5 to £1000 bearing various dates between 1925 and 1928 were issued with the signature of C.P. Mahon. The banknotes are of the traditional design and dimensions, measuring 214 x 135mm. They were plate-printed at St. Luke's Works, Old Street, London, in horizontal pairs then guillotined, leaving one straight edge and three deckled edges. 99,999 banknotes per perfix. Portals Ltd made the paper. Bankotes of £10 and above were legal tender until 1st May 1945 and £5 banknotes without metal thread were legal tender until 1st March 1946 - no doubt to allow wartime hoarders time to pay them in.

LONDON BANKNOTES			VF	EF	UNC
B215	**£5**		450	800	1300
B216	**£10**		500	1000	1500
B217	**£20**		3000	4400	6000
B218	**£50**		2500	3500	4800
B219	**£100**		2500	3500	4800
B220	**£200**	only exists as a specimen			
B221	**£500**		-	29000	-
B222	**£1000**		-	34000	-

B215s **£5** Specimen
Prefix/Serial/Date: 001/Q 00000 9 April 1925
Red solid capitals printed twice diagonally 1400 2600 3600

Mahon white banknotes overprinted SPECIMEN in all the denominations were produced for the benefit of foreign central banks. They should have been returned and destroyed when no longer needed for reference, but this was not always the case. As with Harvey, a few examples have come on to the market. They are rare and to avoid repetition in the numbering only the £5 has been listed. The £10 is prefixed 002/Q 00000 and higher values from 03/Q 00000 to 08/Q 00000.

LONDON FIVE POUNDS Prefixes/Serials/Dates

Printed/Dated from the 1st to 17th in even years and 18th to 30th/31st in odd years.

099/E	18 Apr 1925	*to*	201/E	31 Dec 1925
202/E	1 Jan 1926	*to*	376/E	17 Dec 1926
377/E	18 Jan 1927	*to*	399/E	19 Mar 1927
001/H	21 Mar 1927	*to*	115/H	31 Dec 1927
116/H	2 Jan 1928	*to*	150/H	7 Mar 1928
151/H	1 May 1928	*to*	198/H	6 Aug 1928

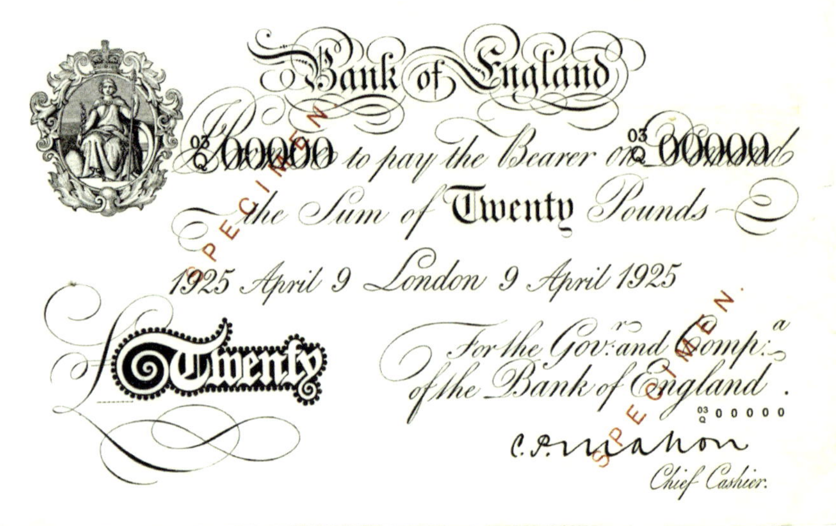

B217s £20 Specimen, paper maker's notch

B218 £50 London, paper maker's notch

BRANCH BANKNOTES

A fair survival rate for Mahon branch banknotes means that collectors with sufficient means should be able to obtain examples of the £5 from most of the eight branches. Denominations of £20, £50 and £100 are rare. The following VF price chart should be taken as general guidance. A dash (−) indicates examples of banknotes not currently known to be in collectors hands. NI indicates: None Issued.

		B215	B216	B217	B218	B219	B221
	VF	£5	£10	£20	£50	£100	£500
a	BIRMINGHAM	5000	2200 *	–	–	–	–
b	BRISTOL	5000	–	NI	–	–	NI
c	HULL	2500	–	NI	–	–	–
d	LEEDS	900	2000	–	3800	8000	–
e	LIVERPOOL	2500	1800	7000	–	–	–
f	MANCHESTER	1500	1700	6000	4000	9000	–
g	NEWCASTLE	3000	7000	–	–	–	NI
h	PLYMOUTH	4000	–	NI	–	–	NI

∗ Also exists as a Bernhard forgery, See page 376: From £600 VF
For detailed Bernhard prefix information: www.britishnotes.co.uk News & Info

B215a £5 Birmingham

B216d £10 Leeds, paper maker's notch

B216g £10 Newcastle on Tyne

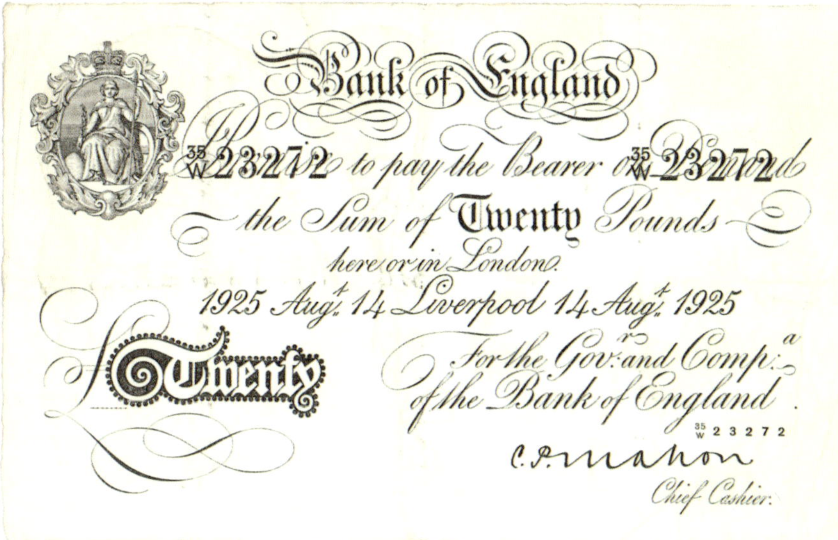

B217e £20 Liverpool

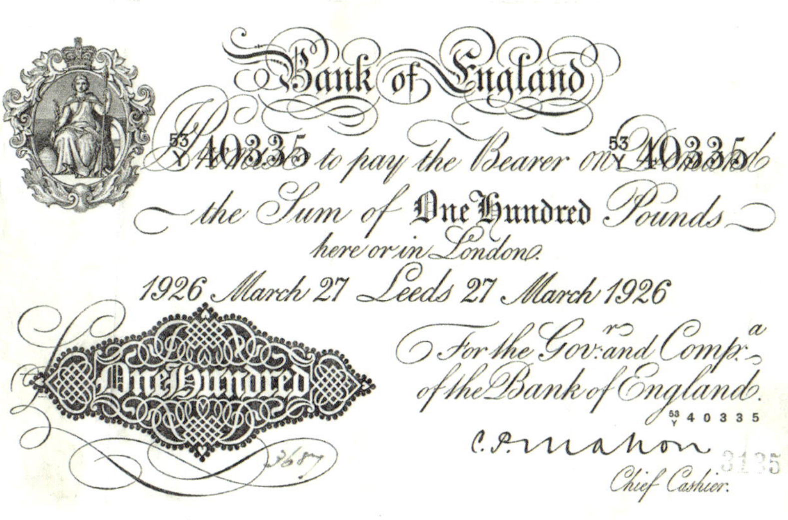

B219d £100 Leeds

BASIL
GAGE CATTERNS
1929-1934

Basil Catterns was born on 20th June 1886 at Oswaldtwistle in Lancashire, the son of the Rector, the Rev T.E.S. Catterns. He was educated at Trent College, Nottingham, and after five years with the Manchester and Liverpool District Banking Company (later the District Bank) at Accrington, he entered the Bank's service on 13th February 1908. During the First World War he served as a Second Lieutenant in the Royal Field Artillery but was severely wounded in the legs in 1917. In 1920 he settled permanently in the Chief Cashier's office; he became Assistant Chief in 1923, Deputy Chief in April 1925 and succeeded Cyril Mahon as the 19th Chief Cashier on 27th March 1929. He held this post until 17th April 1934, when he was appointed an Executive Director. In March 1936 he succeeded Sir Ernest Harvey as Deputy Governor and retired in 1945, serving two more years as a non-executive Director. He died on 5th February 1969.

SERIES A BRITANNIA 1928 *to* 1962

TEN SHILLINGS 15 July 1930

Design, watermark and dimensions as for *B210* C.P. Mahon banknotes. Printed at St. Luke's Works, London.

B223 **10s** Red-Brown

Quantity printed: 977 million

Prefixes: (links Mahon B210 V)

		VF	EF	UNC
V14	(first run)	550	1000	-
V--	(first series)	110	240	350
U--	T-- S-- R-- O-- N-- M-- L--	70	120	200
K--	(last series)	90	200	320
K99	(last run)	400	780	-

B223 First V14 & Last K99

B223s **10s** Specimen

Prefix/Serial: Q00 000000

	VF	EF	UNC
Black small solid capitals printed once diagonally	700	1550	2200

B224 **10s** Replacement (none logged)

ONE POUND 15 July 1930

Design, watermark and dimensions as for *B212* C.P. Mahon banknotes. Printed at St. Luke's Works, London.

B225	**£1**	Green								
		Quantity printed: 1,453 million						VF	EF	UNC
		Prefixes: (links Mahon B212 H)								
	H33	(first run)						550	950	-
	H--	(first series)						55	120	220
	J--	K--	L--	M--	N--	O--	R--	30	65	130
	S--	T--	U--	W--	X--	Y--				
	Z--	(last series)						40	80	140
	Z99	(last run)						500	950	-

B225 First series H & Last series Z

B225s	**£1**	Specimen			
		Prefix/Serial: Q00 000000			
		Red small solid capitals printed once diagonally	700	1550	2200

			VF	EF	UNC
B226	**£1**	Green			
		Quantity printed: 99 million	VF	EF	UNC
		Prefixes:			
	01A	(first run)	600	1100	-
	--A		100	220	360
	99A	(last run)	550	980	-

B226 First 01A

B226 Last 99A

B227 **£1** Replacement (none logged)

WHITE BANKNOTES 27 March 1929

White banknotes from £5 to £1000 were issued bearing various dates between 1929 and 1934. Design, watermark and dimensions as for *B215 etc* C.P. Mahon white banknotes. Printed at St. Luke's Works, London.

LONDON BANKNOTES

			VF	EF	UNC
B228	**£5**		300	500	750
B229	**£10**	* (100 VF 150 EF)	400	650	950
B230	**£20**	* (130 VF 180 EF)	1000	1800	3300
B231	**£50**	* (150 VF 200 EF)	1000	1700	2500
B232	**£100**		1800	2800	4000
B233	**£500**		20000	30000	-
B234	**£1000**		-	28000	-

* Also exists as a Bernhard forgery, prices in brackets, 1930 to 1934. See page 376. For detailed Bernhard prefix information visit: www.britishnotes.co.uk *click* News & Info

			VF	EF	UNC
B228s	**£5**	Specimen *Prefix/Serial/Date:* 000/Q 00000 2 July 1929 Red solid capitals printed twice diagonally	1200	2000	2800

The date chosen for the specimens was later than the start date of the normal issue. Catterns white banknotes overprinted SPECIMEN in all denominations were produced for the benefit of foreign central banks. They should have been returned and destroyed when no longer needed for reference, but as with Mahon and Harvey this was not always the case. Catterns specimens are rare and so far no values above the £5 have come to market.

LONDON FIVE POUNDS Prefixes/Serials/Dates

Printed/Dated from the 1st to 17th in even years and the 18th to 30th/31st in odd years. As can be seen from the list there can be months between printings.

199/H	27	Mar	1929	*to*	305/H	31	Dec	1929
306/H	1	Jan	1930	*to*	399/H	8	Jul	1930
001/J	9	Jul	1930	*to*	039/J	2	Oct	1930
040/J	19	Jan	1931	*to*	135/J	22	Sep	1931
136/J	1	Jan	1932	*to*	243/J	8	Aug	1932
244/J	18	Jan	1933	*to*	327/J	23	Aug	1933
328/J	1	Jan	1934	*to*	351/J	10	Feb	1934

B230 £20 London, paper maker's notch

B231 £50 London

BRANCH BANKNOTES

The good survival rate for Catterns branch banknotes means that collectors should be able to obtain examples of the £5 from most of the branches. Surprisingly the £100 is obtainable from seven of the eight branches. The following VF price chart should be taken as general guidance. A Dash (−) indicates examples of banknotes not currently known to be in collectors hands. NI indicates: None Issued.

		B228	B229	B230	B231	B232	B233
	VF	£5	£10	£20	£50	£100	£500
a	BIRMINGHAM	2000	2500	6000	−	9000 aef	−
b	BRISTOL	6500	8000	NI	10000	14000 ef	NI
c	HULL	2000	−	NI	−	9000	NI
d	LEEDS	800	2500 *	NI	5000	7500	−
e	LIVERPOOL	1600	3500	6000	5000	9000	34000
f	MANCHESTER	800	2000	5000	3500	8000	−
g	NEWCASTLE	1800	9000	−	7000	7500	NI
h	PLYMOUTH	8000	9000	NI	−	−	NI

* Also exists as a Bernhard forgery: From £300 VF

B229g £10 Newcastle on Tyne

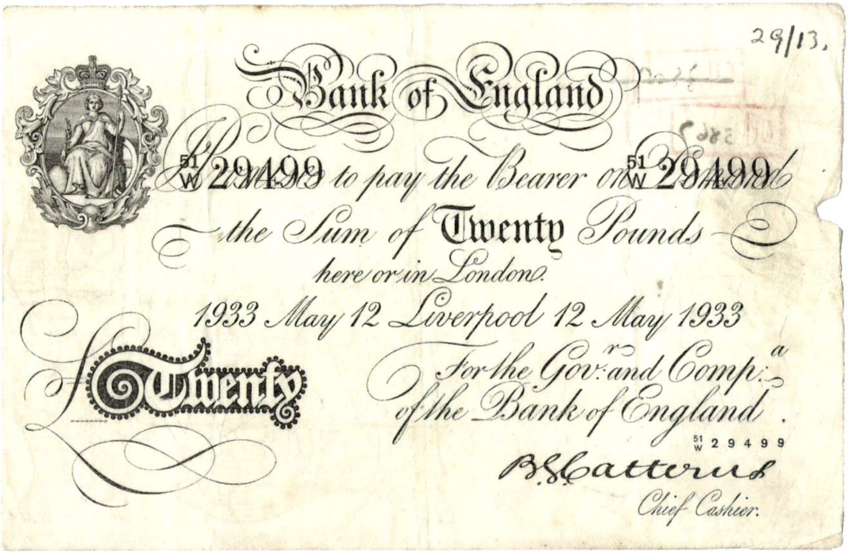

B230e £20 Liverpool, paper maker's notch

B231f £50 Manchester

© Bank of England

KENNETH OSWALD PEPPIATT
1934-1949

Kenneth Peppiatt was born in 1893. He was educated at Bancroft's School and was elected to the staff of the Bank on 9th November 1911. During the First World War he served with the 7th Batallion London Regiment, spending three years in Flanders. He rose to the rank of Major, was wounded twice and awarded the MC and bar. Returning to the Bank after the war he rose to become Principal of the Discount Office in 1928 and the 20th Chief Cashier on 18th April 1934. KOP, as he was known, held the post for fifteen years until 28th February 1949, the second longest period (after Nairne) in the 20th century. Peppiatt was knighted in 1941. From 1949 he was an Executive Director until his retirement in 1957 when he joined Coutts Bank as a Director. He died at the age of ninety on 12th May 1983.

SERIES A BRITANNIA 1928 *to* 1962

Peppiatt notes are subdivided into four periods:

First	1934 *to* 1939	Unthreaded	Continuing from Catterns
Second	1940 *to* 1948	Threaded	War time colour changes
Third	1948	Unthreaded	Using up stockpiled paper
Fourth	1948 *to* 1949	Threaded	Post war banknotes

FIRST PERIOD 1934 *to* 1939

TEN SHILLINGS 5 October 1934

Design, watermark and dimensions as for *B210* C.P. Mahon banknotes. **Unthreaded**. Printed at St. Luke's Works, London.

B235	**10s**	Red-Brown			
		Quantity printed: 693 million	VF	EF	UNC
		Prefixes: (links Mahon B212 A)			
	J01	(first run)	500	1200	-
	J--	(first series)	45	120	240
	H--	E-- D-- C-- B--	40	80	160
	A--	(last series, traced in 02 to 99 [01 Mahon only])	60	120	220
	A99	(last run)	350	700	-

B235 Last A99

B235s	**10s**	Specimen			
		Prefix/Serial: Q00 000000			
		Black small solid capitals printed once diagonally	600	1300	1800

			VF	EF	UNC
B236	**10s**	Red-Brown			
		Quantity printed: 871 million	VF	EF	UNC
		Prefixes: (overlaps B256 O)			
	01Z	(first run)	350	700	1100
	- - Z	(first series)	65	130	260
	- - Y	--X --W --U --T --S --R	35	70	130
	- - O	(last series)	55	110	180
	42O	(traced to 300000)	130	300	-
	49O	(last run, traced to 650000)	250	550	-

B236 First 01Z

B236 Last 49O

Derrick Byatt in an article for Spink's Banknote Circular, January 1997 relating to B236, has confirmed that the prefixes N and M were not used, and the O was cut short at 42O (serials up to 300000) which was produced alongside 49O (serials up to 650000). Unfortunately there is no evidence on whether any or all of the O prefix was actually released or kept in stock until after the war. Printing of 42O was continued and the series eventually ran to 62O, with a gap from 63O to 69O unprinted, and the final run in 70O (serials up to 650000). The balance of the 10s O prefix is listed under B256.

B237 **10s** Replacement (none logged)

ONE POUND 17 October 1934

Design, watermark and dimensions as for *B212* C.P. Mahon banknotes. **Unthreaded**. Printed at St Luke's Works, London.

B238	**£1**	Green			
		Quantity printed: 1,881 million	VF	EF	UNC
		Prefixes:			
	01B	(first run)	650	1100	-
	- - B	(first series)	35	80	130
	- - C --D --E --H - - J --K --L --M --N - - O --R --S --T - - U --W --X - - Y		25	60	100
	- - Z	(last series)	30	70	115
	99Z	(last run)	250	500	800

B238 Last 99Z

B238s	**£1**	Specimen			
		Prefix/Serial: Q00 000000	VF	EF	UNC
		Red small solid capitals printed once diagonally	600	1300	1800

B239	**£1**	Green			
		Quantity printed: 831 million			
		Prefixes:			
	A01A	(first run)	1500	-	
	A--A	(first series)	30	65	90
	B--A	C--A D--A E--A H--A J--A K--A	15	35	75
	L--A	(last series)	25	45	80
	L39A	(last run)	150	300	500

Derrick Byatt in the article quoted has confirmed that the long held view that the prefixes M--A, N--A and O--A were printed but not issued.

B239 First A01A & Last L39A

B240 **£1** Replacement (none logged)

WHITE BANKNOTES 1 May 1934 *to* 1944

Large denomination notes from £5 to £1000, bearing various dates between 1934 and 1944. Design, watermark and dimensions as for C.P. Mahon. Printed at St. Luke's Works, London.

LONDON BANKNOTES		VF	EF	UNC
B241	**£5** * (80 VF 130 EF)	200	350	600
B242	**£10** * (90 VF 140 EF)	350	550	750
B243	**£20** * (110 VF 165 EF)	1100	1650	2500
B244	**£50** * (130 VF 180 EF)	1100	1650	2500
B245	**£100** * (500 VF)	1500	2200	3300
B246	**£500**	-	12000	18000
B247	**£1000**	-	20000	26000

Prices for War dates 1939 to 1943 add up to 30%

* Also exists as a Bernhard forgery, prices in brackets, (1930) 1934 to 1938. See page 376. For a full list of Bernhard prefix/serials visit British Notes website.

B247 £1000 London

B241s	**£5**	Specimen			
		Prefix/Serial/Date: 000/Q 00000 20 April 1934	VF	EF	UNC
		Red solid capitals printed twice diagonally	750	1450	2400

Peppiatt white banknotes overprinted SPECIMEN are found in all denominations produced for the benefit of foreign central banks. They should have been returned and destroyed when no longer needed for reference, but as with previous chief cashiers this was not always the case, a few examples have come on to the market. To avoid repetition only the £5 has been listed. The £10 is prefixed 000/Q 00000 and higher denominations 00/Q 00000. From £3000 EF

LONDON FIVE POUNDS Prefixes/Serials/Dates

Printed/Dated from the 1st to 17th in even years and 18th to 30th/31st in odd years.

352/J	1 May 1934	to	399/J	6 Aug 1934
A/100	7 Aug 1934	to	A/135	13 Oct 1934
A/136	18 Jan 1935	*to*	A/255	23 Nov 1935
A/256	1 Jan 1936	*to*	A/356	17 Jul 1936
A/357	18 Jan 1937	*to*	A/399	30 Apr 1937
B/100	18 May 1937	*to*	B/157	30 Sep 1937

Printed/Dated from the 1st to 16th in even years and 19th to 31st in odd years.

B/158	3 Jan 1938	*to*	B/320	16 Dec 1938
B/321	19 Jan 1939	*to*	B/385	21 Jul 1939
B/386	1 Jan 1940	*to*	B/391	6 Jan 1940
B/392	20 May 1940	*to*	B/394	22 May 1940
B/395	1 Nov 1940	*to*	B/399	6 Nov 1940
C/100	7 Nov 1940	*to*	C/114	9 Dec 1940
C/115	16 Jan 1941	*to*	C/162	26 Apr 1941
C/163	16 Aug 1941	*to*	C/198	27 Oct 1941
C/199	1 Jan 1942	*to*	C/306	8 Sep 1942
C/307	16 Jan 1943	*to*	C/399	4 Aug 1943
D/074	5 Aug 1943	*to*	D/160	13 Nov 1943
D/161	1 Jan 1944	*to*	D/238	31 Mar 1944
D/239	1 Jun 1944	*to*	D/315	29 Aug 1944

D316 to D318 1st September 1944 were printed but not issued.

From 1st August 1943 £5 London issues use the whole of the month. From that point, there are month/months long gaps between dates of issue although the prefixes are consecutive. No banknotes printed in 1946 or 1948

BRANCH BANKNOTES

Peppiatt signature branch banknotes are relatively plentiful, several runs have come on to the market, notably the Liverpool £100. This makes it easier to establish realistic prices for VF banknotes based on auction realisations and other deals. The following price chart should be taken as general guidance.
A Dash (–) indicates examples of banknotes not currently known to be in private hands. NI indicates: None Issued.

		B241	B242	B243	B244	B245	B246
	VF	**£5**	**£10**	**£20**	**£50**	**£100**	**£500**
a	BIRMINGHAM	1100	1200	–	4500	8000	–
b	BRISTOL	4000	4000 *	NI	–	–	NI
c	HULL	1600	RARE	NI	–	–	NI
d	LEEDS	850	3500 *	4000 gf	4500	6000	RARE
e	LIVERPOOL	650	2000 *	3500	3000	1200 gef	9000
f	MANCHESTER	850	2500 *	4000 vg	3000	5000	–
g	NEWCASTLE	1700	3000	–	–	9000	NI
h	PLYMOUTH	3800	RARE	NI	–	–	NI

* Also exists as a Bernhard forgery: From £300 VF
For detailed Bernhard prefix information: www.britishnotes.co.uk News & Info

B241a £5 Birmingham

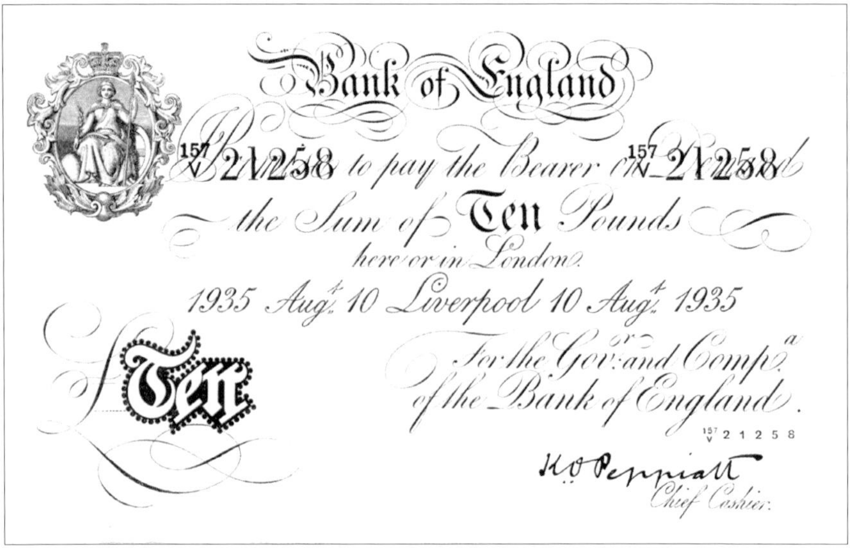

B242e £10 Liverpool

B243e £20 Liverpool

B244e £50 Liverpool

B245d £100 Leeds

SECOND PERIOD 1940 *to* 1948

ONE POUND EMERGENCY ISSUE 29 March 1940

The **Blue/Pink** Emergency Issue incorporating a **Metal Thread**, the invention of the General Manager of the Bank's printing works, S.B. Chamberlain. Basic design unchanged, but a double line surrounds the unprinted watermark area. The banknotes were printed by offset-litho at St. Luke's Works, Old Street, London, and/or at Overton, Hampshire. Legal tender until 28th May 1962. B248 not used.

B249 **£1** **Emergency Issue Blue/Pink** (shades)
Quantity printed: 5,380 million
Prefixes:

Prefix							VF	EF	UNC
A01D	(first run)						190	380	700
A--D	B--D	C--D	D--D	E--D	H--D	J--D			
K--D	L--D	M--D	N--D	O--D	R--D	T--D	12	25	45
U--D	W--D	X--D	Y--D	Z--D					
Z87D	(last run first series)						140	320	-
A01E	(first run sub series)						140	280	470
A--E	B--E	C--E	D--E	E--E	H--E				
J--E	K--E	L--E	M--E	N--E	O--E		12	25	45
R--E	T--E	U--E	W--E						
W48E	(last run sub series)						150	350	520
A01H	(first run last series)						140	280	470
A--H	B--H	C--H	D--H	E--H	H--H				
J--H	K--H	L--H	M--H	N--H	O--H		12	25	45
R--H	T--H	U--H	W--H						
X--H	(last series, shades)						20	35	65
X96H	(last run)						150	350	520

B249 A01H Mid first

			VF	EF	UNC
B249s	£1	Specimen *Prefix/Serial:* A00D 000000 Red small capitals printed once diagonally	600	1300	1800
B250	**£1**	Replacement *Quantity printed:* Not known *Prefixes:*			
	S01D	(first run)	150	400	660
	S--D S--E S--H	(traced to S16D & S16E)	120	280	500
	S13H	(last run, may go higher)	150	400	660

B250 First Replacement S01D

B250 Last Replacement S13H

TEN SHILLINGS EMERGENCY ISSUE 2 April 1940

The **Mauve** Emergency Issue incorporated a **Metal Thread** as in the blue £1. Basic design and dimensions were unchanged. Printed by offset-litho at St. Luke's Works, Old Street, London, and/or at Overton, Hampshire on banknote paper manufactured by Portals Ltd. Legal tender until 29th October 1962.

									VF	EF	UNC
B251	**10s**	Emergency Issue Mauve									
		Quantity printed: 2,100 million							VF	EF	UNC
		Prefixes:									
	Z01D	(first run)							230	430	750
	Z--D	Y--D	X--D	W--D	U--D	S--D	R--D				
	O--D	N--D	M--D	L--D	K--D	J--D	H--D		35	70	130
	E--D	D--D	C--D	B--D	A--D						
	A99D	(last run first series)							100	230	380
	Z01E	(first run last series)							160	350	-
	Z--E	Y--E	X--E (XE18 to 20 not logged)						40	75	145
	X21E	(last run)							200	450	800

B251 Last X21E

			VF	EF	UNC
B251s	**10s**	Specimen			
		Prefix/Serial: Z00D 000000			
		Red small capitals printed once diagonally	600	1300	1800

B252	**10s**	Replacement			
		Quantity printed: Not known	VF	EF	UNC
		Prefixes:			
	T01D	(first run)	460	850	-
	T--D		230	350	600
	T12D	(last run, may go higher)	450	800	-

B252 First Replacement T01D

OBSERVATIONS ON THE PRODUCTION OF WARTIME ISSUES

Anticipating the war, the Bank leased two factories at Overton, Hampshire, near the papermakers Portals and according to Derrick Byatt in 'Promises to Pay' "Future production plans included a project to move all litho printing and threaded paper to Overton by early 1940". Byatt does not elaborate on this statement nor does he give any detailed evidence to support his statement that "Contrary to some reports there was no destruction of, or interruption to, banknote production (at St. Luke's)". We know that St. Luke's suffered bomb damage on four occasions, the worst being through the night of 9th/10th September 1940. It is also reasonable to assume that the true extent of the damage and the contingency plans would have been top secret and that highly sensitive documents would have been destroyed.

It has been implied that '*all*' banknote production continued uninterrupted at St Luke's and may have been what the Bank wanted the public to believe at the time and in his article for Spink's Banknote Circular (January 1997) Byatt subsequently reported his research into the prefixes listed as being printed at St Luke's and Overton respectively. Clearly the ledgers show the extent of the issue, which broadly tallies with English Paper Money. But it does not mean the banknotes were printed or issued in any particular order from either location. Vincent Duggleby was told that some sheets printed at St. Luke's were sent to Overton for numbering, cutting and packing.

FRACTIONALS

FIVE SHILLINGS & TWO SHILLINGS SIX PENCE May 1941

The emergency small denomination (fractional) 5s (crown) and 2s6d (half crown) banknotes were prepared by the Bank of England in 1940, because of a feared shortage of silver coins after the power supply to the Royal Mint had been seriously damaged. The original plan was for just under three million pounds in banknotes: five million 5s, twelve million 2s and ten million 1s. In the event the order on the 4th October 1940 was for eight million 5s (six million printed by Bradbury Wilkinson and two million at St. Luke's) and six million 2s6d (divided equally between Bradbury Wilkinson and Waddingtons). The 2s and 1s banknotes only reached the essay stage.

The banknotes were printed on unwatermarked paper with the same design on both sides, incorporating a metal thread. They measure 114 x 73mm and were distributed to the clearing banks in May 1941. In the event the crisis passed, the banknotes were not authorised for issue to the public and were supposedly destroyed in the late 1940s.

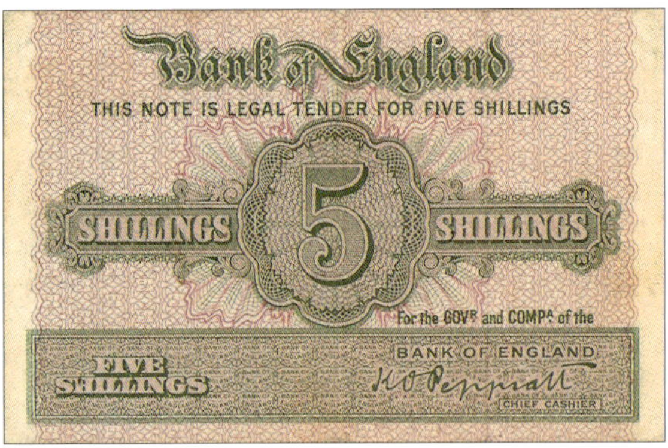

B253 5s Fractional

B253	**5s**	Unissued Olive-Green on Pale Pink			
		Quantity printed: 8 million	VG	F	VF
		Prefixes: None used	2000	3400	6000
B251s	**5s**	Cancelled			UNC
		Prefixes: None used			
		Perforated capitals once horizontally over signature		-	5000
B254	**2s6d**	Unissued Black on Pale Blue			
		Quantity printed: 6 million	VG	F	VF
		Prefixes: None used	2000	3400	6000

B254 2s6d Fractional

2s Essay © Bank of England

1s Essay © Bank of England

WHITE FIVE POUNDS 1945

Design and dimensions as for *B215 etc* C.P. Mahon, but a **Metal Thread** is now incorporated, heavier **Thick Paper** is used and a new prefix numbering system is brought in, the watermark shows five figures instead of four. The banknotes were printed in sheets of four, all straight edges, at St. Luke's Works, Old Street, London and were legal tender until 13th March 1961. Many banknotes have 1944 dates, although not issued until 1945. No banknotes printed in 1946.

B255 **£5** Black on White Thick Paper

Quantity printed: 39·8 million

Prefixes/Dates: (overlaps B264 L)

Prefix	Date		Prefix	Date	VF	EF	UNC
E01	2 Sep 1944 (first run)				350	750	1300
E02	4 Sep 1944	*to*	E99	27 Dec 1944	140	220	370
H01	28 Dec 1944	*to*	H99	23 Apr 1945			
J 01	24 Apr 1945	*to*	J99	16 Aug 1945	130	220	350
K01	17 Aug 1945	*to*	K99	10 Dec 1945			
L01	11 Dec 1945				180	300	450
L02	12 Dec 1945 (last run)				350	750	1300

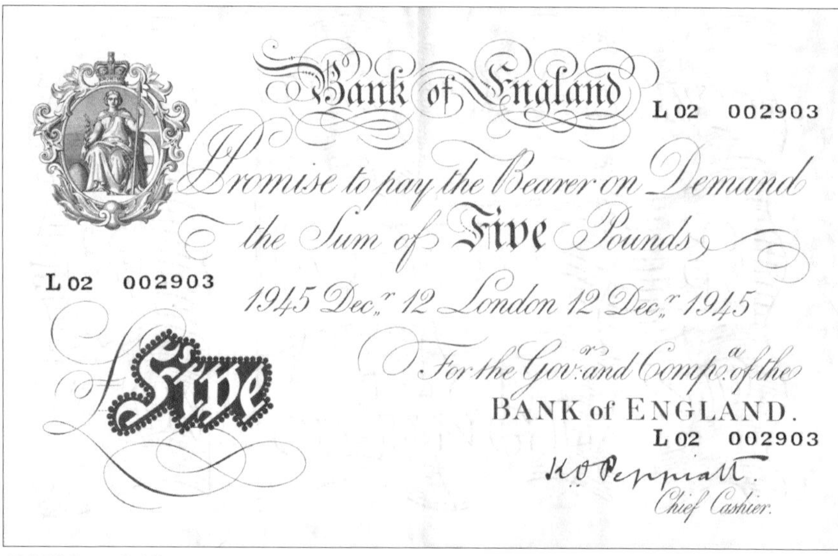

B255 Last L02

B255s **£5** Specimen Thick Paper

Prefix/Serial/Date: E00 000000 5 Dec 1944

Red solid capitals printed twice diagonally 750 1450 2400

THE STATES OF GUERNSEY OVERPRINTS

When the Germans occupied the Channel Islands in the Second World War, German money was made legal tender. As a result almost all British and Channel Islands currency '*disappeared under the floorboards*'. Because of the shortage of small change the Guernsey authorities obtained permission from the Germans in 1941 to issue small denominations 6d, 1s, 1s3d, 2s6d and 5s banknotes. The Germans agreed subject to the withdrawal of £5,000 worth of Guernsey £1's, by handing over soiled banknotes being held for destruction, but not before they had been overprinted front and reverse: **Withdrawn from Circulation......** When these emergency low denomination banknotes also began to run short, agreement was obtained for a further issue of £5,000 except that this time the Germans demanded that £5,000 of Bank of England £1's should be withdrawn. Again the banknotes were overprinted and after the liberation in 1945 £2,000 worth were discovered in Jersey and returned to the Bank of England. The balance of £3,000 came to light in 1980. Most of these were sold to collectors in the USA. They include the green unthreaded £1 signed by Mahon, Catterns and Peppiatt, also the blue wartime £1. The overprints in blue read:

Withdrawn from Circulation September 18th, 1941.	**Withdrawn from Circulation November 10th, 1941.**
Type A front	*Type B front & C reverse*

Type **A**	**September**	Full stop after year	- front only
Type **B**	**November**	Full stop after year	- front & reverse
Type **C**	**November**	Full stop after year	- reverse only

B226A Catterns Overprint

ONE POUND GUERNSEY OVERPRINTS 1941

Withdrawn from Circulation September 18th, 1941. *Type A*

					Recorded	VF	EF	UNC
B212A	Mahon	A--	*to*	H--	*48*	1600	2600	-
B225A	Catterns	H--	*to*	Z--	*69*	950	1600	-
B226A	Catterns	--A	*only*		*5*	6000	-	
B238A	Peppiatt	--B	*to*	--Z	*328*	400	800	-
B239A	Peppiatt	A--A	*to*	L--A	*1901*	250	450	550
B249A	Peppiatt (blue)	A--D	*&*	C--D	*126*	500	980	1400

Withdrawn from Circulation November 10th, 1941. *Types B & C*

B239B	Peppiatt	E03A	*only*	*80*	450	680	950
B239C	Peppiatt	E15A	*only*	*398*	270	460	700

Fake overprints on genuine banknotes are a problem. A complete listing of all genuine prefix/serials can be found on the:

London IBNS website: www.ibnslondon.org.uk

British Notes website: www.britishnotes.co.uk

B249A Peppiatt Overprint, C--D last prefix

THIRD PERIOD 1948

TEN SHILLINGS 17 June 1948

Continuation of the **Unthreaded** pre-war banknotes. This enabled the Bank of England to use up stockpiled banknotes and supplies of paper without the metal thread. The design, dimensions and watermark are the same as for *B210* C.P. Mahon banknotes. Printed at St. Luke's Works, London.

B256	**10s**	Red-Brown Unthreaded			
		Quantity printed: 70 million	VF	EF	UNC
		Prefixes: (overlaps B236 O & B262 L)			
	42O	(first run, traced from 300001)	260	600	850
	49O	(traced from 650001)	180	400	-
	--O	(traced to 70O 650000, 63O to 69 not printed)	70	140	270
	--L	(traced in 05 to 71)	75	150	280
	71L	(last run)	400	700	1100

B256 First 42O & Last 71L

B257 **10s** Replacement (none logged)

The existence of replacement banknotes for the post war unthreaded issue is problematical. It might be assumed that because the Bank had introduced specific replacements for the wartime issue, there would be a dedicated prefix. However, this has not been established until threaded green £1 banknotes were printed/issued.

ONE POUND 17 June 1948

Continuation of the **Unthreaded** pre-war banknotes. This enabled the Bank to use up stockpiled banknotes and supplies of paper without the metal thread. The design, dimensions and watermark were the same as for *B212* C.P. Mahon banknotes. Printed at St. Luke's Works, London.

			VF	EF	UNC
B258	**£1**	Green Unthreaded			
		Quantity printed: 147 million	VF	EF	UNC
		Prefixes: (overlaps B260 SA)			
	R01A	(first run)	110	220	400
	R--A S--A		18	45	70
	S48A	(last run)	100	220	360

B258 First R01A & Last S48A

B259 **£1** Replacement (none logged)

FOURTH PERIOD 1948 *to* 1949

ONE POUND 13 September 1948

It took little more than three months to use up the supply of pre-war unthreaded paper, whereupon the Bank reverted to the newer **Threaded** variety. The banknotes were printed at St. Luke's Works, London.

B260	**£1**	Green Threaded			
		Quantity printed: 1,185 million	VF	EF	UNC
		Prefixes: (overlaps B258 SA & links Beale B268 HB)			
	S39A	(first run)	550	-	
	S--A	(first series)	18	50	80
	T--A	U--A W--A X--A Y--A Z--A	10	22	40
	Z99A	(last run first series)	100	200	350
	A01B	(first run last series)	100	200	350
	A--B	B--B C--B D--B E--B	10	22	40
	H--B	(last series)	12	25	50
	H36B	(last run)	110	220	400

B260 First S39A

B260s	**£1**	Specimen Threaded			
		Prefix/Serial: R00 000000			
		Red thick solid capitals printed once diagonally	600	1300	1800
B261	**£1**	Replacement Threaded			
		Quantity printed: 9 million			
		Prefixes: (links Beale B269)			
	S01S	(first run)	280	500	850
	S--S		120	230	440
	S09S	(last run)	250	450	800

TEN SHILLINGS 25 October 1948

It took little more than four months to use up the supply of pre-war unthreaded paper, whereupon the Bank reverted to the newer **Threaded** variety. The banknotes were printed at St. Luke's Works, London.

			VF	EF	UNC
B262	**10s**	Red-Brown Threaded			
		Quantity printed: 415 million			
		Prefixes: (overlaps B256 L & links Beale B265 E)			
	71L	(first run)	380	700	1150
	-- L	(first series)	100	200	350
	-- K	--J --H	30	70	120
	-- E	(last series)	35	95	150
	91E	(last run)	320	620	950
B262s	**10s**	Specimen Threaded			
		Prefix/Serial: R00 000000			
		Black thick solid capitals printed once diagonally	600	1300	1800
B263	**10s**	Replacement Threaded			
		Quantity printed: 3 million			
		Prefixes: (links Beale B267)			
	01A	(first run)	800	1550	2200
	02A		500	1200	1800
	03A	(last run)	650	1300	-

B263 Replacements 01A - 02A - 03A

WHITE FIVE POUNDS 1948

Design, watermark and dimensions as for *B255* K.O. Peppiatt £5 banknotes of the Second Period, except that **Thin Paper** is used. All banknotes are dated 1947, though not issued until 1948. No banknotes were printed in 1948.

B264	**£5**	Black on White Thin Paper			
		Quantity printed: 16·8 million	VF	EF	UNC
		Prefixes: (links B255 L & Beale B270 M)			
	L03	1 Jan 1947 (first run)	350	750	1350
	L04	2 Jan 1947 *to* L99 24 Apr 1947	130	220	350
	M01	25 Apr 1947 *to* M70 15 Jul 1947			
	M71	16 Jul 1947 (last run)	230	450	720

B264 Last M71

B264s	**£5**	Specimen Thin Paper			
		Prefix/Serial/Date: L00 000000 24 Jan 1947			
		Red solid capitals printed twice diagonally	750	1450	2400

It is not obvious why the date chosen for specimens was later than the start date of the issued banknotes.

© Bank of England

PERCIVAL SPENCER BEALE
1949-1955

Percival Beale was born on 14th September 1906 and entered Bank service on 27th October 1924. He was the 21st Chief Cashier from 1st March 1949 to 16th January 1955, when he retired. Beale died on 4th February 1981 aged 75.

SERIES A BRITANNIA 1928 *to* 1962

TEN SHILLINGS 17 March 1950

Design, watermark and dimensions as for *B262* K.O. Peppiatt banknotes of the Fourth Period. Printed at St. Luke's Works, London.

			VF	EF	UNC
B265	**10s**	Red-Brown			
		Quantity printed: 305 million	VF	EF	UNC
		Prefixes: (links Peppiatt B262 E)			
	92E	(first run)	320	650	1100
	- - E	(first series)	90	170	300
	- - D	- - C	18	35	75
	- - B	(last series)	25	45	90
	99B	(last run)	320	600	-
B265s	**10s**	Specimen			
		Prefix/Serial: 00 000000			
		Black large solid capitals printed once diagonally	600	1300	1800

B266 **10s** Red-Brown

Quantity printed: 1,669 million

Prefixes:

		VF	EF	UNC
Z01Z	(first run)	220	500	850
Z--Z	(first series)	15	30	60
Y--Z X--Z W--Z U--Z T--Z S--Z R--Z O--Z N--Z M--Z L--Z K--Z J--Z H--Z E--Z		12	25	50
D--Z	(last series)	15	35	70
D85Z	(last run)	140	350	650

B266 First Z01Z

B267 **10s** Replacement

Quantity printed: 32 million

Prefixes: (links Peppiatt B263 & overlaps O'Brien B272)

		VF	EF	UNC
04A	(first run)	500	1100	-
--A		80	170	320
35A	(last run)	320	550	900

B267 First Replacement 04A

ONE POUND 17 March 1950

Design, watermark and dimensions as for *B260* K.O. Peppiatt threaded banknotes of the Fourth Period. Printed at St. Luke's Works, London.

			VF	EF	UNC
B268	**£1**	Green			
		Quantity printed: 4,284 million			
		Prefixes: (links Peppiatt B260 HB & O'Brien B273 LJ)			
	H37B	(first run)	170	300	520
	H--B	(first series)	10	24	45
	J--B	K--B L--B M--B N--B O--B R--B			
	S--B	T--B U--B W--B X--B Y--B Z--B	5	15	25
	Z99B	(last run first series)	50	130	260
	A01C	(first run sub series)	50	130	260
	A--C	B--C C--C D--C E--C H--C J--C			
	K--C	L--C M--C N--C O--C R--C S--C	5	15	25
	T--C	U--C W--C X--C Y--C Z--C			
	Z99C	(last run sub series)	50	130	260
	A01J	(first run last series)	50	130	260
	A--J	B--J C--J D--J E--J H--J J--J K--J	7	15	28
	L--J	(last series)	9	22	40
	L63J	(last run)	70	180	340

B268 Last L63J

B268s	**£1**	Specimen			
		Prefix/Serial: 00 000000	VF	EF	UNC
		Red large solid capitals printed once diagonally	600	1300	1800

B269	**£1**	Replacement			
		Quantity printed: 61 million			
		Prefixes: (links Peppiatt B261 & O'Brien B274)			
	S10S	(first run)	220	420	750
	S--S		20	45	85
	S70S	(last run)	180	400	680

B269 First Replacement S10S

B269 Last Replacement S70S

LONDON WHITE FIVE POUNDS 1 March 1949

Design, watermark and dimensions as for *B264* K.O. Peppiatt banknotes of the Fourth Period. Printed at St. Luke's Works, London.

B270 **£5** Black on White

Quantity printed: 108·8 million

Prefixes: (links Peppiatt B264 M & O'Brien B275 Y)

Prefix	From		To	Date	VF	EF	UNC
M72	1 Mar 1949 (first run)				320	750	-
M73	2 Mar 1949	*to*	M99	1 Apr 1949	120	180	350
N 01	2 Apr 1949	*to*	N99	27 Jul 1949			
O 01	28 Jul 1949	*to*	O99	19 Nov 1949			
P 01	21 Nov 1949	*to*	P99	15 Mar 1950			
R 01	16 Mar 1950	*to*	R99	10 Jul 1950			
S 01	11 Jul 1950	*to*	S99	2 Nov 1950			
T 01	3 Nov 1950	*to*	T99	27 Feb 1951	110	160	330
U 01	28 Feb 1951	*to*	U99	23 Jun 1951			
V 01	25 Jun 1951	*to*	V99	17 Oct 1951			
W01	18 Oct 1951	*to*	W99	11 Feb 1952			
X 01	12 Feb 1952	*to*	X99	6 Jun 1952			
Y 01	7 Jun 1952	*to*	Y69	26 Aug 1952	120	180	350
Y 70	27 Aug 1952 (last run)				350	800	-

B270 Last Y70

B270s **£5** Specimen

Prefix/Serial/Date: M00 000000 1 March 1949

Red solid capitals printed twice diagonally 750 1650 2400

SERIES B HELMETED BRITANNIA 1957 *to* 1967

By the time Percival Beale took on the job of Chief Cashier, the Series A banknotes had been circulating for twenty two years. However, it should not be thought that the Bank of England were not interested in replacing the 1928 issue. In June 1931, the Bank began discussions for a new series of banknotes with three designers George Kruger Gray (who had designed the modified head coinage of 1927), Frederick Griggs and Stephen Gooden. Kruger Gray and Griggs soon dropped out, leaving Gooden toying with various different ideas, including a William and Mary portrait, St. George and the Dragon and a bareheaded Britannia holding a spear. The design which found favour with the Court of Directors in December 1933 featured Sir John Houblon, the first Governor of the Bank (who finally turned up on the £50 banknote sixty years later). The essays of the 'Houblon' series reached the proof stage in April 1936, but as the war clouds darkened it was deemed prudent to keep them in reserve.

After the war the Bank still intended to go into production, possibly designating them as a belated 250th anniversary issue and a target date was tentatively set for September 1949, by which time Beale had taken over from Peppiatt as Chief Cashier. It is Beale's signature that appears on essays of the 10s, £1 and £5, which are in the Bank's archives. Yet again the project faltered for a variety of reasons not least because Beale didn't like them. Meanwhile Gooden who had already been asked to design a £2 Houblon (see page 150/1), refused to consider different portraits for his notes. Instead, in 1950, he agreed to start again on a proposal for a new series based on Britannia. Despite ill health Gooden succeeded in completing his task, but in the event only the £5 (B277 / B280) was issued, with the signature of Beale's successor, L.K. O'Brien.

Sadly Gooden himself did not live to see the issue of the £5 in February 1957. The banknote was already in production when it was announced in July 1956 that The Queen had consented to her portrait appearing on Bank of England banknotes. As a result plans to bring in Series B 10s and £1 (B278 / B279) were shelved, and Gooden's successor, Robert Austin, set to work on Series C Portrait banknotes. For further information read 'In Search of Stephen Gooden' by John Deacon in 'The Old Lady' of Threadneedle Street' September 1980. Also 'The Search for the Inimitable Note' by Clive Goodacre in the 'Penrose' 1982 Vol 74 page 195, the international review of graphic arts.

© Bank of England

LESLIE
KENNETH O'BRIEN
1955-1962

Leslie O'Brien was born on 8th February 1908, he was educated at Wandsworth School, and entered Bank service in 1927. He was private secretary to the Governor for two years which included the last year of Lord Norman's term and the first year of Lord Catto. O'Brien was appointed Deputy Chief Cashier in 1951 and was the 22nd Chief Cashier from 17th January 1955 to 28th February 1962. He became an Executive Director in 1962 and Deputy Governor from 1964-66. His term as Governor lasted from 1966-73 and he was the first member of the Bank's ordinary staff to attain this top position. O'Brien was knighted in 1967 and became Lord O'Brien of Lothbury in 1973. He died on 24th November 1995, aged 87.

SERIES A BRITANNIA 1928 *to* 1962

TEN SHILLINGS 21 November 1955

Design, watermark and dimensions as for *B262* K.O. Peppiatt post-war banknotes of the Fourth Period. Printed at St. Luke's Works, London.

			VF	EF	UNC
B271	**10s**	Red-Brown			
		Quantity printed: 2,415 million	VF	EF	UNC
		Prefixes: (links Beale B266 DZ)			
	D86Z	(first run)	130	250	450
	D--Z	(first series)	20	50	120
		C--Z B--Z A--Z	12	25	50
	A99Z	(last run first series)	50	110	230
	Z01Y	(first run sub series)	50	110	230
	Z--Y	Y--Y X--Y W--Y U--Y T--Y S--Y			
	R--Y	O--Y N--Y M--Y L--Y K--Y J--Y	6	15	35
	H--Y	E--Y D--Y C--Y B--Y A--Y			
	A99Y	(last run sub series)	50	110	230
	Z01X	(first run last series)	50	110	230
	Z--X	Y--X	12	25	50
	Y25X	(last run)	95	200	400

B271 Last Y25X

			VF	EF	UNC
B271s	**10s**	Specimen			
		Prefix/Serial: A00A 000000			
		Type 1: Black solid capitals printed twice diagonally	650	1450	2000
		Type 2: A00A 123456/567890 (in Bank's archive)			

			VF	EF	UNC
B272	**10s**	Replacement			
		Quantity printed: 35 million			
		Prefixes: (overlaps Beale B267)			
	35A	(first run)	220	490	700
	--A		55	110	230
	69A	(last run)	220	450	-

ONE POUND 21 November 1955

Design, watermark and dimensions as for *B260* K.O. Peppiatt banknotes of the Fourth Period. Printed at St. Luke's Works, London.

			VF	EF	UNC
B273	**£1**	Green			
		Quantity printed: 3,811 million	VF	EF	UNC
		Prefixes: (links Beale B268 LJ)			
	L64J	(first run)	95	200	350
	L--J	M--J N--J O--J R--J S--J			
	T--J	U--J W--J X--J Y--J Z--J	6	12	20
	Z99J	(last run first series)	30	90	200
	A01K	(first run sub series)	30	90	200
	A--K	B--K C--K D--K E--K H--K J--K			
	K--K	L--K M--K N--K O--K R--K S--K	6	12	20
	T--K	U--K W--K X--K Y--K Z--K			
	Z99K	(last run sub series)	30	90	200
	A01L	(first run last series)	40	100	200
	A--L	B--L C--L D--L E--L H--L J--L	6	12	25
	K--L	(last series)	16	30	65
	K13L	(last run)	140	300	480

B273 A01L Mid first

			VF	EF	UNC
B273s	**£1**	Specimen			
		Prefix/Serial: A00A 000000			
		Type 1: Black solid capitals printed twice diagonally	650	1450	2000
		Type 2: A00A 123456/567890 (in Bank's archive)			

			VF	EF	UNC
B274	**£1**	Replacement *Quantity printed:* 52 million *Prefixes:* (links Beale B269 SS)			
	S71S	(first run)	120	250	450
	S--S		25	50	80
	S99S		100	180	300
	S01T		110	200	400
	S--T		35	60	90
	S23T	(last run, four logged)	-	Rare	-

B274 First Replacement S71S

B274 Last Replacement S23T

LONDON WHITE FIVE POUNDS 17 January 1955

Design, watermark and dimensions as for *B264* K.O. Peppiatt banknotes of the Fourth Period. Printed at St. Luke's Works, London.

B275	**£5**	Black on White			
		Quantity printed: 12·8 million	VF	EF	UNC
		Prefixes/Dates: (links Beale B270 Y)			
	Y71	17 Jan 1955 (first run)	500	1000	1500
	Y72	18 Jan 1955 *to* Y99 18 Feb 1955	120	210	330
	Z01	19 Feb 1955 *to* Z98 14 Jun 1955			
	Z99	15 Jun 1955 (last run)	320	750	1300

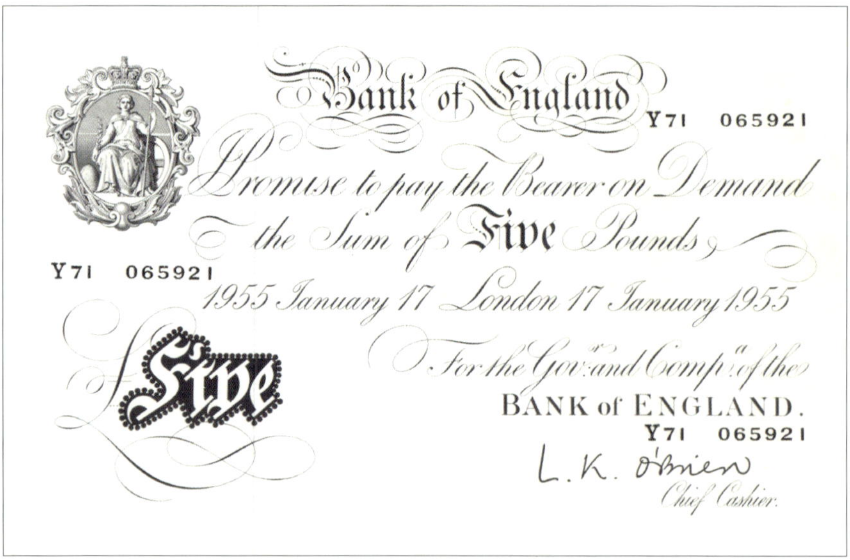

B275 First Y71

B275s	**£5**	Specimen			
		Prefix/Serial/Date: Y71 000000 17 January 1955			
		Red solid capitals printed twice diagonally	750	1450	2400

B276 **£5** Black on White

Quantity printed: 39·6 million

Prefixes/Dates:

Prefix	Date			Prefix	Date	VF	EF	UNC
A01A	16 Jun 1955	(first run)				550	1200	1800
A02A	17 Jun 1955		*to*	A99A	8 Oct 1955	120	210	360
B01A	10 Oct 1955		*to*	B99A	1 Feb 1956	110	170	350
C01A	2 Feb 1956		*to*	C99A	28 May 1956			
D01A	29 May 1956		*to*	D98A	19 Sep 1956	120	210	360
D99A	20 Sep 1956	(last run)				700	1300	2000

Prefixes E01A to E68A were printed, after 20th September 1956, but not issued. White banknotes with metal threads were legal tender until 13th March 1961.

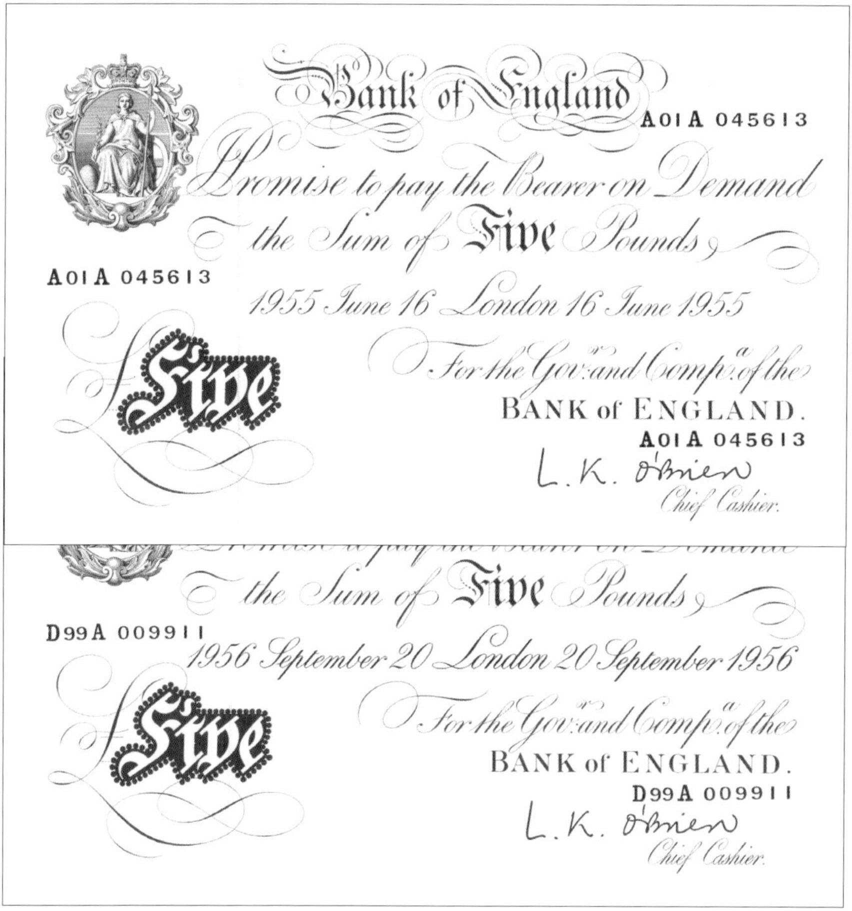

B276 First A01A & Last D99A

SERIES B HELMETED BRITANNIA 1957 *to* 1967

FIVE POUNDS 21 February 1957

Designed by Stephen Gooden R.A. featuring on the front the helmeted head of Britannia, St. George and the Dragon and on the reverse a lion holding a key and chain, also two dark blue **£5 Shaded Symbols**. Plate-printed in sheets of 21 (3 x 7) with watermark incorporating the helmeted head of Britannia. The banknotes measure 159 x 75mm and were legal tender until 27th June 1967. According to the Bank, a total of 649 million Series B £5 banknotes were issued, but this is not necessarily the same as the number printed or that they all went into circulation. Quantities printed have been revised on the basis of 960,000 banknotes per prefix (not 1,000,000).

			VF	EF	UNC
B277	**£5**	Blue Shaded Symbols reverse			
		Quantity printed: 415·68 million	VF	EF	UNC
		Prefixes:			
	A01	(first run)	160	300	550
	A--	(first series)	25	60	105
	B--	C-- D--	22	45	90
	E--	(last series)	30	65	110
	E37	(last run)	350	750	-

B277 First low serial

B277s	**£5**	Specimen Shaded Symbols reverse			
		Prefix/Serial: A00 000000			
		Red cameo capitals printed twice diagonally & perforated capitals horizontally	750	1450	2000

B277 Lion & Key, Shaded Symbols *reverse*

B277 **£5** Shaded Symbol reverse

B280 £5 White Symbol reverse

B278 **£1** Essay Blue & Lilac
Prefix/Serial: A01Z 234567
Beale signature Unissued design

£1 Gooden Essay © Bank of England

B279 **10s** Essay Purple & Orange
Prefix/Serial: A01Z 234567
Beale signature Unissued design

10s Gooden Essay © Bank of England

FIVE POUNDS 12 July 1961

Design, watermark and dimensions as *B277*. Reverse printed in offset-lithography, with the £5 symbols in outline only (£5 **White Symbols**) instead of shaded, at the Bank of England Works, Debden, Essex.

B280 First H01

			VF	EF	UNC
B280	**£5**	Blue White Symbols reverse			
		Quantity printed: 232·5 million	VF	EF	UNC
		Prefixes:			
	H01	(first run)	410	850	1300
	H--	(first series)	25	55	100
	J --	K--	22	45	90
	K45	(last run, to 165000)	300	500	780

B280 Lion & Key White, Symbols *reverse*

			VF	EF	UNC
B280s	**£5**	Specimen White Symbols reverse			
		Prefix/Serial: A00 000000			
		Red solid capitals printed twice diagonally	750	1450	2000

SERIES C PORTRAIT 1960 to 1979

In July 1956 it was announced that H.M. The Queen had agreed to her portrait being included on a new series of banknotes. Stephen Gooden had died on 21st September 1955 and the designs for Series C, known to collectors as the Portrait series were undertaken by Robert Austin R.A. Professor of Engraving at the Royal College of and President of both the Royal Society of Painters in Water-Colours and the Royal Society of Painter-Etchers and Engravers. On 19th November 1959 the Bank announced that the new banknotes would be ready early in 1960 and on 17th March that year the £1 appeared, followed some eighteen months later by the 10s. Then in 1963 came the £5 and the £10 in 1964. These last two were the work of Reynolds Stone who was retained by the Bank from 1959, and on the £5 banknote he used his daughter as the model for the child Britannia on the reverse. A £2 banknote was also designed by Professor Austin, and reached the production stage but was never issued.

£2 Austin's unissued design © Bank of England

Up to 1960 all banknotes were printed on sheet-fed presses by the intaglio process (recess or line-engraved). Sheets of paper were fed one at a time into the machines; the sheets were then stacked and stored so the ink could dry before the next stage of printing was undertaken. All this took several weeks and was clearly unsustainable at a time when the banknote issue had jumped from 939 million in 1950 to 1,627 million by 1960. The peak year was 1965, partly due to the new £5 and £10 issues, when it reached 2,222 million. 99 million banknotes per prefix.

£2 Reverse design © Bank of England

Back in 1951, the Bank had purchased a green field site for a new printing works at Debden in Essex. When it became fully operational a team of engineers assembled to develop a machine which would print and number banknotes in a single process from a reel (or web) of paper into sheets of finished banknotes. A prototype was built by Masson, Scott Thrissell Engineering Ltd, of Bristol, and the first run, the so called **R** notes B283, appeared in 1960 with O'Brien's signature. In 1962 another web press built by the West German company Goebel Darmstad was installed and Hollom and Fforde banknotes from this machine can be identified by a small capital **G** appearing on the reverse. A few years later the Bank opted for MST machines, six of which were installed by the mid 1970s and which continued in use until 1993. According to official figures, a total of 3,759 million Series C 10s and 20,350 million £1 banknotes were issued. Unnoficial estimates for quantities printed have been revised on the basis of 960,000 banknotes per prefix until 1970, and one million thereafter.

ONE POUND 17 March 1960

Designed by Robert Austin R.A. featuring the Queen's portrait on the front in a complex blend of machine-engraved geometric patterns and on the reverse the figure of Britannia seated. Plate-printed in sheets of 24 (3 x 8) at the Bank of England Works, Debden, Essex, on banknote paper manufactured by Portals Ltd., with watermark of continuous laureate heads running vertically on the left. The banknotes measure 151 x 72mm, highest serial is 960000, ceasing to be legal tender after 31st May 1979.

B281 **£1** Green

Quantity printed: 1,711 million

Prefixes:

Prefix		VF	EF	UNC
A01	(first run)	100	240	400
A--	(first series)	5	10	18
B-- C-- D-- E-- H-- J-- K-- L-- N-- R-- S-- T-- U-- W-- X-- Y--		2	4	8
Z--	(last series)	3	7	14
Z99	(last run)	130	300	-

B281 First low serial A01

B281 Britannia in circle surrounded by engine turning *reverse*

B281s	**£1**	Specimen			
		Prefix/Serial: A00 000000	VF	EF	UNC
		Red solid capitals printed twice diagonally	850	-	

B281s Specimen

B282	**£1**	Green			
		Quantity printed: 1,711 million			
		Prefixes:			
	01A	(first run)	120	250	450
	--A	(first series)	5	10	18
	--B --C --D --E --H --J --K --L --N --R --S --T --U --W --X --Y		2	4	8
	--Z	(last series)	3	7	14
	99Z	(last run)	160	350	-

B282 01A First

			F	VF	EF
B283	**£1**	Experimental Issue **R** reverse Green			
		Quantity printed: 3 million	F	VF	EF
		Prefixes: (links Hollom B292)			
	A01N	(first run)	125	250	500
	A05N		140	270	550
	A06N	(last run)	140	270	550

B283 First A01N

These experimental £1 banknotes were produced in sheets of 21 (3 x 7) on a reel-fed press, developed by Masson, Scott, Thrissell Engineering Ltd. of Bristol. To identify them from other banknotes in circulation they had a small capital letter **R** (standing for 'research') on the reverse. A01N low serial banknotes have the original long legged R. Subsequently one leg of the R shortened, then both legs shortened R, thus B283 (A01N, A05N and A06N) can be found with a progressively stubbier R. It is believed that A02N, A03N and A04N were not printed.

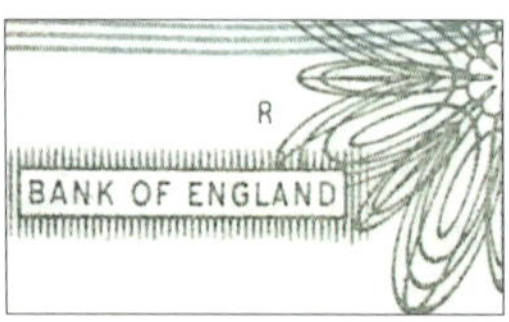

A01N low serial

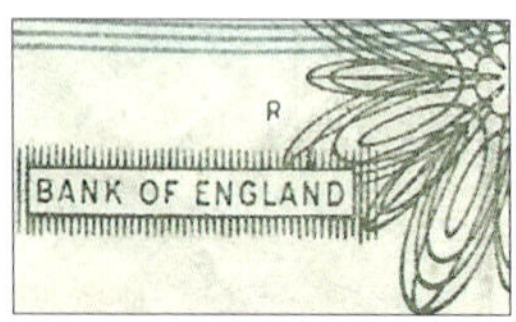

A01N high serial

A05N

A06N

Trials on pink paper with A00N & A01N prefix, 011341/50 serials: From £400 AUNC

			VF	EF	UNC
B284	**£1**	Green			
		Quantity printed: 73 million			
		Prefixes: (links Hollom B288)			
	B01N	(first run)	150	320	-
	B--N		7	16	30
	B76N	(last run)	110	260	450

B284 First B01N

			VF	EF	UNC
B285	**£1**	Replacement			
		Quantity printed: under 65 million			
		Prefixes: (overlaps Hollom B289)			
	M01	(first run)	120	260	500
	M--		8	18	40
	M68	(last run)	180	350	-

B285 First Replacement M01

TEN SHILLINGS 12 October 1961

Designed by Robert Austin R.A. featuring the Queen's portrait on the front in a complex blend of machine-engraved geometric patterns, and on the reverse the figure of Britannia seated. Plate-printed in sheets of 24 (3 x 8) at the Bank of England Works, Debden, on banknote paper manufactured by Portals Ltd., with watermark of continuous laureate heads running vertically on the left. The banknotes measure 140 x 67mm, highest serial is 960000, ceasing to be legal tender after 22nd November 1970.

B286	**10s**	Red-Brown			
		Quantity printed: 727 million	VF	EF	UNC
		Prefixes: (links Hollom B294 K)			
	A01	(first run)	100	220	350
	A--	(first series)	4	8	14
	B--	C-- D-- E-- H-- J--	2	4	9
	K--	(last series)	5	10	22
	K64	(last run)	100	200	350

B286 First A01

B286 Britannia in circle surrounded by engine turning *reverse*

B286s	**10s**	Specimen			
		Prefix/Serial: A00 000000	VF	EF	UNC
		Type 1: Black cameo capitals printed twice diagonally	600	1300	1800
		Type 2: As type 1 but solid capitals (in Bank's archive)			
		Type 3: As type 1 but no overprint (in Bank's archive)			

B286s Specimen

B287	**10s**	Replacement			
		Quantity printed: 17 million			
		Prefixes: (links Hollom B296)			
	M01	(first run)	100	230	440
	M--		25	60	120
	M18	(last run)	150	280	-

B287 Last Replacement M18

© Bank of England

JASPER QUINTUS HOLLOM
1962-1966

Jasper Hollom was born on 16th December 1917, Quintus 5th son. He took his first job as an insurance clerk at the age of seventeen. He entered Bank service in 1936. During the war he served in the infantry in the Middle East and the Western Desert but was captured in 1942 and sent to a prisoner of war camp in Italy. Hollom rejoined the Bank after the war and worked as assistant to O'Brien. In 1956 he was made Deputy Chief Cashier and the 23rd Chief Cashier from 1st March 1962 to 30th June 1966. He was appointed to the Court of Directors in 1966 and succeeded Sir Maurice Parsons as Deputy Governor in March 1970, a position he held until 1980. He was knighted in 1975. Sir Jasper Quintus Hollom retired on 29th February 1984 after serving a further four years as a non-executive Director. He died on 29th August 2014.

SERIES C PORTRAIT 1960 *to* 1979

ONE POUND 27 February 1963

Design, watermark and dimensions as for *B281* L.K. O'Brien Series C banknotes. Plate-printed at the Bank of England Works, Debden, Essex. B292 and B293 carry a small capital letter **G** on the reverse indicating that they were printed on an experimental German Goebel printing press.

G on reverse

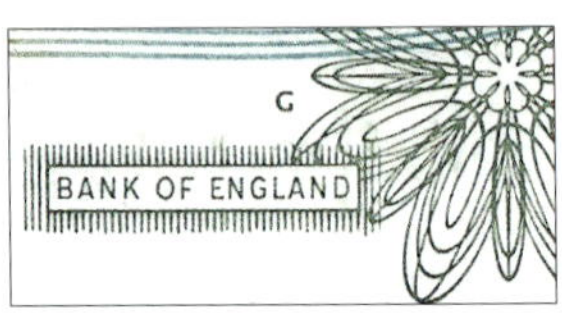

B288 **£1** Green (gaps (**) see B292)

Quantity printed: 5,544 million

Prefixes: (links O'Brien B284 BN & Fforde B301 BY)

									VF	EF	UNC
B77N	(first run)								150	300	550
B--N	(first series)								20	45	80
**		C--N	D--N	E--N	H--N	J--N	K--N	L--N			
A--R	B--R	C--R	D--R	E--R	H--R	J--R	K--R	L--R			
A--S	B--S	C--S	D--S	E--S	H--S	J--S	K--S	L--S			
	B--T	C--T	**	E--T	H--T	J--T	K--T	L--T			
A--U	B--U	C--U	D--U	E--U	H--U	J--U	K--U	L--U	2	4	8
A--W	B--W	**	D--W	E--W	H--W	J--W	K--W	L--W			
A--X	B--X	C--X	D--X	E--X	H--X	J--X	K--X	**			
A--Y											
B--Y	(last series)								20	50	100
B10Y	(last run)								100	230	400

There is some doubt whether the A--T prefix was issued as no examples have been recorded. Bank of England records state: 'reserved for Thrissell'

B288 The First B77N 000001

B288s **£1** Specimen

Prefix/Serial: A00 000000

	VF	EF	UNC
Red solid capitals printed twice diagonally	600	1300	1800

B289 **£1** Replacement

Quantity printed: 30 million

Prefixes: (overlaps O'Brien B285)

		VF	EF	UNC
M68	(first run)	55	120	350
M--		16	30	50
M99	(last run)	75	150	380

B290 **£1** Replacement

		VF	EF	UNC
	Quantity printed: 95 million			
	Prefixes:			
01M	(first run)	120	270	500
--M		12	22	40
99M	(last run)	100	200	420

B291 **£1** Replacement

Quantity printed: 7·68 million

Prefixes: (links Fforde B302)

M01R	(first run)	120	270	500
M--R		45	100	200
M08R	(last run)	110	300	550

B291 First Replacement M01R

B292 **£1** Green **G** reverse

Quantity printed: 310 million

Prefixes: (overlaps O'Brien B283 AN)

A09N	(first run)	140	350	650
A--N	(first series)	5	12	25
C--W	D--T	3	8	18
L--X	(last series)	5	12	25
L34X	(last run, should go higher)	65	140	270

B293 **£1** Replacement **G** reverse

Quantity printed: 26·88 million

Prefixes: (links Fforde B304)

M01N	(first run)	130	320	500
M--N		20	35	80
M28N	(last run)	140	320	550

TEN SHILLINGS 4 April 1963

Design, watermark and dimensions as for L.K. O'Brien Series C banknotes. Printed at the Bank of England Works, Debden, Essex.

			VF	EF	UNC
B294	**10s**	Red-Brown			
		Quantity printed: 984 million	VF	EF	UNC
		Prefixes: (links O'Brien B286 K)			
	K65	(first run)	80	180	360
	K--	(first series)	4	10	22
	L-- N-- R-- S-- T-- U-- W-- X-- Y-- Z--		2	4	8
	Z99	(last run)	70	150	300

B294 The First K65 000001

			VF	EF	UNC
B294s	**10s**	Specimen			
		Prefix/Serial: A00 000000			
		Black cameo capitals printed twice diagonally	600	1300	1800

			VF	EF	UNC
B295	**10s**	Red-Brown			
		Quantity printed: 974 million			
		Prefixes: (overlaps Fforde B309 R)			
	01A	(first run)	95	190	380
	--A --B --C --D --E --H --J --K --L --N		2	4	8
	--R	(last series)	6	12	25
	25R	(last run)	100	250	-

26R excluded until such time as one emerges, B309 26R lowest serial logged 152727.

			VF	EF	UNC
B296	**10s**	Replacement			
		Quantity printed: 35·5 million			
		Prefixes: (links O'Brien B287 & Fforde B311)			
	M19	(first run)	100	230	380
	M--		12	28	70
	M55	(last run)	110	250	380

FIVE POUNDS 21 February 1963

Designed by Reynolds Stone CBE, RDI. Portrait Series C banknotes featuring the Queen's portrait on the front and the figure of a child Britannia on the reverse, modelled by the artist's daughter. Plate-printed in sheets of 18 (3 x 6) at the Bank of England Works, Debden, Essex, on banknote paper manufactured by Portals Ltd., with watermark of continuous laureate head. The banknotes measure 140 x 85mm, highest serial 960000 upto 1970 and were legal tender until 31st August 1973. 2,200 million Series C £5 banknotes were issued.

B297 **£5** Blue

Quantity printed: 968·5 million

Prefixes: (links Fforde B312 R)

		VF	EF	UNC
A01	(first run)	85	150	220
A-- B-- C-- D-- E-- H-- J-- K-- L-- N--		12	25	60
R--	(last series)	20	50	90
R19	(last run)	170	350	600

B297 First A01 low serial

B297s **£5** Specimen

Prefix/Serial: A00 000000

	VF	EF	UNC
Red solid capitals printed twice diagonally	600	1300	1800

B297 Figure of a child Britannia *reverse*

B298	**£5**	Replacement			
		Quantity printed: under 9 million	VF	EF	UNC
		Prefixes: (overlaps Fforde B313)			
	M01	(first run)	280	500	750
	M--	(not all prefixes issued)	120	230	380
	M14	(last run)	300	550	-

B298 First Replacement M01

TEN POUNDS 21 February 1964

Designed by Reynolds Stone CBE, RDI. Portrait C Series, featuring the Queen's portrait on the front together with a figure of Britannia seated; and on the reverse a lion holding a double sided key in its paw with the words Ten Pounds in a scroll issuing from its mouth. Plate-printed in sheets of 15 (3 x 5) at the Bank of England Works, Debden, Essex, on banknote paper manufactured by Portals Ltd., with watermark of the Queen's head. The banknotes measure 150 x 93mm, highest serial 960000 upto 1970 and were legal tender until 31st May 1979. 250 million Series C £10 banknotes were issued. Thus we conclude that blocks of numbers were not used within the given prefixes.

B299	**£10**	Brown			
		Quantity printed: 38·4 million	VF	EF	UNC
		Prefixes: (links Fforde B316)			
	A01	(first run)	40	85	160
	A--		18	35	70
	A40	(last run)	50	110	200

B299 First A01 & Last A40

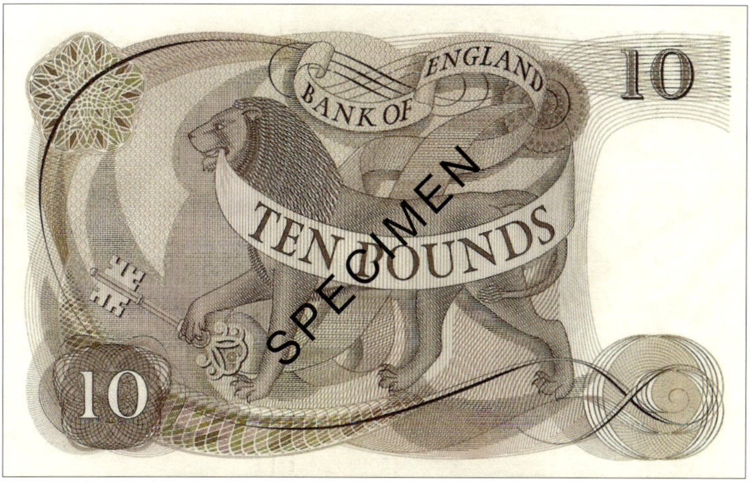

B299 Lion holding a double sided key in its paw *reverse*

B299s	**£10**	Specimen			
		Prefix/Serial: A00 000000	VF	EF	UNC
		Red solid capitals printed twice diagonally	600	1300	1800

B299s Specimen

B300 Previously allocated to a £10 presentation folder. See page 371

© Bank of England

JOHN
STANDISH FFORDE
1966-1970

John Fforde was born on 16th November 1921. He was educated at Rossall School and Christ Church College, Oxford. After serving as a pilot in the RAF during the war he returned to Oxford where he became a Fellow of Nuffield College. Fforde entered Bank service in 1957 and spent four years as Deputy Head of the Central Banking Information Department. In 1964 he became Advisor to the Governor and was appointed the 24th Chief Cashier on 1st July 1966 a position he held to 28th February 1970. He was an Executive Director from 1970-82 and was again Advisor to the Governor from 1982-84. He died on the 19th April 2000.

SERIES C PORTRAIT 1960 *to* 1979

ONE POUND 15 February 1967

Design, watermark and dimensions as for *B281* L.K. O'Brien Portrait Series C banknotes. Plate printed at the Bank of England Works, Debden, Essex. Banknotes B303, B304, B307 and B308 carry a small capital letter **G** on the reverse indicating that they were printed on an experimental German Goebel printing press in sheets of 21 (3 x 7). By 1968 the existing prefix combinations from A--N to L--Z B301 had been exhausted so the Bank reversed the process and restarted the sequence at N--A B305 through to J.B. Page Z--L B320.

When banknote production was switched from Fforde to Page, there were not enough signature blocks available, so Fforde banknotes continued to be produced concurrently with Page for well over a year. **Signature Sequence Pair** prefixes have been logged, sixty-two on £1 B305p / B306p, seventeen on £5 B314p / B315p and three pairs on £10 B316p. See page 370.

B301 **£1** Green (gaps/links (**) B303)

Quantity printed: 1,416 million

Prefixes: (links Hollom B288 BY)

Prefix		VF	EF	UNC
B11Y	(first run)	140	300	650
B--Y	(first series)	12	30	55
	C--Y D--Y ** H--Y J--Y K--Y L--Y A--Z B--Z C--Z D--Z E--Z H--Z J--Z **	2	5	12
L--Z	(last series)	5	12	32
L99Z	(last run)	100	300	500

B301 First B11Y

B301s **£1** Specimen

Prefix/Serial: A00 000000

	VF	EF	UNC
Red solid capitals printed twice diagonally	600	1300	1800

B302 **£1** Replacement

Quantity printed: 40 million

Prefixes: (links Hollom B291)

Prefix		VF	EF	UNC
M09R	(first run)	160	340	550
M--R		25	60	110
M50R	(last run)	110	250	450

B303 **£1** Green **G** reverse (gaps/links B301)

Quantity printed: 190 million

Prefixes:

Prefix		VF	EF	UNC
E01Y	(first run)	65	180	300
E--Y	K--Z	4	8	15
K99Z	(last run)	65	180	300

B304 **£1** Replacement **G** reverse

Quantity printed: 13·5 million

Prefixes: (links Hollom B293)

		VF	EF	UNC
M29N	(first run)	120	230	420
M--N		25	60	110
M42N	(last run)	90	180	400

B305 **£1** Green (gaps/links (**) B307 & Page B320)

Quantity printed: 4,398 million

Prefixes: (overlaps Page B320 x18)

									VF	EF	UNC
N01A	(first run)								-	Rare	-
N--A	(first series)								25	70	120
	N--B	N--C	N--D	N--E	N--H	N--J	N--K	N--L			
R--A	**	R--C	R--D	R--E	R--H	R--J	R--K	**			
S--A	S--B	S--C	S--D	S--E	S--H	S--J	S--K	S--L			
T--A	T--B	T--C	T--D	T--E	T--H	T--J	T--K	T--L	2	4	8
U--A	U--B	U--C	U--D	**	U--H						
W--A	W--B	W--C	W--D								
**	X--B										
X--C	(last series)								12	30	45
X42C	(last run)								200	450	-

B305 Last X42C

B305p **£1** Signature Sequence Pair

		VF	EF	UNC
	Pair with consecutive serials	-	340	650

Banknotes with signature of J.S. Fforde B305 were issued concurrently with those of J.B. Page B320. Sixty-two different prefixes in S--L to X--C have been logged for B305p. For more details see page 370.

B306	**£1**	Replacement			
		Quantity printed: 96 million	VF	EF	UNC
		Prefixes: (links B308 TM & overlaps Page B321 RM SM)			
	R01M	(first run)	110	350	600
	R--M		5	14	30
	R54M		70	160	400
	S01M		100	280	500
	S--M		4	12	25
	S78M	(logged in Signature Sequence Pair)		-	650
	T01M		160	400	600
	T--M		90	220	400
	T04M		160	450	600
	U01M	(only - last run)	260	550	900

B306 First R01M & Last U01M

B306p	**£1**	Replacement Signature Sequence Pair		
		Pair with consecutive serials	360	750

Banknotes with signature of J.S. Fforde B306 were issued concurrently with those of J.B. Page B321. Thirteen prefixes in R--M and S--M have been logged.

B307	**£1**	Green **G** reverse (gaps/links B305 & Page B320)			
		Quantity printed: 224 million	VF	EF	UNC
		Prefixes:			
	R01B	(first run)	140	220	450
	R--B		3	6	16
	R99B		40	85	200
	R01L		45	90	180
	R--L		3	6	16
	R99L		40	85	200
	U01E		50	110	250
	U--E	(traced to 29)	4	8	20
	U45E	(last run)	170	380	-

B307 First R01B

B307 Last U45E

B308 **£1** Replacement **G** reverse

		VF	EF	UNC
	Quantity printed: 14·64 million			
	Prefixes: (links B306 TM)			
N01M	(first run)	150	330	540
N--M		20	45	90
N14M		65	160	270
T29M		55	110	220
T--M		60	120	240
T32M	(last run)	160	350	-

B308 First Replacement N01M

B308 Last Replacement T32M

TEN SHILLINGS 15 February 1967

Design, watermark and dimensions as for *B286* L.K. O'Brien Series C portrait banknotes. Printed at the Bank of England Works, Debden, Essex.

B309	**10s**	Red-Brown			
		Quantity printed: 736 million	VF	EF	UNC
		Prefixes: (links Hollom B295 R)			
	26R	(first run)	150	280	550
	--R	(first series)	4	8	15
	--S	--T --U --W --X --Y --Z	2	4	8
	99Z	(last run)	90	180	380

B309 First 26R

B309 Last 99Z

B309s	**10s**	Specimen			
		Prefix/Serial: A00 000000			
		Black solid capitals printed twice diagonally	600	1300	1800

B310	**10s**	Red-Brown			
		Quantity printed: 322 million	VF	EF	UNC
		Prefixes:			
	A01N	(first run)	65	110	220
	A--N	B--N C--N	2	4	8
	D--N	(last series)	4	7	12
	D38N	(last run)	20	40	80

Bank records show the last prefix printed as D57N (in Bank's museum), but nothing higher than D38N has come to light in private hands.

B310 First A01N

B311	**10s**	Replacement			
		Quantity printed: 24 million			
		Prefixes: (links Hollom B296)			
	M56	(first run)	75	170	320
	M--		4	8	14
	M80	(last run)	12	25	50

B311 First Replacement M56

FIVE POUNDS 9 January 1967

Design, watermark and dimensions as for *B297* J.Q. Hollom banknotes. Printed at the Bank of England Works, Debden, Essex.

B312	**£5**	Blue			
		Quantity printed: 742 million	VF	EF	UNC
		Prefixes: (links Hollom B297 R)			
	R20	(first run)	160	310	520
	R--	(first series)	14	32	70
	S--	T-- U-- W-- X-- Y-- Z--	12	25	60
	Z99	(last run)	100	250	400

B312 Last Z99

B312s	**£5**	Specimen			
		Prefix/Serial: A00 000000			
		Red solid capitals printed twice diagonally	600	1300	1800

B313	**£5**	Replacement			
		Quantity printed: 19 million			
		Prefixes: (overlaps Hollom B298)			
	M08	(first run)	120	300	550
	M--		100	250	450
	M28	(last run)	120	300	550

B314	**£5**	Blue			
		Quantity printed: 285 million	VF	EF	UNC
		Prefixes: (overlaps Page B324 C D E H)			
	01A	(first run)	140	320	560
	--A	--B --C --D --E --H	12	25	60
	--L	(last series)	65	130	240
	40L	(last run)	180	400	650

Prefixes J and K may have been printed but were probably never issued as none have come to light.

B314p	**£5**	Signature Sequence Pair			
		Pair with consecutive serials (D E H)	-	550	950

Banknotes with signature of J.S. Fforde B314 were issued concurrently with those of J.B. Page B324. Seventeen prefixes in C, D, E and H were shared by both cashiers.

B315	**£5**	Replacement			
		Quantity printed: 9 million			
		Prefixes: (overlaps Page B325)			
	01M	(first run)	180	350	550
	--M		100	220	400
	15M	(last run)	180	350	550

B315 First Replacement 01M

B315p	**£5**	Replacement Signature Sequence Pair			
		Pair with consecutive serials (08/10/13M)	-	Rare	-

Banknotes with signature of J.S. Fforde B315 were issued concurrently with those of J.B. Page B325. Four pairs have been logged for B315p.

TEN POUNDS 9 January 1967

Design, watermark and dimensions as for *B299* J.Q. Hollom banknotes. Printed at the Bank of England Works, Debden, Essex.

			VF	EF	UNC
B316	**£10**	Brown			
		Quantity printed: 49·5 million	VF	EF	UNC
		Prefixes: (links Hollom B299 & overlaps Page B326)			
	A41	(first run)	65	160	260
	A--		18	35	70
	A95	(last run)	65	150	280
B316p	**£10**	Signature Sequence Pair			
		Pair with consecutive serials		-	8000

Banknotes with signature of J.S. Fforde B316 were issued concurrently with those of J.B. Page B326. Three pairs logged in prefix A shared by both cashiers.

B316p Signature Sequence Pair

			VF	EF	UNC
B316s	**£10**	Specimen			
		Prefix/Serial: A00 000000			
		Red solid capitals printed twice diagonally	600	1300	1800

B317 10s/50p Reserved for a Sir Walter Raleigh essay if one surfaces.

SERIES D PICTORIAL 1970 *to* 1994

The Pictorial Series D banknotes, 10s, £20, £5, £10, £1, £50 in order of preparation, were the work of Harry N. Eccleston OBE, assisted by Roger Withington and David Wicks. Eccleston joined the Bank in January 1958 and later became the first full time banknote designer. By the time the £50 banknote was issued in 1981, nearly twenty years work had gone into the series with a great deal of innovation in both design and production. In fact Eccleston's earliest work was on a new 10s banknote (later amended to 50p). As he recalled in an interview for 'The Moneymakers International': "It was a beautiful note to design···· all offset in various shades of brown and orange with Sir Walter Raleigh as the historical figure on the reverse···· but in 1964 when the design was approved and production was just getting underway, the Government decided to bring out the 50p coin instead, so my first English banknote was stillborn."

10s Sir Walter Raleigh *reverse* Eccleston's unissued design

H. Eccleston OBE retired in January 1983. He died on the 30th April 2010. Roger Withington took over as chief designer and in 1985 the Bank introduced a computer to help with design. The CAD software package enabled complex designs and patterns to be stored and reproduced on a high-resolution screen. The £1, £5 and £10 banknotes started life on the sheet-fed presses but were subsequently switched to the web presses. They were marked with the small letter **W** (standing for web) in the case of the £1, and **L** (standing for litho) on the £5 and £10. The reels of paper used on the web presses were two miles long, which meant they had to be particularly durable, the watermark could no longer be matched exactly to each banknote.

TWENTY POUNDS William Shakespeare 9 July 1970

Designed by Harry Eccleston OBE, featuring on the front the Queen's portrait with a vignette of St. George and the dragon; the reverse shows the statue of William Shakespeare from the Kent Memorial in Westminster Abbey and a scene from Romeo and Juliet. Plate-printed in sheets of 15 (3 x 5) at the Bank of England Works, Debden, Essex, on banknote paper manufactured by Portals Ltd, with watermark of the Queen's head. The banknotes measure 160 x 90mm, highest serial 960000 and ceased to be legal tender after 19th March 1993. Although the first issue was signed by J.S. Fforde, he had ceased to be Chief Cashier on 28th February 1970.

			VF	EF	UNC
B318	**£20**	Purple			
		Quantity printed: ~ 5 million	VF	EF	UNC
		Prefixes: (links Page B328)			
	A01	(first run)	170	300	500
	A--		180	320	400
	A05	(last run)	200	340	620

B318 First A01

B318s	**£20**	Specimen			
		Prefix/Serial: A00 000000			
		Red cameo capitals printed twice diagonally	1200	2000	3400

B318 William Shakespeare *reverse*

B319	**£20**	Replacement			
		Quantity printed: 0·5 million	VF	EF	UNC
		Prefix: (overlaps Page B329)			
	M01	(only)	160	320	550

B319 Replacement First M01

© Bank of England

JOHN
BRANGWYN PAGE
1970-1980

John Page was born on 23rd August 1923 (he was named Brangwyn after the artist Sir Frank Brangwyn). He was educated at Highgate School and King's College, Cambridge. Having served as a pilot in the RAF during the war he joined the Bank in 1948 and was seconded for two years to the IMF in 1953. He was appointed Assistant Chief Cashier in 1966 and First Deputy Chief Cashier in March 1968. Page held the post of the 25th Chief Cashier from 1st March 1970 to 29th February 1980 (which he said "he enjoyed more than anything else he had ever done"). He even agreed to appear on the television programme in response to a request from a boy to "meet the man who signs the pound notes". Page became an Executive Director of the Bank in 1980 until his retirement in 1982. He died on the 2nd February 2005.

SERIES C PORTRAIT 1960 *to* 1978

ONE POUND 1970

Design, watermark and dimensions as for *B281* L.K. O'Brien portrait banknotes. Printed on sheet-fed or continuous reel-fed machines at the Bank of England Printing Works, Debden, Essex. Sheet size 24 (3 x 8) subsequently in sheets of 21 (3 x 7).

When banknote production was switched from Fforde to Page, there were not enough signature blocks available, so Fforde £1 B305, £5 B314 and £10 B316 banknotes continued to be produced concurrently with Page for well over a year. For the £1 alone sixty-two **Signature Sequence Pairs** prefixes have been logged.

			F	VF	EF
B320	**£1**	Green (gaps/links (**) Fforde B305 & B307)			
		Quantity printed: 3,870 million	F	VF	EF
		Prefixes: (overlaps Fforde B305 x18 prefixes)			
	S87L	(first run)	950	1450	2200
	S--L	(first series, traced in 89 & 90)	850	1300	1800

B320 First low serial S87L

									VF	EF	UNC
**	T--B	**	T--D	T--E	T--H	**	T--K	T--L			
U--A	U--B	U--C	U--D	**	U--H				2	4	8
W--A	W--B	W--C	W--D	W--E	W--H						

Sheet size from here 21 (3 x 7) banknotes, with the highest prefix now 84.

X--A	X--B	X--C	X--D	X--E	X--H	X--J	X--K	X--L			
Y--A	Y--B	Y--C	Y--D	Y--E	Y--H	Y--J	Y--K	Y--L	-	3	6
Z--A	Z--B	Z--C	Z--D	Z--E	Z--H	Z--J	Z--K	Z--L			
Z84L	(last run)								70	160	350

B320 Solid serial 888888

B321	**£1**	Replacement			
		Quantity printed: ~ 170 million	VF	EF	UNC
		Prefixes: (overlaps Fforde B306 RM SM)			
	R44M	(first run, may go lower)	85	180	380
	R--M		10	28	50
	R99M	S32M (mid last/first)	110	280	360
	S--M		6	15	30
	S98M	(last run)	120	220	380

Sheet size from here 21 (3 x 7) banknotes, with the highest prefix now 84.

W01M	(first run)	65	150	280
W--M		5	12	25
W84M	(mid last)	25	55	130
X01M	(mid first)	25	55	130
X--M		5	12	25
X84M	(last run)	120	250	-

B321 Last sheet size 24 (3 x 8)

B321 First sheet size 21 (3 x 7)

B322 **£1** Green

Quantity printed: 3840 million

Prefixes:

Prefix									VF	EF	UNC
AN01	(first run)								110	240	380
AN--	(first series, old size sheets, traced to 96)								3	8	15
	AR--										
BN--	BR--	BS--	BT--	BU--	BW--	BX--	BY--	BZ--			
CN--	CR--	CS--	CT--	CU--	CW--	CX--	CY--	CZ--	-	3	6
DN--	DR--	DS--	DT--	DU--	DW--	DX--	DY--				
EN--	ER--	ES--	ET--	EU--	EW--	EX--	EY--	EZ--			
HN--	HR--	HS--	HT--	HU--	HW--	HX--	HY--				
HZ--	(last series)								3	6	12
HZ63	(last run)								45	120	250

AS to AZ and DZ prefixes have not been seen and were probably not issued.

B322 First AN01

B323 **£1** Replacement (not all were used as such)

Quantity printed: 185 million

Prefixes:

Prefix					VF	EF	UNC
MR01	(first run)				90	220	380
MR--					10	22	40
MR48					90	200	350
MS01	MS84	MT01	(mid first/last/first)		32	65	140
MS--	MT--	MU--	MW--		3	8	15
MT23					45	120	230
MU01					14	32	60
MU19					200	-	-
MW01					30	65	140
MW19	(last run)				40	110	200

FIVE POUNDS 1971

Design watermark and dimensions as for *B297* J.Q. Hollom banknotes. Printed at the Bank of England Works, Debden, Essex. At some stage (date unknown) the sheet size was changed from 18 (3 x 6) to 21 (3 x 7). Highest serial now to 1 million.

			VF	EF	UNC
B324	**£5**	Blue			
		Quantity printed: 210 million	VF	EF	UNC
		Prefixes: (overlaps Fforde B314 C D E H)			
	03C	(first run)	220	450	-
	--C	(first series)	18	35	70
	--D	--E	16	30	65
	--H	(last series)	65	150	260
	41H	(last run, probably to 42)	130	300	-

B324 First 03C

B325	**£5**	Replacement			
		Quantity printed: 8 million			
		Prefixes: (overlaps Fforde B315)			
	04M	(first run)	220	450	650
	--M		180	380	550
	18M	(last run)	250	480	-

TEN POUNDS 1971

Design, watermark and dimensions as for *B299* J.Q. Hollom banknotes. Printed at the Bank of England Works, Debden, Essex.

			VF	EF	UNC
B326	**£10**	Brown			
		Quantity printed: 167 million	VF	EF	UNC
		Prefixes: (overlaps Fforde B316)			
	A--	(first series, traced in 89 to 95)	720	1300	-
	B--	C--	16	35	65
	C90	(last run)	185	400	700

B326 Last C90

			VF	EF	UNC
B326s	**£10**	Specimen			
		Prefix/Serial: A00 000000			
		Red cameo capitals printed twice diagonally		-	3000
		Prefix/Serial: B00 000000			
		Type 1: Black cameo capitals printed twice diagonally	600	1300	1800
		Type 2: No overprint, in the Bank's archive			

			VF	EF	UNC
B327	**£10**	Replacement			
		Quantity printed: 14 million			
		Prefixes:			
	M01	(first run)	60	140	280
	M--		25	45	80
	M14	(last run)	110	250	450

The M15 M16 M17 prefixes excluded until such time as one emerges.

SERIES D PICTORIAL 1970 *to* 1994

TWENTY POUNDS William Shakespeare 1970

Design, dimensions and watermark as for *B318* J.S. Fforde banknotes. Printed at the Bank of England Works, Debden, Essex.

B328	**£20**	Purple			
		Quantity printed: 250 million	VF	EF	UNC
		Prefixes: (links Fforde B318)			
	A06	(first run)	130	280	500
	A--	(first series)	30	50	95
	B--	(scarcer prefix, traced in 01 to 14 [15])	60	150	300
	C--	D--	28	45	90
	D80	(last run)	200	400	-

B328 First A06

B328s	**£20**	Specimen		
		Prefix/Serial: A00 000000		
		Red cameo capitals printed twice diagonally	-	3000

B329	**£20**	Replacement			
		Quantity printed: 4 million			
		Prefixes: (overlaps Fforde B319)			
	M01	(first run)	130	260	480
	M--		55	100	180
	M04	(last run)	160	330	550

TEN POUNDS Florence Nightingale 20 February 1975

Designed by Harry N. Eccleston OBE, Pictorial Series D banknotes, the front features H.M. The Queen's portrait in State Robes, a medallion of Britannia and a vignette derived from the lily symbol used by Florence Nightingale. On the reverse a portrait of F. Nightingale was created from photographs taken on her return from the Crimean War. It is set beside a vignette based on a contemporary lithograph showing her at work in the Barracks Hospital, Scutari. Printed in sheets of 20 (4 x 5) at the Bank of England Works, Debden, Essex, on banknote paper manufactured by Portals Ltd., with watermark of Nightingale's head. The banknotes measure 151 x 85mm and ceased to be legal tender after 20th May 1994.

In a letter to Vincent Duggleby in 1994, the Bank revealed that a total of 6,533 million Series D £10 banknotes were issued, 1,911 million from sheet-fed presses and 4,622 million from the web presses. Quantities printed for each prefix are estimates and must be regarded as approximate within the overall total.

B330	**£10**	Brown			
		Quantity printed: 980 million	VF	EF	UNC
		Prefixes:			
	A01	(first run)	55	110	220
	A--	(first series)	15	30	50
	B -- C-- D-- E-- H-- J-- K-- L-- N-- R-- S--		14	25	45
	T --	(last series)	28	55	120
	T20	(officially the last run)	320	700	-
	U--	(last run, traced in 34 to 39)	-	3000	-

B330 T20 Officially the last run

Three examples of B330 are known with prefixes U34, U35 and U39, two in signature sequence pairs. Presumably a small quantity of old stock with Page's signature, after he ceased to be Chief Cashier, went into the Somerset printing run B346.

B330 Florence Nightingale *reverse* (no L)

B330p	**£10**	Signature Sequence Pair (two recorded)	VF	EF	UNC
		Pair with consecutive serials	-	10000	-

Banknotes with signature of J.B. Page B330 were issued concurrently with those of D.H.F. Somerset B346. Only two pairs recorded, prefix U35 and U39.

B330s	**£10**	Specimen			
		Prefix/Serial: A00 000000			
		Type 1: Red cameo capitals printed twice diagonally	600	1300	1800
		Type 2: No overprint	650	1450	2000

			VF	EF	UNC
B331	**£10**	Replacement			
		Quantity printed: ~ 50 million	VF	EF	UNC
		Prefixes:			
	M01	(first run)	100	230	360
	M--	(not inclusive)	40	80	150
	M50	(last run)	70	160	330

B331 First Replacement M01

FIVE POUNDS **Duke of Wellington** 11 November 1971

Designed by H. Eccleston OBE, Pictorial Series D banknotes. The front features the Queen's portrait, a medallion of Britannia and a vignette depicting a winged Victory. The reverse has a portrait of the first Duke of Wellington and a vignette of a scene based on a 19th century engraving of the Battle of Fuentes de Onoro, which took place in 1811 during the Peninsular War. Initially printed in sheets of 18 (3 x 6) at the Bank of England Works, Debden on banknote paper with **0·5mm metal thread**, manufactured by Portals Ltd., with continuous watermark of Wellington's head. From 1973 (B334) printed on the web presses, intaglio on the front and offset lithography on the reverse (identified by a small capital **L**). The banknotes measure 146 x 78mm and ceased to be legal tender after 29th November 1991.

The Bank revealed to Vincent Duggleby in 1994, that a total of 9,400 million Series D £5 banknotes were issued, 2,100 million from sheet-fed presses and 7,300 million from the web presses. Quantities printed for each prefix are estimates and must be regarded as approximate within the overall total.

B332 **£5** Blue

Quantity printed: 1,725 million

Prefixes:

		VF	EF	UNC
A01	(first run)	70	160	340
A--	(first series)	8	18	40
B-- C-- D-- E-- H-- J-- K--		-	14	30
L--	(last series)	12	22	50
L94	(last run)	100	250	500

B332 Last L94

B332 Duke of Wellington *reverse* (no L)

			VF	EF	UNC
B332s	**£5**	Specimen			
		Prefix/Serial: A00 000000	VF	EF	UNC
		Type 1: Red cameo capitals printed twice diagonally	600	1300	1800
		Type 2: Black solid capitals printed twice diagonally	-	1450	2000

B333	**£5**	Replacement			
		Quantity printed: 4·5 million			
		Prefixes:			
	M01	(first run)	200	380	550
	M--		125	200	380
	M05	(last run)	220	400	600

B333 M01 First Replacement

L on reverse B334

FIVE POUNDS **Duke of Wellington** August 1973

Design, dimensions and watermark as for *B332*, but printed on web presses in sheets of 24 (4 x 6). The front main design is by intaglio and the reverse by offset lithography. The banknotes are distinguished by a small capital letter **L** (standing for litho) on the reverse next to the £5 sign at the bottom left corner.

B334 **£5** Blue **L** reverse

Quantity printed: 1,600 million

Prefixes:

								VF	EF	UNC
01A	(first run)							75	160	350
--A	(first series)							8	18	40
--B	--C	--D	--E	--H	--J	--K	--L	-	14	30
--N	--R	--S	--T	--U	--W	--X	--Y			
--Z	(last series)							12	22	45
96Z	(last run)							100	250	500

Matched First prefixes low serial pair A01 & 01A

Matched low serial pairs A01 B332 / 01A B334 occasionally appear on the market.
From £1250 UNC

B334s	**£5**	Specimen **L** reverse			
		Prefix/Serial: 00A 000000	VF	EF	UNC
		Type 1: Red cameo capitals printed twice diagonally	600	1300	1800
		Type 2: Black solid capitals printed twice diagonally	-	1450	2000

B335	**£5**	Replacement **L** reverse			
		Quantity printed: 8 million			
		Prefixes:			
	01M	(first run)	180	380	650
	--M		80	170	320
	08M	(last run)	180	380	550

B335 First & Last Replacements 01M & 08M

B336	**£5**	Blue **L** reverse			
		Quantity printed: 2,250 million			
		Prefixes: (overlaps Somerset B343 EZ)			
	AN01	(first run)	100	220	400
	AN--	(first series)	8	16	35
		AR-- AS-- AT-- AU-- AW-- AX-- AY-- AZ--			
	BN--	BR-- BS-- BT-- BU-- BW-- BX-- BY-- BZ--	-	12	28
	CN--	CR-- CS-- CT-- CU-- CW-- CX--			
	EZ--	(last series)	25	55	120
	EZ56	(last run)	160	340	600

ONE POUND Sir Isaac Newton 9 February 1978

Designed by Harry N. Eccleston OBE, Pictorial Series D banknotes. The front has the same portrait of the Queen as used on the £5 banknote (B332), and features a medallion of Britannia, a vignette of a design comprising a caduceus, cornucopia and an olive branch, combined in multicoloured patterns of green, yellow and blue. On the reverse is a portrait in green of Sir Isaac Newton specially created from a number of contemporary portraits, together with multicoloured machine-engraved patterns suggesting the solar system, overlaid by a geometric diagram from Newton's Principia. Initially printed in sheets of 40 (5 x 8), and subsequently from B340 in sheets of 21 (3 x 7) on the web machines, at the Bank of England Works, Debden, Essex, on banknote paper manufactured by Portals Ltd., with watermark of Newton's head. The banknote has only one serial number, printed at the bottom right hand corner. The top left hand side was left blank for encoding marks used by electronic banknote sorting machines. The banknotes measure 135 x 67mm and ceased to be legal tender after 11th March 1988. According to the Bank about 5,770 million Series D £1 banknotes were issued.

B337	**£1**	Green			
		Quantity printed: 1,440 million	VF	EF	UNC
		Prefixes:			
	A01	(first run)	3	6	20
	A-- B-- C-- D-- E-- H-- J-- K-- L-- N-- R-- S-- T-- U-- W-- X-- Y--		-	3	6
	Z --	(last series)	4	7	16
	Z80	(last run)	110	240	400

B337 Last Z80

B337s	**£1**	Specimen			
		Prefix/Serial: A00 000000			
		Red cameo capitals printed twice diagonally	600	1300	1800

B337 Sir Isaac Newton *reverse* (no W)

B338	**£1**	Replacement			
		Quantity printed: possibly 1 million	VF	EF	UNC
		Prefix:			
	M01	(only)	95	220	400

B338 M01 Replacement

B339	**£1**	Green									
		Quantity printed: 1,280 million									
		Prefixes:									
	01A	(first run)							10	35	80
	--A	--B	--C	--D	--E	--H	--J	--K	-	3	6
	--L	--N	--R	--S	--T	--U	--W	--X			
	--Y	(last series)							-	5	16
	80Y	(last run)							100	200	-

B339 Last 80Y

B339a **£1** Experimental Issue Green

Quantity printed: fewer than 5 million

Prefixes:

									VF	EF	UNC
	81A	(first run)							240	450	-
	81B	81C	81D	81E	81H	81J	81K	81L	120	240	380
	81N	81R	81S	81T	81U	81W	81X	81Y			
	81Z	(last run)							140	360	520
						82J	82K		300	500	-

B339a Experimental Issue 82J

All B339a have an 81 or 82 prefix which is outside the normal range, B339 sheets (5 x 8 = 40) times two = 80.

			VF	EF	UNC
B340	**£1**	**Green**			
		Quantity printed: 420 million	VF	EF	UNC
		Prefixes:			
	A01N	(first run)	20	45	90
	A--N	B--N C--N D--N	-	4	8
	E--N	(last series)	3	8	18
	E84N	(last run)	120	260	-

B340 First A01N

B340p	**£1**	Signature Sequence Pair		
		Pair with consecutive serials	-	Rare

B340p Page AN01 from Signature Sequence Pair

A single example of B340 prefix/serial AN01 431011 in the new colours used for D.H.F. Somerset B341 exists with the signature of J.B. Page. It is supported on each side by Somerset banknotes AN01 431010/2. The Bank of England Works, Debden retains good banknotes from experimental and normal runs. A Page £1 sheet was probably set aside without anyone realising the signature had changed to Somerset in the meantime.

© Bank of England

DAVID HENRY FITZROY SOMERSET
1980-1988

David Somerset was born on 19th June 1930. Educated at Wellington College and Peterhouse, Cambridge. He joined the Bank in 1952 and from 1959-62 was seconded as personal assistant to the Managing Director of the IMF. On his return he became private secretary to the Governor, Lord Cromer. Nicknamed 'Boomer', he was appointed Deputy Chief Cashier in 1973 and was promoted to become the 26th Chief Cashier on 1st March 1980. Somerset remained in office until his retirement on 28th February 1988.

SERIES D PICTORIAL 1970 *to* 1994

ONE POUND Sir Isaac Newton 20 March 1981

Design, dimensions and watermark as for *B337* J.B. Page Pictorial Series D banknotes, but the general appearance is enhanced by the inclusion of additional background colours, mainly lilac, light green, pink and yellow. The Queen's portrait is more sharply defined and the portrait of Sir Isaac Newton appears rather more lively. Printed on web presses in sheets of 21 (3 x 7) at the Bank of England Works, Debden on banknote paper manufactured by Portals Ltd. The main design on the front is printed by intaglio and the reverse by offset lithography, indicated by a small capital **W** (standing for web-press) on the bottom left reverse.

B341	**£1**	Green **W** reverse		
		Quantity printed: 2,877 million		
		Prefixes:	VF	EF	UNC
		AN01 (first run)	18	35	80
		AN-- AR-- AS-- AT-- AU-- AW-- AX-- AY-- AZ-- BN-- BR-- BS-- BT-- BU-- BW-- BX-- BY-- BZ-- CN-- CR-- CS-- CT-- CU-- CW-- CX-- CY-- CZ-- DN-- DR-- DS-- DT-- DU-- DW-- DX-- DY--	-	3	6
		DY21 (last run)	8	25	50

The highest prefix/serial printed was DY21 999997, in the Bank's museum. A single copy, with the signature of J.B. Page, with the prefix/serial AN01 431011 B340p in the new colours used for B341 is known. See page 257.

B341 First low serial

Web-press **W** on reverse

B341s	**£1**	Specimen **W** reverse			
		Prefix/Serial: A00 000000			
		Type 1: Red cameo capitals printed twice diagonally	-	1300	1800
		Type 2: Black cameo capitals printed twice diagonally (in Bank's archive)			
		Prefix/Serial: AN00 000000			
		Red cameo capitals printed twice diagonally	700	-	

B342	**£1**	Replacement Green **W** reverse			
		Quantity printed: Not known	F	VF	EF
		Prefixes:			
	MN--	(traced in 03 [01] to 18 [21])	1400	2400	4000
	MX65	(only one recorded)	2000 VG		

Only nine examples of MN-- have been reported all with serials above 900000.

B342 MN04

Only one examples of MX65 has been reported, serial 737090.

B342 MX65

FIVE POUNDS Duke of Wellington June 1980

Design, dimensions and watermark as for *B332* J.B. Page Pictorial Series D banknotes. Printed on web presses in sheets of 18 (3 x 6) at the Bank of England Works, Debden, Essex. The banknotes are distinguished by a small capital letter **L** (standing for Litho) on the bottom left of the reverse.

B343 **£5** Blue **L** reverse

Quantity printed: 5,130 million

Prefixes: (overlaps Page B336 EZ)

		VF	EF	UNC
DN01	(first run)	55	110	230
DN-- DR-- DS-- DT-- DU-- DW-- DX-- DY-- DZ-- EN-- ER-- ES-- ET-- EU-- EW-- EX-- EY-- EZ-- HN-- HR-- HS-- HT-- HU-- HW-- HX-- HY-- HZ-- JN-- JR-- JS-- JT-- JU-- JW-- JX-- JY-- JZ-- KN-- KR-- KS-- KT-- KU-- KW-- KX-- KY-- KZ-- LN-- LR-- LS-- LT-- LU-- LW-- LX-- LY--		-	10	25
LZ--	(last series)	8	22	40
LZ90	(last run)	160	380	600

Prefix now reversed to combine letters from the second half of the alphabet with those of the first half. DN is a continuation of B336.

		VF	EF	UNC
NA01	(first run)		-	Rare
NA--	(first series, probably 01 to 18)	350	600	-
NB--	NC--	-	12	25
NC90	(last run)	16	35	70

B343a **£5** Error Signature Omitted

Quantity printed: ~ 61,500

Prefixes:

		VF	EF	UNC
DU--	(traced in 55 to 72)	-	110	200

This remarkable error has been recorded in the DU55 to DU72 prefix range. A survey of actual serials taken from banknotes in collector's hands has produced a range from 445787 to 449402 (~ 61,500 banknotes).

B343a Error Somerset signature omitted

B344	**£5**	Experimental Issue OCR Blue **L** reverse			
		Quantity printed: Not known	VF	EF	UNC
		Prefixes:			
	AN91	(first run)	650	1100	1700
	BR91	CS91 DT91 EU91 HW91 JX91 KY91	550	900	1600
	LZ91	(last run)	650	1100	1700

Optical Character Recognition (OCR) banknotes used for circulation trials. All have a 91 prefix outside the normal range (18 x 5 = 90). AN - BR - CS are Page prefixes.

B344 OCR Experimental Issue Last LZ91

FIVE POUNDS **Duke of Wellington** 16 July 1987

Design, dimensions and watermark as for *B332* J.B. Page Pictorial Series D Pictorial banknotes. A wider **1mm Thread** added, making more pronounced. Printed on web presses in sheets of 18 (3 x 6) at the Bank of England Works, Debden, Essex.

B345	**£5**	Blue **L** reverse			
		Quantity printed: 270 million			
		Prefixes:			
	RA01	(first run)	16	38	80
	RA--	RB-- RC--	-	14	30
	RC90	(last run)	16	38	80
B345s	**£5**	Specimen **L** reverse			
		Prefix/Serial: RA00 000000			
		Red cameo capitals printed twice diagonally	-	1300	1800
		Prefix/Serial: A00 000000			
		Black cameo capitals printed twice diagonally (in Bank's archive)			

TEN POUNDS Florence Nightingale December 1980

Design, dimensions and watermark as for *B330* J.B. Page Pictorial Series D banknotes. Plate-printed in sheets of 20 (4 x 5) at the Bank of England Works, Debden, Essex.

			VF	EF	UNC
B346	**£10**	Brown			
		Quantity printed: 400 million	VF	EF	UNC
		Prefixes:			
	U01	(first run)	320	750	1350
	U--	(first series)	18	35	85
	W--	X-- Y-- Z--	16	32	80
	Z80	(last run)	250	600	-

B346 Last Z80

			VF	EF	UNC
B347	**£10**	Brown			
		Quantity printed: 680 million			
		Prefixes:			
	01A	(first run)	110	260	450
	--A	--B --C --D --E --H --J --K	-	28	60
	--L	(last series)	25	55	115
	40L	(last run)	320	600	-

TEN POUNDS **Florence Nightingale** 20 February 1984

Design, dimensions and watermark as for *B330* J.B. Page Pictorial Series D banknote. Printed on web presses in sheets of 15 (3 x 5) with the front main design by intaglio and the reverse by offset lithography. The banknotes are distinguished by a small capital letter **L** (standing for Litho) on the bottom left of the reverse.

			VF	EF	UNC
B348	**£10**	Brown **L** reverse			
		Quantity printed: 1,800 million	VF	EF	UNC
		Prefixes:			
	AN01	(first run)	60	130	280
	AN-- AR-- AS-- AT-- AU-- AW-- AX-- AY-- AZ-- BN-- BR-- BS-- BT-- BU-- BW-- BX-- BY-- BZ-- CN-- CR--		-	22	45
	CR90	(last run)	110	240	400

B348 First AN01 low serial

Litho **L** on reverse

TEN POUNDS Florence Nightingale 16 July 1987

Design, dimensions and watermark as for *B330*, but now incorporating a **1mm Windowed Thread** (Stardust). There are also some minor changes to the background behind the Queen's portrait.

B349 **£10** Brown **L** reverse

			VF	EF	UNC
		Quantity printed: 660 million			
		Prefixes:			
	CS01	(first run)	55	110	230
	CS--	CT-- CU-- CW-- CX-- CY-- CZ--	-	28	60
	DN--	(last series)	22	45	80
	DN30	(last run)	150	320	-

B349 First CS01

B349s **£10** Specimen **L** reverse

Prefix/Serial: A000 000000

Red cameo capitals printed twice diagonally - 1300 1800

Prefix/Serial: A00 000000

Black cameo capitals printed twice diagonally (in Bank's archive)

TWENTY POUNDS William Shakespeare March 1981

Design, dimensions and watermark as for *B318* J.S. Fforde Pictorial Series D banknotes. Plate-printed in sheets of 20 (4 x 5) at the Bank of England Works, Debden, Essex.

B350 **£20** Purple

Quantity printed: 200 million

Prefixes:

		VF	EF	UNC
E01	(first run)	250	480	800
E--	(first series)	40	90	240
H--		30	50	110
J --	(last series)	40	70	130
J40	(last run)	420	850	1400

B350 Last J40

B350s **£20** Specimen

Prefix/Serial: A00 000000

Black cameo capitals printed twice diagonally (in Bank's archive)

TWENTY POUNDS William Shakespeare 15 November 1984

Design and dimensions as for *B318* J.S. Fforde Pictorial Series D banknotes, but now incorporating a **New Watermark** 'William Shakespeare's head' and a (Stardust) **1mm Windowed Thread**. There are also some changes in the ink colours with more emphasis on green and brown areas and the banknote has a more sharply defined appearance. Plate-printed in sheets of 20 (4 x 5) at the Bank of England Works, Debden, Essex. The banknotes ceased to be legal tender after 19th March 1993.

B351	**£20**	Purple & Green			
		Quantity printed: 360 million	VF	EF	UNC
		Prefixes:			
	01A	(first run)	45	110	220
	--A	--B --C --D --E --H --J	25	55	110
	--K	(officially last series)	30	60	130
	40K	(officially last run)	120	250	-
	78L	(last run, only one recorded)	-	Rare	-

A single copy of B351 prefix 78L, presumably old paper stock with Somerset's signature used for Gill B355.

B351 Last 78L only one recorded

B351s	**£20**	Specimen			
		Prefix/Serial: 00A 000000			
		Red cameo capitals printed twice diagonally	-	1400	1900

B351 William Shakespeare revised colours *reverse*

FIFTY POUNDS Sir Christopher Wren 20 March 1981

Designed by Harry N. Eccleston OBE and Roger Withington, the front has the same portrait of H.M. The Queen, as used on the £10 and £20 Pictorial Series D banknotes and features a Phoenix based on a design by Sir Christopher Wren and patterns derived from various design features in St Paul's Cathedral. A medallion of Britannia completes the picture. On the reverse is a portrait of Sir Christopher Wren created from contemporary portraits by J.B. Closterman 1695 and Sir Godfrey Kneller 1711. The background shows a view of St Paul's from the River Thames, a floor plan and a decorative guilloche developed from the wood carvings by Grinling Gibbons in the south choir aisle. Printed in sheets of 15 (3 x 5) on banknote paper manufactured by Portals Ltd., with a **Contoured Thread** and watermark of H.M. The Queen. The banknotes measure 169 x 95mm and ceased to be legal tender after 20th September 1996.

			VF	EF	UNC
B352	**£50**	Brown			
		Quantity printed: 180 million	VF	EF	UNC
		Prefixes:			
	A01	(first run)	65	100	220
	A--	B--	-	85	140
	B90	(last run)	85	160	300

B352 Sir Christopher Wren *reverse*

B352s **£50** Specimen

Prefix/Serial: A00 000000

	VF	EF	UNC
Type 1: Red cameo capitals printed twice diagonally	-	1500	2200
Type 2: Black cameo capitals printed twice diagonally (in Bank's archive)			

B352s Specimen red cameo capitals

© Bank of England

GEORGE MALCOLM GILL
1988-1991

Malcolm Gill was born on 23rd May 1934. He was educated at Cambridgeshire High School and Sidney Sussex College, Cambridge. After National Service in the RAF, he joined the Bank in 1957. He was seconded to the office of the UK delegation at the IMF in Washington from 1966-68, seconded to H.M. Treasury from 1977-80 and was private secretary to the Governor, Lord O'Brien, from 1970-72. Gill became Head of the Foreign Exchange Division in 1982 and was the 27th Chief Cashier from 1st March 1988 until his retirement on 24th November 1991. In December 1991 he joined the Bank for International Settlements.

Collectors should be aware that earlier and/or later alphabetical prefixes were sometimes printed for general circulation. From 1990 certain first, last and special prefixes were made available by Debden Security Printing (DSP) in presentation packs. See page 340.

SERIES D PICTORIAL 1970 *to* 1994

FIVE POUNDS Duke of Wellington 1 March 1988

Design, dimensions and watermark as for *B322* J.B. Page Pictorial Series D banknotes, but incorporating **1mm Security Thread** as in *B345* D.H.F. Somerset. Printed on web presses in sheets of 18 (3 x 6) at the Bank of England Works, Debden, Essex. Ceased to be legal tender after 29th November 1991.

			VF	EF	UNC
B353	**£5**	Blue **L** reverse			
		Quantity printed: 990 million	VF	EF	UNC
		Prefixes:			
	RD01	(first run)	18	40	80
		RD-- RE-- RH-- RJ-- RK-- RL-- SA-- SB-- SC-- SD--	-	10	25
	SE--	(last series)	8	15	28
	SE90	(998500 on, in C100)		-	100
	SE90	(last run, from circulation)	30	70	150

B353 First low serial RD01 & Last high serial

TEN POUNDS Florence Nightingale 1 March 1988

Design, dimensions and watermark as for *B330* J.B. Page Pictorial Series D banknotes, but incorporating a **Windowed Thread** as in *B349* D.H.F. Somerset. Printed on web presses in sheets of 15 (3 x 5) at the Bank of England Works, Debden.

B354 **£10** Brown **L** reverse

Quantity printed: 2,500 million

Prefixes:

		VF	EF	UNC
DR01	(first run)	22	50	100
	DR-- DS-- DT-- DU-- DW-- DX-- DY-- DZ--			
EN--	ER-- ES-- ET-- EU-- EW-- EX-- EY-- EZ--	-	20	40
HN--	HR-- HS-- HT-- HU-- HW-- HX-- HY-- HZ--			
JN--				
JR --	(last series)	16	35	75
JR60	(officially last run)	160	440	800
KN52	(last run, only one recorded)	Rare	-	

Officially the last run was JR60, but the Bank has confirmed that a small quantity of banknotes with the KN prefix were issued from old stock with Gill's signature after he had ceased to be Chief Cashier. So far only one example has come to light.

B354 KN52 only one recorded

TWENTY POUNDS William Shakespeare 1 March 1988

Design dimensions and watermark as for *B351* D.H.F. Somerset Pictorial Series D banknotes. Printed on sheet-fed presses in sheets of 20 (4 x 5) at the Bank of England Works, Debden. The banknotes ceased to be legal tender after 19th March 1993.

			VF	EF	UNC
B355	**£20**	Purple & Green			
		Quantity printed: 580 million	VF	EF	UNC
		Prefixes:			
	01L	(first run)	60	130	275
	--L	--M --N --R --S --T --U --W --X	30	65	130
	20X	(998500 on, in C102)		-	200
	20X	(last run, from circulation)	95	210	420

A £20 prefix 78L with Somerset's signature has surfaced, listed under B351.

B355 First 01L & Last 20X

FIFTY POUNDS Sir Christopher Wren 21 July 1988

Design, dimensions and watermark as for *B352* D.H.F. Somerset Pictorial Series D banknotes, but incorporating a **Windowed Security Thread** (Stardust). The banknotes also include new colours, in particular a light olive green in the text, the Britannia symbol and the denomination numerals. Printed on sheet-fed presses in sheets of 15 (3 x 5) at the Bank of England Works, Debden, Essex.

			VF	EF	UNC
B356	**£50**	Brown			
		Quantity printed: Not known	VF	EF	UNC
		Prefixes: (overlaps Kentfield B361 E)			
	C01	(first run)	110	230	420
	C--	D--	65	100	180
	D90	(officially last run)	70	140	280
	E--	(last series, from E13)	-	120	250
	E30	(last run)	90	200	-
B356cs	*Column Sort:*				
	D--	(traced in 91 to 95)	70	130	250

Although the last production run Gill £50 was supposed to be to D90, banknotes have been found with prefixes D91 to D95, the **first noted Column Sort**. Kentfield £50 B361 also in the E prefix overlapping with Gill. The Bank has confirmed E prefix Gill old stock was used after he had ceased to be Chief Cashier.

B356 First low serial C01

			VF	EF	UNC
B356s	**£50**	Specimen			
		Prefix/Serial: A00 000000			
		Red cameo capitals printed twice diagonally	-	1500	2200

SERIES E FIRST HISTORICAL 1990 *to* 1999

In October 1988 the Bank of England announced that a new series of English banknotes, designed by Roger Withington would be introduced between 1990 and 1994, starting with the £5. The banknotes feature historical figures on the reverse, with a new portrait of H.M. The Queen's portrait engraved by Alan Dow. They incorporated the latest security devices, including a **Windowed Security Thread** and a redesigned watermark. They also have **Ascending Serials** and a **Coloured Denomination Symbol** to aid the partially-sighted.

FIVE POUNDS George Stephenson 7 June 1990

Designed by Roger Withington, H.M. The Queen's portrait with a vignette of Britannia and **round symbol** to assist the partially-sighted, the reverse shows the engineer, George Stephenson 1781-1848 and early railway history. This includes the Skerne Bridge with The Rocket, built by his son Robert, on the Stockton and Darlington Railway. Printed in sheets of 18 (3 x 6) at the Bank of England Works, Debden, Essex, on banknote paper manufactured by Portals with watermark of the Queen's head in registration. **Copyright Line** introduced, © Copyright 1990. The banknotes measure 135 x 70mm, ceasing to be legal tender after 21st November 2003.

			VF	EF	UNC
B357	**£5**	Turquoise			
		Quantity printed: 1,000 million	VF	EF	UNC
		Prefixes: (overlaps Kentfield B362 R S T U)			
	A01	(first run, from circulation & C101 C116)	8	20	35
	A01	(998500 on, in C100)		-	30
	A--	B-- C-- D-- E-- H-- J-- K-- L--	-	12	25
	N--	(officially last run, traced to 54)	10	25	60
	R--	S-- T--	20	55	100
	U--	(last series)	45	85	160
	U17	(last run, probably to U18)	150	360	-

B357 Officially last run N54 Light £5 top left

B357 George Stephenson *reverse*

Although the last run was supposed to be prefix N, leading on to Kentfield R01 B362, the Bank has confirmed that old stocks of Gill £5 banknotes continued to be numbered and issued after he had ceased to be Chief Cashier. As a result there are overlaps with Kentfield in the R, S, T and U prefixes. See text after B358.

B357s **£5** Specimen

Prefix/Serial: A00 000000	VF	EF	UNC
Red cameo capitals printed once horizontally	-	1300	1800

B357s Specimen

B357p **£5** Signature Sequence Pair (two recorded)

Pair with consecutive serials	-	3500

Banknotes with signature of G.M. Gill B357 were issued concurrently with those of G.E.A. Kentfield B362. Two pairs recorded with prefix/serial S05 994197/8 and S05 994215/6.

TWENTY POUNDS **Michael Faraday** 5 June 1991

Designed by Roger Withington, featuring on the front H.M. The Queen's portrait with a vignette of Britannia and **square symbol** to assist the partially-sighted. The reverse shows a portrait of the physicist and chemist, Michael Faraday 1791-1867, together with a scene of him giving one of a series of lectures at the Royal Institution. Printed by intaglio on sheet-fed presses in sheets of 35 (5 x 7) at the Bank of England Works, Debden, Essex on banknote paper manufactured by Portals with watermark of the Queen's head in registration. The banknotes measure 149 x 80mm and ceased to be legal tender after 28th February 2001. Copyright 1991.

			VF	EF	UNC
B358	**£20**	Purple & Black			
		Quantity printed: Not known			
		Prefixes: (overlaps Kentfield B371 E H J L R S U)			
	A01	(first run, from circulation & C116)	30	65	110
	A01	(998500 on, in C102)		-	95
	A-- B-- C-- D-- E-- H-- J--		-	45	90
	L-- R-- S--		40	80	140
	U--	(last series)	45	90	150
	U19	(last run, probably to U35)	100	250	-
B358cs	*Column Sort:*				
	A--	(first run, traced in 71 to 98)	60	100	200
	B--	(traced in 71 to 98)	60	100	200
	C--	(last run, traced in 71 to 98)	120	250	-

Prefixes L, R and S are scarcer than A to J. No K, N or T prefixes have surfaced.

B358 Column Sort Mid First B71

B358 Michael Faraday *reverse* Copyright 1991

Originally Gill £20 B358 ended on the D prefix with Kentfield B371 starting at E01. However, sometime during 1993 prior to the introduction of the new £20 B374 there was a '*spring clean*' of old un-numbered stock with Gill's signature as well as that of Kentfield. The Gill banknotes were mixed up with Kentfield and as a result were printed with later alphabetical prefixes. Hence, overlaps may be found. The same thing happened with the B Ream recovery system which meant that column sort prefixes A, B and C appeared, with prefixes above 70, outside the usual run of both cashiers. Most have been found in low grade from circulation. Collectors will find it easier to make sense of the situation if they regard B358, B359, B371 and B372 as a whole, rather than separately. To a lesser extent the same applies to the £5 in B357 and B362.

			VF	EF	UNC
B358s	**£20**	Specimen *Prefix/Serial:* A00 000000 Red solid capitals printed once horizontally	-	1300	1800

			EF	UNC
B358p	**£20**	Signature Sequence Pair (only one recorded) Pair with consecutive serials	-	Rare

Banknotes with the signature of G.M. Gill (B358) were issued concurrently with those of Kentfield (B371). Only one pair recorded with prefix/serial E68 675378/9.

B358p Signature Sequence Pair

B359	**£20**	Experimental Issue Purple & Black			
		Quantity printed: Not known	VF	EF	UNC
		Prefix:			
	Z13	(only one recorded)		-	Rare

© Bank of England

GRAHAM EDWARD ALFRED KENTFIELD
1991-1998

Graham Kentfield was born on 3rd September 1940. He was educated at Bancroft's School, Essex (as was Kenneth Peppiatt) and at St Edmund Hall, Oxford where he read classics. He joined the Bank in 1963 and worked in the Economics Division (including a spell as Editor of the Bank's Quarterly Bulletin) and in the International Division. Kentfield was in the Financial Statistics Division from 1980-84 when he joined the Banking Department. In 1985 he became Deputy Chief Cashier and was appointed the 28th Chief Cashier from 25th November 1991. Graham retired on 31st December 1998.

SERIES D PICTORIAL 1970 *to* 1994

TEN POUNDS Florence Nightingale 25 November 1991

Design, dimensions and watermark as for *B330* J.B. Page Pictorial Series D banknotes, but incorporating the **Windowed Security Thread** as in D.H.F. Somerset £10 banknotes B349. Printed on web presses in sheets of 15 (3 x 5) at the Bank of England Works, Debden, Essex. Ceased to be legal tender after 20th May 1994.

			VF	EF	UNC
B360	**£10**	Brown **L** reverse			
		Quantity printed: 120 million			
		Prefixes:			
	KN01	(first run, also in C106)	30	60	120
	KN--	KR--	22	40	80
	KR30	(998500 on, in C104)	-	65	120
	KR30	(last run, from circulation & C109)	50	110	200

B360 First low serial KN01

B360 Last KR30

FIFTY POUNDS Sir Christopher Wren 25 November 1991

Design, dimensions and watermark as for *B352* D.H.F. Somerset Pictorial Series D banknotes, but incorporating further security devices as for B356 G.M. Gill £50 banknotes. Plate-printed in sheets of 15 (3 x 5) at the Bank of England Works, Debden, Essex. Ceased to be legal tender after 20th september 1996

			VF	EF	UNC
B361	**£50**	Brown			
		Quantity printed: 30 million	VF	EF	UNC
		Prefixes: (overlaps Gill B356)			
	E01	(first run, from circulation)	75	130	280
	E01	(500001 to 502000 in C106)		-	200
	E--		70	95	180
	E30	(998500 on, in C113 & C114)		-	220
	E30	(last run, from circulation & C109)	75	130	260

Prefixes from E16 to E30 have been recorded with the signature of G.M. Gill B356. The Bank has confirmed that these were issued from old stock after Gill had ceased to be Chief Cashier.

B361 The First 000001 serial

£50 production is meticulous and more labour intensive than other denominations. Column Sort numbering was probably used to achieve the full quotas on later issues.

SERIES E FIRST HISTORICAL 1990 *to* 1999

The first Kentfield issues were printed in the same format as Gill, but following public criticism that the banknotes were not sufficiently distinctive, the Bank in 1993 made design changes. This meant sharpening up the outlines of the value symbols and thus providing new varieties and prefix/serials for collectors. Mr Kentfield said: "We are not too proud to admit we got it wrong. It is the first time that we have made changes in a note in response to public demand". When designer Roger Withington retired in January 1994 he was succeeded by Andrew Ward, who was responsible for modifications evident in the Series E Second Historical. See Page 305.

By the late eighties it had become clear that the reel-fed machines, some of which were more than twenty years old were no longer adaptable to technological change. The new Simultan machines were manufactured by De La Rue Giori and came into use following a major programme of refurbishment at Debden between 1993 and 1996 aimed at concentrating all work within a single building. They are known in-house as 'Superkits' and are twice as fast as the old web presses. Seven different processes are involved: Off-set litho (x 3); intaglio (x 3); foiler (x 1); sheet examiner (x 43); numerota (x 3); cutpacks (x 3); packing machines (x 3). Most of the printing is offset litho, except for H.M. The Queen's portrait and some lettering which is intaglio, giving the '*raised feel*' to the banknote.

FIVE POUNDS George Stephenson 25 November 1991

Design, dimensions and watermark as for *B357* G.M. Gill Series E banknotes. Printed on web presses in sheets of 18 (3 x 6) at the Bank of England Works, Debden.

B363s Specimen black capitals

			VF	EF	UNC
B362	**£5**	Turquoise			
		Quantity printed: 450 million	VF	EF	UNC
		Prefixes: (overlaps Gill B357 R S T U)			
	R01	(first run, also in C106)	12	26	60
	R--	S-- T-- U-- W--	-	20	45
	W18	(998500 on, in C110)		-	110
	W18	(last run, from circulation)	30	80	150

B362 First low serial R01 Light £5 top left

Prefixes R, S, T and U have been recorded with the signature of G.M. Gill B357. The Bank has confirmed that these were issued concurrently from old stock after Gill had ceased to be Chief Cashier. For more information see B357/71.

B362 Last W18 high serial *from* C110

FIVE POUNDS George Stephenson 1 March 1993

Design, dimensions and watermark as for *B357* G.M. Gill Series E banknotes, but top left the **£5 Denomination Darker** and more sharply defined. Printed on web presses in sheets of 18 (3 x 6) at the Bank of England Works, Debden.

			VF	EF	UNC
B363	**£5**	Turquoise			
		Quantity printed: 100 million	VF	EF	UNC
		Prefixes:			
	AA01	(first run, from circulation)	10	20	35
	AA01	(998500 on, in C110)		-	30
	AA--	AB--	-	12	25
	AB18	(998500 on, in C107)	-	40	90
	AB18	(last run, from circulation)	25	70	140

B363 Last AB18 *from* C107 Dark £5 top left

			EF	UNC
B363s	**£5**	Specimen		
		Prefix/Serial: AA00 000000		
		Red cameo capitals printed once horizontally	-	1800
		Black capitals printed once horizontally	-	2200

FIVE POUNDS George Stephenson 1993

Design, dimensions and watermark as for *B363* but printed on sheet-fed presses in sheets of 40 (5 x 8) and later, from the CC prefix, in sheets of 45 (5 x 9) at the Bank of England Works, Debden, Essex.

			VF	EF	UNC
B364	**£5**	Turquoise			
		Quantity printed: 2,200 million	VF	EF	UNC
		Prefixes:			
	AC01	(first run, from circulation)	40	95	180
	AC01	(first run in C108)	15	40	90
		AC-- AD-- AE-- AH-- AJ-- AK-- AL--			
	BA-- BB--	BC-- BD-- BE-- BH-- BJ-- BK-- BL--	-	10	20
	CA-- CB--	CC-- CD-- CE-- CH-- CJ-- CK--			
	DA-- DB--	DC--			
	DC90	(last production run)	65	120	200
	DL99	(last, special run in C142 & C146)		-	45
B364cs	*Column Sort:* (overlaps Lowther B380cs)				
	CL01	(first run)	55	110	220
	CL--		8	20	50
	CL45	(last run)	80	180	-
	Special Prefixes in Presentation Packs:	BH & BJ 25-28		-	18
	BE98 HK97 HM50	HM70 PW50 YR19		*from*	35

B364 HM70 is the first Special Prefix issued in C119.

B364 DL99 Last low serial Special Run

B364 HK97 Special Prefix Hong Kong handover *from* C122

B365	**£5**	Replacement			
		Quantity printed: 1·57 million	VF	EF	UNC
		Prefixes: (overlaps Lowther B381)			
	LL01	(first run)	50	110	220
	LL--		25	55	100
	LL40 / LL45	(last runs)	80	180	-

B365 Replacement First LL01

Serials 980001 to 999999 were printed 40 (5 x 8) to a sheet, to LL40 and 45 (5 x 9) to a sheet, to LL45. B365 is the first LL replacement.

TEN POUNDS Charles Dickens 29 April 1992

Designed by Roger Withington, featuring on the obverse H.M. The Queen's portrait with a vignette of Britannia and diamond shaped symbol to assist the partially-sighted. The reverse shows a portrait of novelist Charles Dickens beside a scene from the cricket match at Dingley Dell, based on an illustration from the first edition of The Pickwick Papers. Printed on web presses in sheets of 40 (5 x 8) at the Bank of England Works, Debden, Essex on banknote paper manufactured by Portals with watermark of the Queen's head in registration. Copyright 1992. The banknotes measure 142 x 75mm and ceased to be legal tender after 31st July 2003.

B366	**£10**	Orange-Brown			
		Quantity printed: 1,280 million	VF	EF	UNC
		Prefixes:			
	A01	(first run, also in C104 C105 C117)	-	22	50
	A--	B-- C-- D-- E-- H-- J-- K--	-	18	35
	L--	N-- R-- S-- T-- U-- W-- X--			
	X40	(998501 on, in C111)		-	120
	X40	(officially last run, from circulation)	45	110	200
	Y--	(traced in 41 to 80)	22	50	110
	Y80	(last run)	60	140	-
B366cs	*Column Sort:*				
	Y81	(first run)	60	140	-
	Y--		22	50	110
	Y96	(last run)	50	120	250

B366 Last X40 *from* C111

The Y prefix run was printed to use up the old paper before the introduction of the enhanced security features on B369. It appears that some or all of these banknotes were put through the column sort numbering process.

B366 Charles Dickens *reverse*

			VF	EF	UNC
B366s	**£10**	Specimen *Prefix/Serial:* A00 000000			
		Red cameo capitals printed once horizontally	-	1300	1800
B367	**£10**	Experimental Issue Orange-Brown *Quantity printed:* Not known *Prefix:*			
	Z90	(only)	75	120	250
B368	**£10**	Replacement *Quantity printed:* Not known *Prefixes:*			
	M01	(first run)	60	150	350
	M--		45	100	180
	M40	(last run)	60	160	380

B368 Replacement First M01

TEN POUNDS Charles Dickens 22 November 1993

Design, dimensions and watermark as for *B366*, but **£10 Denomination** added at the top right hand corner front and reverse (crown replaced on the front). Denominations now darker and more sharply defined. Copyright 1993. Printed on sheet-fed presses in sheets of 40 (5 x 8) at the Bank of England Works.

			VF	EF	UNC
B369	**£10**	Orange-Brown			
		Quantity printed: 3,500 million	VF	EF	UNC
		Prefixes:			
	DD01	(officially first run, from circulation)	-	22	50
	DD01	(998500 on, in C111)		18	45
	DA01	(later printing, earlier cypher)	75	160	350
	DA-- DB-- DC-- DD-- DE-- DH-- DJ-- DK-- DL--				
	EA-- EB-- EC-- ED-- EE-- EH-- EJ-- EK--				
	HA-- HB-- HC-- HD-- HE-- HH-- HJ-- HK--		-	16	35
	JA-- JB-- JC-- JD-- JE-- JH-- JJ-- JK--				
	KA-- KB-- KC-- KD-- KE-- KH-- KJ-- KK--				
	KK80	(last production run)	85	200	400
	KK99	(last, special run in C143 C146)		-	60
B369cs	*Column Sort:*	(overlaps Lowther B382cs EL)			
	DL81	(first run)	50	100	200
	DL--	EL--	15	40	80
	DL96	EL01 (mid last & first)	70	130	200
	EL40	(last run)	70	135	220
	Special Prefixes in Presentation Packs:				
	BE98 HM50 HM70 PW50 YR19			*from*	45

B369 Last production run KK80

Charles Dickens *reverse* £10 added top right

			VF	EF	UNC
B369a	**£10**	Crown Top Right Orange-Brown *Quantity printed:* A few sheets? *Prefix:*			
	DD01	(only one recorded)	-	Rare	-

B369a Crown top right DD01

A single £10 banknote with the cypher DD01 has been discovered with the previous design B366 showing the Crown instead of the £10 symbol in top right corner. This suggests that one or more old sheets went through at the beginning of the new numbering system by accident or design. So far only one example with the serial 994035 is known.

			VF	EF	UNC
B369s	**£10**	Specimen *Prefix/Serial:* DD00 000000 Red cameo capitals printed once horizontally	-	1300	1800
		Prefix/Serial: AA00 000000 Black solid capitals printed twice diagonally		-	2200

			VF	EF	UNC
B369r	**£10**	Registration Banknote *Prefix/Serial:* AA00 000000			
		No overprint	300	600	1000

Can be found with orange phosphor ink line 3mm wide.

B369r Registration Banknote

B370	**£10**	Replacement *Quantity printed:* 3·52 million *Prefixes:* (overlaps Lowther B383)			
	LL01	(first run)	90	220	450
	LL--		65	120	200
	LL40	(last run)	90	220	-

B370 Replacement First LL01

TWENTY POUNDS Michael Faraday 25 November 1991

Design, dimensions and watermark as for *B358* G.M. Gill Series E banknotes. Printed on sheet-fed presses in sheets of 35 (5 x 7) at the Bank of England Works, Debden, Essex.

			VF	EF	UNC
B371	**£20**	Purple & Black			
		Quantity printed: Not known	VF	EF	UNC
		Prefixes: (overlaps Gill B358 E H J L R S U)			
	E01	(first run from circulation)	45	95	220
	E01	(first run in C106 & C118)	40	80	180
	E-- H-- J-- K-- L-- N-- R-- S-- T-- U-- W--		-	45	95
	W35	(998500 on, in C112)		-	175
	W35	(last run, from circulation)	60	120	230
B371cs	*Column Sort:*				
	A--	(first run, traced in 71 to 98)	50	95	200
	B--	(traced in 71 to 98)	55	100	220
	C--	(traced in 71 to 98)	150	250	-
	N--	(traced in 84 to 94)	100	160	-
	R--	(last run, traced in 91)	100	160	-

B371cs Column Sort First A71

Originally Gill £20 B358 ended on the D prefix with Kentfield B371 starting at E01. However, sometime during 1993 prior to the introduction of the new £20 B374 there was a 'spring clean' of old unnumbered stock with Gill's signature as well as that of Kentfield. The Gill sheets were mixed up with Kentfield and as a result were printed with later alphabetical prefixes. The L prefix seems to be scarcer. Hence, overlaps may be found. The same thing happened with the B Ream recovery system which meant that column sort prefixes were used with prefixes above 70.

			VF	EF	UNC
B372	**£20**	Experimental Issue Purple & Black			
		Quantity printed: Not known			
		Prefixes:			
	Z01	(first run)	70	180	350
	Z--	(traced in 01 to 35)	60	130	250
	Z90	(last run)	70	180	350

B372 Experimental Issue First Z01

B373	**£20**	Replacement			
		Quantity printed: Not known			
		Prefixes:			
	M01	(first run)	90	200	350
	M--		80	160	280
	M35	(last run)	100	220	-

B373 Replacement First M01

TWENTY POUNDS Michael Faraday 27 September 1993

Design, dimensions and watermark as for *B358* G.M. Gill Series E Historical banknotes, but **£20 Denomination** added at the top right hand corner front and reverse (crown replaced on the front). Denominations now darker and more sharply defined Copyright 1993. Printed on sheet-fed presses in sheets of 35 (5 x 7) at the Bank of England Works, Debden, Essex.

			VF	EF	UNC
B374	**£20**	Purple & Black			
		Quantity printed: 140 million	VF	EF	UNC
		Prefixes:			
	X01	(first run, from circulation, first 1000 not issued)	30	60	120
	X01	(998500 on, in C112)		-	100
	X--	Y-- (production runs to 70)	-	40	90
	Y70	(last run)	60	200	360
B374cs	*Column Sort:*				
	X--	Y-- (both traced in 71 to 98)	50	100	180

B374 Last Y70

Michael Faraday *reverse* £20 added top right

B374s	**£20**	Specimen			
		Prefix/Serial: X00 000000			
		Red cameo capitals printed once horizontally	600	1300	1800

TWENTY POUNDS Michael Faraday 1994

Design, dimensions and watermark as *B374*. Printed in sheets of 35 (5 x 7) and later, from prefix BA in sheets of 40 (5 x 8).

			VF	EF	UNC
B375	**£20**	Purple & Black			
		Quantity printed: 2,000 million	VF	EF	UNC
		Prefixes:			
	AA01	(first run)	80	170	350
	AA-- AB-- AC-- AD-- AE-- AH-- AJ-- AK-- AL--				
	BA-- BB-- BC-- BD-- BE-- BH-- BJ-- BK-- BL--		-	35	70
	CA-- CB-- CC-- CD-- CE-- CH-- CJ--				
	CJ80	(last production run)	80	180	350
	CL99	(last, special run in C144 C146)		-	80
B375cs	*Column Sort:*				
	CL01	(first run)	80	180	-
	CL--	(traced in 01 to 40)	28	65	130
	CL55	(last run)	110	220	430
	Special Prefixes in Presentation Packs: BE98 YR19			*from*	75

B375 Last Special Run CL99 low serial

			VF	EF	UNC
B376	**£20**	Replacement			
		Quantity printed: 1·24 million			
		Prefixes:			
	LL01	(first run)	70	150	270
	LL--		45	80	160
	LL40	(last run)	55	120	240

FIFTY POUNDS Sir John Houblon 20 April 1994

Designed by Roger Withington. H.M. The Queen's portrait with a vignette of Britannia and triangular shaped symbol to assist the partially-sighted on the front. Reverse shows a portrait of Sir John Houblon, first Governor of the Bank of England, appearing beside a scene of his house in Threadneedle Street together with an 18th century Bank gatekeeper. Additional security devices are a medallion, **Silver Foil Tudor Rose** with the serial printed over it. Printed in sheets of 28 (4 x 7) and later, from prefix E in sheets of 35 (5 x 7) at the Bank of England Works, Debden, Essex, on banknote paper manufactured by Portals with watermark of the Queen's head in registration and a **Windowed Thread**. The banknotes measure 156 x 85mm.

			VF	EF	UNC
B377	**£50**	Red			
		Quantity printed: Not known	VF	EF	UNC
		Prefixes:			
	A01	(first run, also in C113 C115 C117)	65	95	160
	A--	B-- C-- D-- E-- H--	-	70	120
	H70	(last production run)	80	120	-
	H99	(last, special run in C145, C146)		-	150
B377cs	*Column Sort:* (overlaps Lowther B385 L & Bailey B404 L)				
	A--	(first run traced in 85 to 98)	80	120	-
	B--	(traced in 85 to 98)	70	100	-
	H--	(traced in 71 to 98)	70	100	120
	L01	(first run)	75	110	200
	L--		-	70	120
	L35	(last run)	80	120	-
	Special Prefixes in Presentation Packs:	EP50 PW50 YR19		*from*	160

B377 Last Special Run 000001 serial

B377 Sir John Houblon *reverse* Copyright 1994

CANCELLED (on the reverse) B377's from the Millenium Dome one million pound display can be obtained slabbed, usually found in charity auctions. £300 UNC

B377s	**£50**	Specimen	VF	EF	UNC
		Prefix/Serial: A00 000000			
		Black cameo capitals printed once horizontally	-	1500	2200
		Black solid capitals printed once horizontally		-	2400

B377s Specimen

			VF	EF	UNC
B378	**£50**	Experimental Issue Red *Quantity printed:* A99 1 million M99 50,000 *Prefixes:*			
	A99	(only)	70	140	250
	M99	(only)	120	200	380

B378 Experimental Issue M99

B379	**£50**	Replacement *Quantity printed:* 210,000 *Prefixes:*			
	LL01	(first run)	220	400	-
	LL--		80	140	250
	LL35	(last run)	180	350	-

B379 Replacement

© Bank of England

MERLYN VIVIENNE LOWTHER
1999-2003

Merlyn Lowther was born on 3rd March 1954. She was educated at Manchester High School for Girls and at the University of Manchester where she graduated with first class honours in mathematics in 1975. She gained her MSc (Economics) from the London Business School in 1981. Ms Lowther has spent her entire working life at the Bank, joining direct from university as an analyst in the Economics Division. Over the following fifteen years she worked variously in Money Market Operations, Foreign Exchange and the Gilt Edged Division. In 1991 she was appointed Head of Banking and Deputy Chief Cashier and in 1996 became Personnel Director. Merlyn Lowther was appointed the 29th Chief Cashier and a Deputy Director of the Bank on 1st January 1999, the first woman to hold the position in the Bank's 300 year history. She retired on 31st December 2003.

B380cs First Column Sort CL01

SERIES E FIRST HISTORICAL 1990 *to* 1999

FIVE POUNDS George Stephenson 1 January 1999

Design, dimensions and watermark as for *B357* G.M. Gill Series E notes, but incorporating modifications as in G.E.A. Kentfield £5 banknotes B363. Printed on sheet-fed presses in sheets of 45 (5 x 9). Ceased to be legal tender after 21st November 2003.

			VF	EF	UNC
B380	**£5**	Turquoise			
		Quantity printed: 512 million	VF	EF	UNC
		Prefixes:			
	EA01	(first run from circulation)	-	25	60
	EA01	(first run, in C142 998501 on & C147 to 001000)	-	-	45
	EA46	(first production run, 02 to 45 not seen)		-	30
	EA--	EB-- EC-- ED-- EE-- EH-- EJ--	-	10	20
	E J45	(last production run)	-	140	330
	E J90	(special run in C162, 999001 on)		-	180
B380cs	*Column Sort:* (overlaps Kentfield B364cs)				
	CL01	(first run)	30	70	120
	CL--		-	10	25
	CL45	(last run)	55	120	-
	Special Prefixes in Presentation Packs:				
	GJ20 QE50 QM10 QM20 QV20 VR10 YR20			*from*	25
B381	**£5**	Replacement			
		Quantity printed: 2·12 million			
		Prefixes: (overlaps Kentfield B365)			
	LL01	(first run)	25	65	110
	LL--		12	30	70
	LL45	(last run)	25	65	110

B381 Last Replacement LL45

TEN POUNDS Charles Dickens 1 January 1999

Design, dimensions and watermark as for *B366* G.E.A. Kentfield Series E banknotes, incorporating modifications as in Kentfield £10 banknotes B369. Printed on sheet-fed presses in sheets of 40 (5 x 8) at the Bank of England Works, Debden, Essex.

			VF	EF	UNC
B382	**£10**	Orange-Brown			
		Quantity printed: 160 million	VF	EF	UNC
		Prefixes:			
	KL01	(first run, from circulation & C147)	25	45	75
	KL01	(998500 on, in C143)		-	50
	KL--	LA--	-	25	45
	LA80	(999000 on, in C157)		-	45
	LA80	(last run, from circulation)	-	60	135
B382cs	*Column Sort:* (overlaps Kentfield B369cs)				
	EL01	(first run)	70	160	-
	EL--		30	60	90
	EL40	(last run)	70	160	-
	Special Prefixes in Presentation Packs: QM10 YR20			*from*	35

B382 First low serial KL01 & B383 First LL01

			VF	EF	UNC
B383	**£10**	Replacement			
		Quantity printed: 840,000			
		Prefixes: (overlaps Kentfield B370)			
	LL01	(first run)	80	180	-
	LL--		45	85	170
	LL40	(last run)	80	180	350

TWENTY POUNDS Michael Faraday 1 January 1999

Design, dimensions and watermark as for *B358* G.M. Gill Series E banknotes, but incorporating modifications as in G.E.A. Kentfield £20 banknotes B374. Printed on sheet-fed presses in sheets of 40 (5 x 8) at the Bank of England Works, Debden, Essex. Ceased to be legal tender after 28th February 2001.

			VF	EF	UNC
B384	**£20**	Purple & Black			
		Quantity printed: Less than 1·5 million	VF	EF	UNC
		Prefixes:			
	DA01	(first run, from circulation & C144 + C147)	50	75	125
	DA41	(first production run)	50	85	150
	DA--		40	60	100
	DA80	(999000 on, in C148)		-	110
	DA80	(last run, from circulation)	50	85	150

This was a very short run. An unknown number of DA01 notes were printed followed by 34,000 sheets in the DA41 to 80 range from 966001 to 999999, a total of 1·36 million. Very few replacement banknotes were needed and it is understood that B376 Kentfield LL's were used. None were produced with Lowther's signature.

B384 First DA01 & Last DA80

FIFTY POUNDS Sir John Houblon 1 January 1999

Design, dimensions and watermark as for *B377* G.E.A. Kentfield Series E banknotes. Printed on sheet-fed presses in sheets of 35 (5 x 7) at the Bank of England Works, Debden, Essex.

			VF	EF	UNC
B385	**£50**	Red			
		Quantity printed: Not known	VF	EF	UNC
		Prefixes: (overlaps Bailey B404 M)			
	J01	(first run, lowest available 000011, from circ & C146 + C147)	-	110	180
	J01	(J in 01 only - 998500 on, in C145)		-	140
	K--	M--	-	70	120
	M35	(last run)	60	95	190
B385cs	*Column Sort:*	(overlaps Kentfield B377cs L & Bailey B404cs L)			
	K71	(first run)	75	180	-
	K--	L--	-	75	150
	K98	L01 (mid last/first)	65	140	275
	L70	(last run)	75	180	-

B385 Low serial First & B385cs L01 Column Sort

SERIES E SECOND HISTORICAL 1999 *continuing*

On 22nd December 1998, ten years after the original Series E was launched, the Bank announced that the existing historical figures would be replaced over the next few years, and that additional security devices would be used. In fact Roger Withington had produced a short list of fifteen, including Darwin, Elgar, Purcell, Tennyson, Keats, Shelley, Gainsborough, Turner and Grace Darling. The original choice for the £10 had been Charles Darwin but his views were held to be 'inappropriate at the time'. No longer, it seems! The banknotes were to retain their size and basic format, including the same portrait of H.M. The Queen, hence staying with Series E and not moving on to Series F.

The first of the new releases was the £20 on 22nd June 1999 with a portrait of the composer Sir Edward Elgar to replace Michael Faraday. On 17th May 2000, the Bank announced a new version of the £10 banknote featuring a portrait of the naturalist and scientist Charles Darwin to replace Charles Dickens. This was released on 7th November 2000 and as with the £20, the banknotes are the same size and broadly follow the original Series E design.

On 18th December 2001 the Bank announced a new version of the £5 banknote with the Quaker philanthropist and 19th century prison reformer, Elizabeth Fry replacing George Stephenson. The banknote was issued on 21st May 2002 but had to be suspended a week later to sort out problems with the varnish coating. The banknotes were re-issued on 19th August 2002. The other important change which occurred in April 2003 was the transfer of the printing contract to De La Rue, which took over the Debden works and the trade name Debden Security Printing.

TWENTY POUNDS Sir Edward Elgar 22 June 1999

Original design by Roger Withington, showing H.M. The Queen's portrait on the obverse and a square symbol to assist the partially-sighted. Modified by Andrew Ward with new features including a **Foil Hologram** which switches from an image of Britannia to the figure 20 when viewed at different angles; also a fluorescent red and green number 20 is clearly visible under ultra-violet light. The reverse of the banknote contains a portrait of Sir Edward Elgar together with the west face of Worcester Cathedral and other vignettes relating to his life and work. The metallic security **Windowed Thread** is now visible from the reverse instead of the front of the banknote, and appears as a continuous line when held up to the light. Copyright 1999. Printed on sheet-fed presses in sheets of 40 (5 x 8) at the Bank of England Works, Debden, Essex. The banknotes ceased being legal tender after 30th June 2010.

			VF	EF	UNC
B386	**£20**	Purple & Black			
		Quantity printed: 2,320 million	VF	EF	UNC
		Prefixes: (overlaps Bailey B402 DE41-80)			
	AA01	(first run, lowest 000031, from circulation & C170)	-	40	60
	AA01	(999000 on, in C148)		-	50
	AA-- AB-- AC-- AD-- AE-- AH-- AJ-- AK-- BA-- BB-- BC-- BD-- BE-- BH-- BJ-- BK-- CA-- CB-- CC-- CD-- CE-- CH-- CJ-- CK-- DA-- DB-- DD-- DE--		-	25	40
	DE80	(last run)	70	150	260
B386cs	*Column Sort:* (overlaps Bailey B402cs BL)				
	AL01	(first run)	50	95	170
	AL-- BL--		-	30	65
	AL80 BL01	(mid last/first)	35	60	120
	BL40	(last run)	50	110	-
	Special Prefixes in Presentation Packs:				
	ER50 QC50 QM10 VR10 YR20			*from*	65

The DB prefix was the first run to be printed, picking up from the last Faraday £20 DA B384, before the prefix/cypher machines were reset to AA. The DC prefix has not been seen and may not exist.

B386 First AA01 low serial

B386cs Column Sort AL01

B386 Sir Edward Elgar *reverse*

			VF	EF	UNC
B386s	**£20**	Specimen			
		Prefix/Serial: AA00 000000			
		Red solid capitals printed once horizontally	-	1300	1800
		Black solid capitals printed once horizontally	-	1600	-

			VF	EF	UNC
B386p	**£20**	Signature Sequence Pair (only one recorded Pair with consecutive serials		-	Rare

Banknotes with signature of M.V. Lowther B386cs were issued concurrently with those of A.J. Bailey B402cs. One pair recorded with a column sort prefix BL23 718783/4.

B386p Signature Sequence Pair

			VF	EF	UNC
B387	**£20**	Replacement *Quantity printed:* 5·6 million *Prefixes:* (overlaps Bailey B403)			
	LL01	(first run)	60	140	330
	LL--		35	60	110
	LL40	(last run)	60	140	330

TEN POUNDS Charles Darwin 7 November 2000

Original design by Roger Withington, showing H.M. The Queen's portrait on the obverse and a diamond shaped symbol to assist the partially-sighted. Modified by Andrew Ward with new features including a **Foil Hologram** which switches from an image of Britannia to the figure 10 when viewed at different angles; also a fluorescent red and green number 10 is clearly visible under ultra-violet light. The reverse of the banknote contains a portrait of Charles Darwin together with vignettes relating to his life and work. The metallic **Windowed Thread** is now visible from the reverse instead of the front of the banknote, and appears as a continuous line when held up to the light. Printed on sheet-fed presses in sheets of 40 (5 x 8) at the Bank of England Works, Debden. There are two versions of the 'Copyright 2000' wording around the central watermark area:

THE GOVERNOR AND **THE COMPANY** OF THE BANK OF ENGLAND

THE GOVERNOR **AND COMPANY** OF THE BANK OF ENGLAND

THE COMPANY B388

AND COMPANY B390

			VF	EF	UNC
B388	**£10**	Orange-Brown THE COMPANY			
		Quantity printed: 450 million			
		Prefixes: (overlaps B390 AD)			
	AA01	(first run, lowest 000031, also in C170)	-	25	45
	AA--	AB-- AC-- AD-- AE-- AH--	-	16	32
	AH80	(last run)	100	210	450
B388cs	*Column Sort:*	(overlaps B390cs & Bailey B400cs)			
	EL01	(first run)	50	110	220
	EL--		15	30	70
	EL40	(last run)	45	100	180

The Bank has confirmed that the first copyright was used for the AA to AH prefixes. However, the AD prefix was used with both types of copyright, and overlaps may be found. The first production run of the new copyright started at AJ. Subsequently a special run of AA01 was produced by Debden Security Printing for use in presentation packs, serials 999001 to 999999. LL replacements and EL column sorts are found in both types. Several Darwin £10 column sorts have been discovered with a mismatched prefix error, showing DL24 in one position and EL24 in the other. This and similar '*mistakes*' are usually put down to '*operator error*'.

B388 Charles Darwin THE COMPANY *reverse*

			VF	EF	UNC
B389	**£10**	Replacement THE COMPANY			
		Quantity printed: 1·96 million	VF	EF	UNC
		Prefixes: (overlaps B391 & Bailey B401)			
	LL01	(first run)	60	120	280
	LL--		35	75	165
	LL40	(last run)	60	140	320

B389 First Replacement LL01

			VF	EF	UNC
B390	**£10**	Orange-Brown AND COMPANY			
		Quantity printed: 1,045 million	VF	EF	UNC
		Prefixes: (overlaps Bailey B400 CC41-80)			
	AA01	(first, special run in C157, 999000 on)		-	60
	AD--	(later printing, earlier prefix overlaps B388 to AD40)	40	90	180
	AJ01	(first production run)	50	110	200
		AJ-- AK--			
	BA-- BB-- BC-- BD-- BE-- BH-- BJ-- BK--		-	16	30
	CA-- CB-- CC--				
	CC80	(last run)	40	110	200
B390cs	*Column Sort:* (overlaps B388cs & Bailey B400cs)				
	EL01	(first run)	50	100	200
	EL--		-	16	32
	EL80	(last run)	80	170	320

Special Prefixes in Presentation Packs:
ER50 QC50 QV10 VR10 — *from* 35

B390 Last CC80 & B390cs First EL01

			VF	EF	UNC
B390s	**£10**	Specimen AND COMPANY *Prefix/Serial:* AA00 000000			
		Red solid capitals printed once horizontally	-	1300	1800

B390s Specimen

B391	**£10**	Replacement AND COMPANY *Quantity printed:* 3 million *Prefixes:* (overlaps B389 & Bailey B401)			
	LL01	(first run)	50	110	220
	LL--		25	60	95
	LL40	(last run)	70	170	320

B391 First Replacement LL01

B392 **£10** Experimental Issue Circulation
Orange-Brown AND COMPANY
Quantity printed: 465,000
Prefixes:

Prefixes	VF	EF	UNC
MH01 (first run)	180	350	-
MH-- MJ-- MK-- MM--	90	160	360
MM40 (last run)	160	350	-

Experimental banknote issue used in circulation trials, issued from February 2004. Serials logged from 999000 down to 996001.

B392 Experimental Issue MK01

B392 Experimental Issue MM01

FIVE POUNDS Elizabeth Fry 21 May 2002

Original design by Roger Withington, showing H.M. The Queen's portrait on the front and a round symbol to assist the partially-sighted. Modified with new historical figure by Andrew Ward and other new features including a **Foil Hologram** which switches from an image of Britannia to the figure 5 when viewed at different angles; also a fluorescent red and green number 5 is clearly visible under ultra-violet light. The reverse of the note contains the portrait of Elizabeth Fry together with vignettes relating to her life and work. The metallic **Windowed Thread** is now visible from the reverse instead of the front of the note, and appears as a continuous line when held up to the light. Copyright 2002. The paper has a varnish coating intended to prolong the life of the banknote in circulation. Printed on sheet-fed presses in sheets of 45 (5 x 9) at the Bank of England Works, Debden, Essex.

The first production run was printed with the prefix HA (picking up from the last Stephenson £5 EJ B380. However, the issue had to be suspended after a week because the prefix/serial could be rubbed off from the unvarnished surface above the hologram. About 3 million out of the 200 million printed were said to be affected. The solution was to reduce the unvarnished area surrounding the hologram. The issue resumed on 19th August. By holding the banknote at an angle to the light, the difference will be apparent as a Full Halo (full oval) unvarnished area on the first type, and a Cut Halo (flat topped oval) unvarnished area on the amended version. Some banknotes were issued with the varnish coating completely omitted.

FULL HALO B393

CUT HALO B395

B393 Elizabeth Fry *reverse*

			VF	EF	UNC
B393	**£5**	Turquoise Full Halo			
		Quantity printed: 200 million	VF	EF	UNC
		Prefixes:			
	HA01	(first run, lowest available 000005, also in C170)	-	15	30
	HA-- HB-- J A--		-	8	18
	J A90	(last run)	20	45	95
B393cs	*Column Sort:* (overlaps B395cs)				
	DL01	(first run)	60	130	-
	DL--		-	12	25
	DL45	(last run)	75	180	350
	Special Prefix in Presentation Packs: ER50			-	40

B393 Last JA90

			VF	EF	UNC
B393s	**£5**	Specimen Full Halo			
		Prefix/Serial: AA00 000000			
		Red solid capitals printed once horizontally	-	1300	1800

			VF	EF	UNC
B394	**£5**	Replacement Full Halo			
		Quantity printed: 4·5 million			
		Prefixes: (overlaps B396 & Bailey B399)			
	LL46	(first run)	55	110	220
	LL--		-	15	30
	LL90	(last run)	75	170	350

B395 **£5** Turquoise Cut Halo

			VF	EF	UNC
		Quantity printed: Not known	VF	EF	UNC
		Prefixes: (overlaps Bailey B398 JB46-90)			
	HA01	(first, special run in C162 999001 on)	-	20	45
	HC01	(first production run)	25	60	120
	HC-- HD-- HE-- HH-- HJ-- JB--		-	8	15
	J B90	(last run)	50	100	200
B395cs	*Column Sort:* (overlaps B393cs DL & Bailey B398cs EL)				
	DL01	(first run)	60	130	260
	DL-- EL--		-	12	25
	DL45 EL01	(mid last/first)	40	80	170
	E L45	(last run)	70	180	-

Special Prefixes in Presentation Packs:
HM02 HM03 QC03 QC50 — *from* 25

B395cs Column Sort DL45

B396 **£5** Replacement Cut Halo (not all were used as such)

			VF	EF	UNC
		Quantity printed: 4·5 million			
		Prefixes: (overlaps B394 & Bailey B399)			
	LL46	(first run)	55	110	220
	LL--		-	15	30
	LL90	(last run)	75	170	320

			F	VF	EF
B397	**£5**	Experimental Issue Durability Turquoise *Quantity printed:* 880,000 *Prefixes:*			
	XA01	(first run, unvarnished)	100	240	-
	XA-- XB-- XC-- XD--	(unvarnished)	85	180	300
	XE-- XH-- XJ-- XK--	(varnished Cut Halo)			
	XK45	(last run, varnished Cut Halo)	100	220	-

B397 Experimental Issue First XA01

B397 Experimental Issue Last XK45

Varnish Coating Trials to test durability are reported to have been issued in tranches, between February and November 2004. XA to XD have no varnish coating. XE to XK are varnished with the Cut Halo unvarnished area. Serials have been noted from 999000 down to 996501. Apart from a small run of banknotes with the prefix XB12 only a few uncirculated banknotes have surfaced. £450 UNC

© Bank of England

ANDREW JOHN BAILEY
2004-2011

Andrew Bailey was born on 30th March 1959. He was educated in Leicester at Wyggeston Boys School, followed by the University of Central England, Birmingham, and Queens' College, Cambridge where he obtained a BA and Ph.D. He was a research officer at the London School of Economics before joining the international division of the Bank on 3rd June 1985. After moving into Banking Services, he became senior manager for Policy, Risk and Special Operations, then was appointed private secretary to the Governor and after that Head of the International Economic Analysis Division in Monetary Analysis. On 1st January 2004, he returned to Banking Services combining the role of Executive Director and the 30th Chief Cashier. Bailey left the post on 1st April 2011 to become Deputy Head of the Prudential Business Unit of the FSA. Mr. Bailey is married with two children and includes among his recreations gardening and supporting West Bromwich Albion.

Release of banknotes bearing the signature of A.J. Bailey was announced in a press notice on Monday 15th March 2004, but there was no official information on the first prefixes and no presentation packs were prepared. The traditional facility at the Bank's HQ in Threadneedle Street for collectors to obtain banknotes on the first day of issue was withdrawn and the press notice merely stated that: 'All banknotes will be issued in the normal way through the day-to-day distribution network operated by the Bank and main commercial cash handlers.'

SERIES E SECOND HISTORICAL 1999 *to* 2017

FIVE POUNDS Elizabeth Fry 15 March 2004

Design, watermark and dimensions as for *B393* M.V. Lowther Series E Second Historical banknotes. As of JJ90 the paper was unvarnished, from JK01 banknotes can be found on both **varnished** paper with the cut halo and **unvarnished** paper. Printed on sheet-fed presses in sheets of 45 (5 x 9) by De La Rue at the Debden Security Printing works, Essex.

			VF	EF	UNC
B398	**£5**	Turquoise Cut Halo & Unvarnished			
		Quantity printed: Not known	VF	EF	UNC
		Prefixes: (overlaps Lowther B395 JB & B407 LE)			
	JB46	(first run)	15	35	75
		JB-- JC-- JD-- JE-- JH-- JJ-- JK--			
	KA--	KB-- KC-- KD-- KE-- KH-- KJ-- KK--	-	8	15
		LB-- LC-- LD-- LE--			
	LE90	(last run)	65	130	260
B398cs	*Column Sort:* (overlaps Lowther B395cs)				
	EL01	(first run)	18	45	80
	EL--		-	10	17
	EL45	(last run)	25	55	100

The LA prefix has not been seen and may not exist.

B398 LE90 Last

B398 EL01 First Column Sort

B399	**£5**	Replacement Cut Halo			
		Quantity printed: Not known	VF	EF	UNC
		Prefixes: (overlaps Lowther B394 & B396)			
	LL46	(first run)	45	90	200
	LL--		-	12	25
	LL90	(last run)	65	130	260

B399 LL90 Replacement Last

TEN POUNDS Charles Darwin 15 March 2004

Design, watermark and dimensions as for *B390* M.V. Lowther Series E Second Historical banknotes. Printed on sheet-fed presses in sheets of 40 (5 x 8) by De La Rue at the Debden Security Printing works, Essex. HK prefix not seen.

			VF	EF	UNC
B400	**£10**	Orange-Brown			
		Quantity printed: Not known	VF	EF	UNC
		Prefixes: (overlaps Lowther B390 CC & B408 KB KC)			
	CC41	(first run)	30	70	150
		CC-- CD-- CE-- CH-- CJ-- CK--			
	DA--	DB-- DC-- DD-- DE-- DH-- DJ-- DK--			
	EA--	EB-- EC-- ED-- EE-- EH-- EJ-- EK--	-	12	18
	HA--	HB-- HC-- HD-- HE-- HH-- HJ--			
	JA--	JB-- JC-- JD-- JE-- JH-- JJ-- JK--			
	KA--	KB-- KC--			
	KC40	(last run)	45	110	240
B400cs	*Column Sort:*	(overlaps Lowther B388cs EL & B390cs EL)			
	EL41	(first run)	60	140	-
	EL--		-	13	28
	HL--		15	30	50
	EL80	HL01 (mid last/first)	20	50	100
	HL40	(last run)	30	80	150

B400 Column Sort HL01

			VF	EF	UNC
B401	**£10**	Replacement			
		Quantity printed: Not known			
		Prefixes: (overlaps Lowther B389 & B391)			
	LL01	(first run)	30	70	140
	LL--		15	25	55
	LL40	(last run)	30	70	140

TWENTY POUNDS Sir Edward Elgar 15 March 2004

Design, watermark and dimensions as for *B386* M.V. Lowther Series E Second Historical banknotes. Printed on sheet-fed presses in sheets of 40 (5 x 8) by De La Rue at the Debden Security Printing works, Essex. Withdrawn from circulation on 30th June 2010.

			VF	EF	UNC
B402	**£20**	Purple & Black			
		Quantity printed: Not known	VF	EF	UNC
		Prefixes: (overlaps Lowther B386 DE)			
	DE41	(first run)	65	130	260
	DE-- DH-- DJ-- DK-- EA-- EB-- EC-- ED-- EE-- EH--		-	25	40
	EH40	(last run)	65	130	260
B402cs	*Column Sort:* (overlaps Lowther B386cs)				
	BL01	(first run)	30	70	140
	BL--		-	25	48
	BL40	(last run)	30	65	130

B402 Last EH40

			VF	EF	UNC
B403	**£20**	Replacement			
		Quantity printed: Not known			
		Prefixes: (overlaps Lowther B387)			
	LL01	(first run)	75	160	-
	LL--		-	35	70
	LL40	(last run)	45	85	145

FIFTY POUNDS **Sir John Houblon** August 2006

Design, dimensions and watermark as for *B377* G.E.A. Kentfield Series E Historical banknotes. Printed on sheet-fed presses in sheets of 35 (5 x 7) by De La Rue at the Debden Security Printing works, Essex. Ceased to be legal tender after 30th April 2014.

			VF	EF	UNC
B404	**£50**	Red			
		Quantity printed: Not known	VF	EF	UNC
		Prefixes: (overlaps Lowther B385 M)			
	L01	(first run)	75	100	180
	L-- M-- N-- R--		-	70	110
	R70	(last run)	75	100	180
B404cs	*Column Sort:* (overlaps Lowther B385cs)				
	L 71	(first run)	90	180	-
	L --		-	80	120
	L 87	(last run, may go higher)	85	160	-

B404 First L01 & Last R70

SERIES F THIRD HISTORICAL 2007 *continuing*

TWENTY POUNDS Adam Smith 13 March 2007

Original design by Roger Withington, showing H.M. The Queen's portrait on the front and £ symbol synchronised with the reverse. New features including a continuous **Foil Hologram Strip**, images which alternate from Adam Smith to a £ symbol and figure 20 when viewed at different angles; also a fluorescent red and green number 20 is clearly visible under ultra-violet light. Adam Smith FRSE 1723-90 depicted on the reverse, a Scottish moral philosopher and regarded as one of the fathers of modern economics, to his right a depiction of pin manufacturing. **Prefixes/Serials switched to the reverse**, the Windowed Thread appearing as a continuous line when held up to the light. Copyright 2006. Dimensions 150 x 80mm. Printed on sheet-fed presses in sheets of 40 (5 x 8) by De La Rue at the Debden Security Printing works.

			VF	EF	UNC
B405	**£20**	Purple			
		Quantity printed: Not known	VF	EF	UNC
		Prefixes: (overlaps Salmon B409 HA HB HD HE)			
	AA01	(first run, lowest available 000007)	-	30	60
	AA-- AB-- AC-- AD-- AE-- AH-- AJ-- AK-- BA-- BB-- BC-- BD-- BE-- BH-- BJ-- BK-- CA-- CB-- CC-- CD-- CE-- CH-- CJ-- CK-- DA-- DB-- DC-- DD-- DE-- DH-- DJ-- DK-- EA-- EB-- EC-- ED-- EE-- EH-- EJ-- EK-- HA-- HB-- HC-- HD-- HE--		-	25	35
	HE80	(last run)	45	110	240
B405cs	*Column Sort:*				
	AL01	(first run)	35	60	120
	AL--		-	26	50
	AL40	(last run)	35	60	120

B405 Front

B405 Last HE80 prefix on *reverse*

			VF	EF	UNC
B406	**£20**	Replacement			
		Quantity printed: Not known	VF	EF	UNC
		Prefixes:			
	LL01	(first run)	32	70	150
	LL--		-	30	60
	LL40	(last run)	35	75	170

B406 Last Replacement LL40 prefix *reverse*

Replacement and Column Sort banknotes have been discontinued on all values after:
B399 £5 - B401 £10 - B406 £20 - B404cs £50

Sheets of forty Bailey £20's sold at a charity auction: BC41 *to* BC80 and BD01 *to* BD40 all with 999999 serials.

© Bank of England

CHRIS SALMON
2011-2014

Chris Salmon was born on 29th August 1968 and joined the Bank in 1991 in the Economics Division. He holds a BSc in Economics from Bristol University and an MSc in Econometrics and Mathematical Economics from LSE. In 2000 he was seconded to the IMF for two years, after which he was appointed Head of the Bank's International Finance Division. Salmon then became the Governor's private secretary for three years before being appointed Head of Sterling Markets Division in 2009. He was appointed the 31st Chief Cashier as of April 1st 2011. Chris's hobbies include running, playing tennis and supporting Manchester United FC.

SERIES E SECOND HISTORICAL 1999 *to* 2017

FIVE POUNDS Elizabeth Fry 12 September 2012

Design, watermark and dimensions as for *B393* M.V. Lowther Series E Second Historical banknotes. Printed on sheet-fed presses in sheets of 45 (5 x 9) by De La Rue at the Debden Security Printing works, Essex. Ceased to be legal tender after 5th May 2017.

B407 **£5** Turquoise

Quantity printed: Not known

Prefixes: (overlaps Bailey B398 LE)

Prefixes	VF	EF	UNC
LE46 (first run, starts 082001)	10	30	70
LE-- LH-- LJ-- LK-- MA-- MB-- MC-- MD--	-	6	10
MD90 (last run)	-	110	200

B407 Low serial First LE46

B407 Last MD90

TEN POUNDS Charles Darwin 12 September 2012

Design, watermark and dimensions as for *B390* M.V. Lowther Series E Second Historical banknotes. Printed on sheet-fed presses in sheets of 40 (5 x 8) by De La Rue at the Debden Security Printing works, Essex.

			VF	EF	UNC
B408	**£10**	Orange-Brown			
		Quantity printed: Not known	VF	EF	UNC
		Prefixes: (overlaps Bailey B400 KB KC & Cleland B411 LH)			
	JH01	(first run, starts 033001)	50	110	200
		JH-- JJ--			
		KB-- KC-- KD-- KE-- KH-- KJ-- KK--	-	12	20
		LB-- LC-- LD-- LE-- LH--			
	LH40	(last run)	30	90	180

The KA and LA prefixs have not been seen and may not exist.

B408 Low serial First JH01

B408 LH40 Last

SERIES F THIRD HISTORICAL 2007 *continuing*

TWENTY POUNDS Adam Smith 12 September 2012

Design, watermark and dimensions as for *B405* A.J. Bailey Series F Third Historical banknotes. Dimensions 150 x 80mm. Printed on sheet-fed presses in sheets of 40 (5 x 8) by De La Rue at the Debden Security Printing works, Essex.

			VF	EF	UNC
B409	**£20**	Purple			
		Quantity printed: Not known	VF	EF	UNC
		Prefixes: (overlaps Bailey B405 HA HB HD HE & Cleland B412 JH)			
	HA01 (first run, lowest available 000001)		60	120	240
	HA-- HB-- HD-- HE-- HH-- HJ-- HK-- JA-- JB-- JC-- JD-- JE-- JH--		-	25	35
	J??? (last run)				

The series may end JH80, further prefixes may also be issued?

HA01 000001 to 000025 sold in a charity auction, HA01 to HA40 scarce, HA41 to HA80 readily available. The HC prefix has not been seen and may not exist.

B409 Low serial First HA01 *reverse*

FIFTY POUNDS Matthew Boulton & James Watt 2 November 2011

Designed and printed by De La Rue, showing H.M. The queen's portrait to the front right with £ symbol synchronised with the reverse to the left. New features include a **Motion Thread** woven into the paper, it has five green windows along its length which contain images of the £ symbol and the number 50, also retains a metallic thread. When the banknote is tilted from side to side, the images move up and down and when tilted up and down the images move from side to side, the 50 and £ symbol switch. Under ultra-violet the 50 appears in bright red and green as do randomly spread bright flecks also visible on both sides the banknote. The watermark incorporates an image of the Queen together with a bright £50. The reverse depicts Matthew Boulton (1728-1809) an Industrialist and Entrepreneur born in Birmingham, renowned for development, production and sale of steam engines and the minting of high quality coins. Alongside James Watt (1736-1819) an Engineer and Scientist from Greenock, Scotland. James was the great improver of the steam engine, he also introduced the term '*horsepower*' and the metric unit of power is named after him. Prefixes/Serials switched to the reverse. Dimensions 156 x 85mm. Printed in sheets of 35 (5 x 7). Copyright 2010.

B410 £50 Red

	VF	EF	UNC
Quantity printed: Not known *Prefixes:* (overlaps Cleland B413 AJ)			
AA01 (first run, lowest available 000013)	-	65	125
AA-- AB-- AC-- AD-- AE-- AH-- AJ--	-	55	85
AJ70 (last run)	-	80	150

Sheets of thirty five Salmon £50's sold at a charity auction:

AB01 *to* AB35 all with 997788 serial
AB01 *to* AB35 all with 997777 serial

B410 Front

B410 Low serial First AA01 *reverse*

© Bank of England

VICTORIA CLELAND

2014 *ongoing*

Victoria Mary Florence Cleland read Philosophy Politics and Economics at Oxford and has an MBA from Imperial College London, following which she joined the Bank of England's graduate programme. Victoria has undertaken a variety of roles at the Bank including: policy analysis of the financing of small businesses, payment systems - working as the Private Secretary to the Deputy Governor - Deputy Head of the Sp ecial Resolution Unit - Head of Notes Division (responsible for banknotes) at the Bank. Victoria was appointed the 32nd Chief Cashier as of 1st June 2014. In 2012 she joined as a Trustee of the RLSB (Royal London Society for Blind people). Victoria's hobbies include: road cycling, wine tasting, theatre and art history.

SERIES E SECOND HISTORICAL 1999 *to* 2017

TEN POUNDS Charles Darwin 3 March 2015

Design and watermark as for *B390* M.V. Lowther Series E Second Historical banknotes. Dimensions 142 x 75mm. Printed on sheet-fed presses in sheets of 40 (5 x 8) by De La Rue at the Debden Security Printing works, Essex.

			VF	EF	UNC
B411	**£10**	Orange-Brown			
		Quantity printed: Ongoing	VF	EF	UNC
		Prefixes: (overlaps Salmon B408 LH)			
	LH01	(first run, lowest available 000001)	80	150	250
	LH--	(first series)	12	18	25
		LJ-- LK-- MA-- MB-- MC-- MD-- ME-- *continuing?*	-	12	18
	M ? ??	(last run)			

The series may end ME40 (or go higher), further prefixes may also be issued?

B411 Low serial First LH01

SERIES F THIRD HISTORICAL 2007 *continuing*

TWENTY POUNDS Adam Smith 3 March 2015

Design and watermark as for *B405* A.J. Bailey Series F Third Historical banknotes. Dimensions 150 x 80mm. Printed on sheet-fed presses in sheets of 40 (5 x 8) by De La Rue at the Debden Security Printing works, Essex.

			VF	EF	UNC
B412	**£20**	Purple			
		Quantity printed: Ongoing	VF	EF	UNC
		Prefixes: (overlaps Salmon B409 JH)			
	JH41	(first run, lowest available 000001)	45	90	180
	JH--	(first series)	-	28	40
	KA-- KB-- KC-- KD-- *continuing*	JJ-- JK--	-	23	32

B412 Low serial First JH41 *reverse*

FIFTY POUNDS Matthew Boulton & James Watt 3 March 2015

Design and watermark as for *B410* C. Salmon Series F Third Historical banknotes. Dimensions 157 x 85mm. Printed on sheet-fed presses in sheets of 35 (5 x 7) by De La Rue at the Debden Security Printing works, Essex.

			VF	EF	UNC
B413	**£50**	Red			
		Quantity printed: Ongoing	VF	EF	UNC
		Prefixes: (overlaps Salmon B410 AJ)			
	AJ36	(first run, lowest available 000001)	75	110	220
	AJ--	(first series)	-	65	90
	AK--	*continuing*	-	60	75

B413 Low serial First AJ36 *reverse*

The Bank of England Governor Sir Mervyn King, announced on 26th April 2013 at Chartwell, that Sir Winston S. Churchill would appear on the next Bank of England £5 banknote. The decision was also taken to produce it in polymer, which smoothly leads the way to further polymer banknote issues, although the selection process for the historical figure chosen has changed dramatically.

SERIES G POLYMER 2016 *continuing*

FIVE POUNDS Sir W.S. Churchill 13 September 2016

The Bank's first polymer banknote Designed by Innovia, De La Rue and the Bank of England. 125 x 65mm (15% smaller), features Churchill from a photograph taken in Ottawa by Yousuf Karsh, along with a view of Westminster and the Elizabeth Tower from the South Bank looking across Westminster Bridge. The Great Clock's hands at 3 o'clock, the approximate time on 13th May 1940 when Churchill declared in a speech to the House of Commons. *"I have nothing to offer but blood, toil, tears and sweat"*. This declaration is quoted beneath his portrait alongside a background image of the Nobel Prize medal for literature, which he was awarded in 1953, together with the wording of the prize citation. Printed in sheets of sixty (6 x 10) by De La Rue at the Debden Security Printing works, the polymer substrate supplied by Innovia of Wigton, Cumbria. Copyright 2015.

			VF	EF	UNC
B414	**£5**	Pale Blue			
		Quantity printed: 590 million *ongoing*			
		Prefixes:			
	AA01	(first run, lowest available 000017)	10	18	45
	AA--	(first series)	-	8	10
		AB-- AC-- AD-- AE-- AH-- AJ-- AK-- AL-- AM--	-	6	8
	BA--	*continuing*			

B414 Polymer Front

B414 Low serial First *reverse*

A £5 sheet of sixty polymer £5 banknotes sold at a charity auction: AM01 *to* AM60 all with serial 428000.

The large see through windows comprise: the Queen’s likeness to the left with ‘£5 Bank of England’ appearing twice around the image - ‘£’ symbol to the right - a foil Elizabeth Tower in gold from the front and silver from the reverse. Above is a silver foil 3D patch of the Coronation Crown, below is a foil patch which alternates between ‘Five’ and ‘Pounds’ when tilted. On the reverse is a green foil circular patch containing the word ‘BLENHEIM’ in between spokes.

TEN POUNDS **Jane Austen** September 2017

It was confirmed on 24th July 2013, that Jane Austen will appear on the £10 banknote printed on polymer in 2017. The design will include: A portrait of Jane Austen, originally drawn by her sister Cassandra Austen, then a painting was commissioned by James Edward Austen Leigh (Jane Austen's nephew) in 1870. An illustration of Miss Elizabeth Bennet undertaking 'The examination of all the letters which Jane had written to her' from a drawing by Isabel Bishop. An image of Godmersham Park, the home of Edward Austen Knight, Jane's brother. It is believed that it was the inspiration for a number of her novels and Jane's writing table. The central design in the background is inspired by the twelve sided writing table and writing quills, used by Jane Austen at Chawton Cottage.

The Bank quotes "As Austen joins Adam Smith, Boulton and Watt, and now, Churchill, our banknotes will celebrate a diverse range of individuals who have contributed in a wide range of fields."

B415	**£10**	Orange-Brown			
		Quantity printed: Ongoing	VF	EF	UNC
		Prefixes:			
	AA01	(first run)			
	AA--	(first series)			

Jane Austen Banknote Concept

Concept design © Bank of England

TWENTY POUNDS Joseph M.W. Turner *expected* 2020

On 22nd April 2016 the Bank of England Governor Mark Carney announced that Joseph Mallord William Turner will appear on the £20 polymer banknote due out by 2020. The decision to feature Turner was by means of a new character selection process adopted by the Bank of England. Stating "Turner is perhaps the single most influential British artist of all time. His work was transformative for the art world. His influence spanned his lifetime and well beyond."

The reverse of the banknotes will depict Turner's self-portrait, painted c.1799 and currently on display in the Tate Britain. One of Turner's most eminent paintings *The Fighting Temeraire*; a tribute to the ship HMS Temeraire which played a distinguished role in Nelson's victory at the Battle of Trafalgar in 1805. Also the quote "*Light is therefore colour*" from an 1818 lecture by Turner referring to his innovative use of light, shade, colour and tone in his paintings with Turner's signature from his will, the document with which he bequeathed many of his paintings to the nation.

B416	**£20**	Purple			
		Quantity printed: Ongoing	VF	EF	UNC
		Prefixes:			
	AA01	(first run)			
	AA--	(first series)			

JMW Turner Banknote Concept

Concept design © Bank of England

DEBDEN SECURITY PRINTING

BRITANNIA GIFTWARE

Debden Security Printing (DSP) was set up in March 1986 to exploit new technical developments at the Bank of England Printing Works. This included storage, banknote destruction, design and security consultancy. From mid 1988 the brief was extended to explore marketing opportunities presented by the Bank's museum, including publications 'The Search for the Inimitable Note' and 'The Moneymakers International' (in collaboration with the Austrian National Bank). Booklets dealing with aspects of the Series E banknotes followed together with paperweights and other desk ornaments.

In June 1990 the first Presentation Pack was issued containing the last £5 banknote in Series D and the first in Series E. With little advance publicity few collectors knew about it and the vast bulk of the issue went to a handful of dealers. Packs were soon changing hands at four times the original issue price. Unfortunately this gave a distorted view of the market and when the £20 pair (C102) was released it cost £200. By comparison, twenty years later the asking price for a Faraday/Elgar pair was only just above the selling price. To complicate matters the original purchasers of the £5 set had the right to buy subsequent matching prefix/serial sets of the £10, £20 and £50. If these later denomination set were not taken up (and many collectors could not afford them) they were allocated to newcomers. So although a total of one thousand five hundred exist of each denomination, far fewer sets of all four exist with identical serials.

It is fair to say that some collectors (and dealers) felt aggrieved and doubted the validity of ensuing issues, especially when it was found that the so-called first and last were at variance with those found in circulation. A particular case in point was the £10 Kentfield DD prefix which was followed by a later run with the DA prefix. DSP argued that they were offering authentic first print runs in good faith and this was quite separate from the Bank's responsibility for mass banknote production. The charitable view might be that somewhere along the line the wires got crossed.

Collectors also began to question whether prefixes claimed to be 'the last' were, in fact, specially created and whether any had been put into circulation. Some dealers decided to break the packs to get hold of a particular prefix unobtainable by any other means. DSP acknowledged that some were column sort banknotes, prefixed 99 when sheet size dictated a top limit of 80, but that the alphabetical prefixes were within the recognised system.

This was not the case with the Special Prefixes on banknotes never intended for circulation, such as the Queen's 50th wedding anniversary (HM50 and EP50), the Prince of Wales' 50th birthday (PW50) and the Queen Mother's 100th birthday (QM10). Meanwhile the year sets could be purchased with birth dates or other anniversaries and some were done as joint ventures with the Royal Mint and the Royal Mail. There were inconsistencies in the denominations made available and in some cases (e.g. the £50) the banknotes were not obtainable without the gold crown. Despite setbacks, Special Prefixes created for the Far East sold well and increasingly the business became focused on such wholesale deals rather than the retail market for individuals. In May 2001 DSP announced that Britannia Giftware (as it was then known) would be operated by the Royal Mint with effect from 1st June. It was not a success and within two years the Bank decided (at the behest of De La Rue who were now running the printing works) that the effort of printing limited edition prefixes was not worth the trouble. Over the thirteen year period 1990 to 2003, there were over eighty special issues and these are listed in full with official confirmation of the quantities actually sold where known. Most of them were issued in presentation folders (or wallets) usually accompanied by certificates and in some cases descriptive booklets. Whether they receive greater recognition and acceptance by collectors with the passage of time remains to be seen.

PRICING: Many prefixes (first, last and special) are only to be found in these presentation sets / packs, as a consequence many have been split up, thus some are scarce. The volatile price of gold makes it difficult to price sets including gold crowns, prices marked ∗ are subject to this. Many gold sets have been split up.

PRESENTATION SETS / PACKS

LAST & FIRST June 1990 — UNC

C100 **£5** Gill **SE90** B353 **A01** B357 — 150
Last Series D, first Series E. Limited edition Blue *leatherette* binder, 1,500 £5 pairs with matching serials 998500 to 999999.

QUEEN MOTHER'S 90th BIRTHDAY 1990

C101 **£5** Gill **A01** B357 + silver proof £5 crown — 95
Limited edition blue box, 1,100 sets (448 sold). Serials traced between 002401 and 003503. The Bank supplied an unspecified quantity of £5 banknotes, believed to be around 1,500. It is not known what happened to the balance.

LAST & FIRST 1991

C102 **£20** Gill **20X** B355 **A01** B358 — 300
Last Series D, first Series E. Limited edition Red *leatherette* binder, 1,500 £20 pairs with matching serials 998500 to 999999.

LATE CYPHERS 1991

C103 **£5** Gill **SE67-69** B353 **£20** **20U** B355 — 165

Limited edition, 400 sets in Black *leatherette* binder with matching serials 722501 to 723000. As the last prefixes were no longer available, the order form stated that both banknotes were drawn 'from a very late cyphers' but did not specify which ones. DSP booked 400 matching serials in advance for the £10 and £50 in C109 for those who wished to obtain a matching set.

	LAST & FIRST 1992		UNC
C104	**£10** Kentfield **KR30** B360 **A01** B366		165
	Last Series D, first E Series. Limited edition Brown *leatherette* binder, 1,500 £10 pairs with matching serials 998500 to 999999.		

FIRST 1992

C105 **£10** Kentfield **A01** B366 + two silver proof 10p coins 85

Limited edition, 1,000 (844 sold) pairs with serials traced between 002402 to 003402. Remarks apply as for C101.

FIRSTS 1993

C106 **£5 R01** B362 **£10 KN01** B360 **£20 E01** B371 **£50 E01** B361 580

Kentfield. Limited edition Red *leatherette* binder, 2,000 sets with matching serials 500001 to 502000.

C106 E01 First

LAST SHEETLET 1993

C107 **£5** Kentfield **AB16/17/18** B363 120

Limited edition folder, 1,500 strip of 3 containing the last Kentfield £5 banknotes printed in sheetlets of three (1 x 3) on the web presses (which ceased production in 1993). Serials 998500 to 999999.

FIRST SHEETLET 1993

C108 **£5** Kentfield **AC01/02/03** B364 120

Limited edition folder, 1,500 strip of 3 containing the first Kentfield £5 banknotes printed in sheetlets of three (1 x 3) on the new sheet-fed presses. Serials 000001 to 001500.

LASTS 1994 UNC

C109 **£10** Kentfield **KR30** B360 **£50** **E30** B361 430

Last Series D. Limited edition Black *leatherette* binder, 400 pairs with matching serials between 722501 to 723000. The relevant prefix/serials were earmarked in advance once the decision had been made to release the £5 and £20 in C103.

C109 KR30 Last

LAST & FIRST PAIRS VARIANT DESIGN 1994

C110 **£5** Kentfield **W18** B362 **AA01** B363 150

C111 **£10** Kentfield **X40** B366 **DD01** B369 180

C112 **£20** Kentfield **W35** B371 **X01** B374 300

Last and first Series E. Limited edition Blue *leatherette* binders, 1,500 pairs with matching serials 998500 to 999999.

LAST & FIRST 1994

C113 **£50** Kentfield **E30** B361 **A01** B377 390

Last Series D, first Series E. Limited edition Green *leatherette* binder, 1,500 £50 pairs with matching serials 998500 to 999999.

LAST + PRINT 1994

C114 **£50** Kentfield **E30** B361 + St Paul's print (56 x 46cm) 240

Last Series D. Limited edition, 100 £50 Kentfield E30 taken from unsold banknotes in the 999--- serial range of C113.

D-DAY LANDINGS COMMEMORATION 1994 UNC

C115 **£50** Kentfield **A01** B377 + silver proof 50p 220
Limited red boxed edition, 750 firsts (649 sold) with serials between 002422 and 003423. Remarks apply as for C101.

FIRSTS 1994

C116 **£5** Gill **A01** B357 **£20 A01** B358 145
First Series E. Limited edition, 400 pairs with matching serials within range 000148 to 003400. Banknotes were drawn from available stock.

FIRSTS 1994

C117 **£10** Kentfield **A01** B366 **£50 A01** B377 220
First Series E. Limited edition (110 sold) pairs with matching serials between 002000 and 003500. These banknotes were drawn from available stock to match those in C116 (if requested).

FIRST UNCUT PAIR 1995

C118 **£20** Kentfield **E01/E02** B371 290
First Series E. Limited edition folder, 1,000 uncut pair containing the first Kentfield £20 banknotes printed. Serials 000001 to 001000.

HM THE QUEEN'S 70th BIRTHDAY 1996

C119 **£5** Kentfield **HM70** B364 + cupro-nickel £5 crown 50
Limited edition packet, 5,000 serials 000001 to 005000.

C120 **£10** Kentfield **HM70** B369 with silver proof £5 crown 100
Limited red boxed edition, 2,000 (1,970 sold) serials within range 000001 to 005000.

C120 HM70

	AS GOOD AS GOLD COLLECTION MINISHEET 1996	UNC
C121	**£5** Kentfield **BH/BJ 25-28** & **33-36** B364	180
	Minisheet of 8 (2 x 4) in gold card packaging (30 x 30cm). Limited edition of 5,000 worldwide.	

The sets were produced jointly by DSP and Money World Asia PTE Ltd. 2,000 were put on sale at Suntec City, Singapore 5th to 8th September 1996. The UK allocation was 200 minisheets BH 000400 to 000599.

	HONG KONG HANDOVER 1997	
C122a	**£5** Kentfield **HK97** B364 single (two packaging sizes)	55
C122b	**£5** Kentfield **HK97** minisheet of 12 (printed card packaging)	620
C122c	**£5** Kentfield **HK97** sheet of 35 (supplied in printed tube)	1500
	Singles - Minisheets of 12 (3 x 4) - Sheets of 35 (5 x 7), the top gutter overprinted in black:	

COMMEMORATING / THE RETURN OF / HONG KONG TO CHINA / ISSUED 23RD MAY 97 / NO 0735

Mainly produced for the Hong Kong market, the sheet of 35 within a glossy £5 money pictured tube. The Bank printed one million banknotes from 000001 to 999999 but certain numbers had to be withdrawn, including all those beginning with '4', in deference to local tradition. All the prefixes on the sheets are the same but each banknote carries a different serial which is a departure from the Bank's normal numbering practice. Total sales were 330,000 sheets of which the UK allocation was 50 sheets, although it is likely that more have been re-imported.

C122 HK97

	HM THE QUEEN'S GOLDEN WEDDING ANNIVERSARY 1997	UNC
C123	**£5** Kentfield **HM50** B364 + cupro-nickel £5 crown Limited edition packet, 5,000 £5 (1,314 sold) serials within range 000001 to 005000.	60
C124	**£10** Kentfield **HM50** B369 + silver proof £5 crown Limited green boxed edition, 1,500 £10 (927 sold) serials within range 000001 to 001500.	110
C125	**£50** Kentfield **EP50** B377 + gold proof £5 crown Limited brown boxed edition, 150 £50 (150 sold) serials within range 000001 to 000150.	*1350

C125 EP50 9 low serial

	YEAR PREFIX 1998	
C126	**£5** Kentfield **YR19** B364	40
C127	**£10** Kentfield **YR19** B369	60
C128	**£20** Kentfield **YR19** B375	90
C129	**£5 £10 £20 £50 YR19** B377 Kentfield Limited edition packets, 1,000 banknotes in lower denominations and 500 sets containing all four denominations. Banknotes could be ordered with special birthday or anniversary prefix/serials, 980001 and following.	340

All year prefix sets C126/29 - C135/38 - C139/41 - C149/51 could be ordered with prefix/serials to match birthdays, anniversaries or special dates.

PRINCE OF WALES 50th BIRTHDAY 1998 — UNC

C130 **£5** Kentfield **PW50** B364 + cupro-nickel £5 crown — 70
Limited edition packet, 1,000 £5 (897 sold) serials within rangc 000001 to 001000.

C131 **£10** Kentfield **PW50** B369 + silver proof £5 crown — 145
Limited green boxed edition, 500 £10 (397 sold) serials within range 000001 to 000500.

C132 **£50** Kentfield **PW50** B377 + gold proof £5 crown — *1450
Limited blue boxed edition, 100 £50 (4 sold) serials within range 000001 to 0000100. (All four may have been split up?)

C133 **£5 £10 £50 PW50** Kentfield + three £5 crowns (as above) — *1500
Wooden boxed set of three banknotes (95 sold).

Orders for C133 were satisfied first and then the remaining banknotes were allocated to C130, C131 and C132.

C131 PW50

THE UK ROYAL TRIPLET 1998

C134 **£5** B364 **£10** B369 **£20** B375 Kentfield (all) **BE98** — 130
Set of three denominations, produced for Money World Asia. Limited edition packet, 1,888 sets. Believed to be numbered from 000001 but the precise upper limit is not known as more banknotes were supplied than actually used. (traced to 000863).

	YEAR PREFIX 1999	UNC
C135	**£5** Kentfield **YR19** B364	40
	Limited edition packet, 1,000 £5 990001 and following.	
C136	**£10** Kentfield **YR19** B369	70
	Limited edition packet, 1,000 £10 990001 and following.	
C137	**£20** Kentfield **YR19** B375	125
	Limited edition packet, 1,000 £20 990001 and following.	
C138	**£5 £10 £20 £50 YR19** B377 Kentfield	280
	Limited edition four denominations packet, 500 sets.	

	YEAR PREFIX + CROWN 1999	
C139	**£5** Kentfield **YR19** B364 + cupro-nickel £5 crown	55
	Limited edition packet £5 (748 sold).	
C140	**£20** Kentfield **YR19** B375 + silver proof £5 crown	155
	Limited red boxed edition £10 (298 sold).	
C141	**£50** Kentfield **YR19** B377 + gold proof £5 crown	*1400
	Limited black boxed edition £50 (91 sold) serials 990400 to 990499. See text at bottom of page 346.	

C141 YR19

	FIRST & SPECIAL RUN 1999					
C142	**£5** Kentfield **DL99**	B364	Lowther **EA01**	B380	90
C143	**£10** Kentfield **KK99**	B369	Lowther **KL01**	B382	140
C144	**£20** Kentfield **CL99**	B375	Lowther **DA01**	B384	210
C145	**£50** Kentfield **H99**	B377	Lowther **J01**	B385	330

Limited edition packets, 1,500 banknote pairs with matching serials 998500 to 999999.

	LASTS SPECIAL RUN 1999		UNC
C146	**£5 £10 £20 £50** Kentfield **DL99 KK99 CL99 H99** As C142 to C145. Limited edition, 1,000 sets with matching serials from 001001 to 002000.		340

A further supply of Kentfield special run 99's was released later in loose leaf form, most of which were bought by dealers. Serials 000001 to 001000.

	FIRSTS 1999	
C147	**£5 £10 £20 £50** Lowther **EA01 KL01 DA01 J01** As in C142 to C145. Limited edition, 1,000 sets with matching serials from 001001 to 002000.	380

A further supply of Lowther first prefixes 01's was released later in loose leaf form, most of which were bought by dealers. Serials 000001 to 001000.

	LAST & FIRST 1999	
C148	**£20** Lowther **DA80** B384 **AA01** B386 Last Faraday, first Elgar. Limited edition packet, 1,000 pairs with matching serials 999000 to 999999.	180

	MILLENNIUM YEAR PREFIX 2000	
C149	**£5** Lowther **YR20** B380	35
C150	**£10** Lowther **YR20** B382 Limited edition packet, 1,500 serials 000001 and following.	55
C151	**£20** Lowther **YR20** B386 + silver £5 proof crown Limited edition, 2,000 £20 serials 000001 and following. Available in a red box or cardboard packet packaging. See text at bottom of page 346.	150

HM THE QUEEN MOTHER'S 100th BIRTHDAY 2000 UNC

C152 **£5** Lowther **QM10** B380 + cupro-nickel £5 crown & stamp Philatelic/Numismatic cover (postmark 4 8 2000). Limited edition, 5,000 serials 000001 to 005000. 45

C153 **£5** Lowther **QM10** B380 + cupro-nickel £5 crown Limited edition, 1,000 (382 sold) serials 010001 to 011000. 45

C154 **£10** Lowther **QM10** B382 + silver proof £5 crown Limited edition, 750 (485 sold) serials 000001 to 000750. 100

C155 **£20** Lowther **QM10** B386 + gold proof £5 crown Limited edition, 200 (98 sold) serials 000001 to 000200. *1400

C156 **£5 £10 £20 QM10** Lowther + gold proof £5 crown Cardboard box with three packets C153/4/5 (87 sold) with matched serials in above ranges. *1500

C154 QM10

C155 QM10

LAST & FIRST 2000 UNC

C157 **£10** Lowther **LA80** B382 **AA01** B390 110
Last Dickens and first Darwin. Limited edition, 1,000 pairs, with matching serials 999000 to 999999.

QUEEN VICTORIA CENTENARY END OF ERA 2001

C158 **£10** Lowther **QV10** B390 + cupro-nickel £5 crown & 26p stamp 60
Limited edition, 5,000 covers serials 000001 to 005000.

C159 **£5** Lowther **VR10** B380 + cupro-nickel £5 crown 70
Limited edition, 400 packets (400 sold) serials in range 000001 to 000650.

C160 **£10** Lowther **VR10** B390 + silver proof £5 crown 130
Limited edition, 700 packets (327 sold) serials 000251 to 000950.

C161 **£5 £10 £20 VR10** Lowther B386 + gold proof £5 crown *1400
Set of three values. Limited edition, 250 cardboard box with three packets C158/9/60 (178 sold) with matching serials 000001 to 000250.

C160 VR10 5 low serial

LAST & FIRST May 2002

C162 **£5** Lowther **EJ90** B380 **HA01** B395 240
Last Stephenson, first Fry. Limited edition, 1,000 pairs with matching serials 999001 to 999999. This is the only source for these two specific prefix / 'B' numbers.

HM THE QUEEN'S GOLDEN JUBILEE June 2002 UNC

C163 **£5** Lowther **QE50** B380 + £5 crown & 1st & 2nd class stamps 50
Philatelic/Numismatic cover (postmark 6-2-2002). Limited edition, 10,000 serials 000001 to 010000.

C164 **£5** Lowther **YR20** B380 + £5 crown 45
Baby Gift Set. Limited edition packet within range 020001 to 029999.

C165 **£5** Lowther **ER50** B393 + cupro-nickel £5 crown 65
Limited edition packet, 1,000 serials 000151 to 0001150.

C166 **£10** Lowther **ER50** B390 + silver proof £5 crown 130
Limited blue boxed edition, 500 serials 000151 to 000650.

C167 **£20** Lowther **ER50** B386 + gold proof £5 crown *1350
Limited wooden cased edition, 100 serials 000151 to 000250.

C168 **£5 £10 £20 ER50** + the three £5 crowns (as above) *1450
Set of three values. Limited wooden cased edition of 100, serials within range 000001 to 000150.

C166 ER50

ROYAL CELEBRATION UNCUT PAIR November 2002

C169 **£5** Lowther **HM02/HM03** B395 80
Uncut £5 pair in packet. Limited edition, 5,000 pairs with matching serials 000001 to 005000.

FIRSTS May 2003

C170 **£5 £10 £20** Lowther **HA01** B393 **AA01** B388 **AA01** B386 135
Fry - Darwin - Elgar. Limited edition packet, 1,000 sets with matching serials within range 001001 to 002100.

According to a Royal Mint Coin Club letter:
'Traditionally whenever a new series of banknotes is authorised, the first 1,000 banknotes are not made available to the general public.'

	CORONATION 50th ANNIVERSARY June 2003	UNC
C171	**£5** Lowther **QC03** B395 + £5 crown & £5 stamp Philatelic/Numismatic cover (postmark 2-6-2003). Limited edition, 10,000 serials within range 000001 to 010000.	50
C172	**£5** Lowther **QC50** B395 + cupro-nickel £5 crown Limited edition packet, 1,000 serials 000151 to 001150.	50
C173	**£10** Lowther **QC50** B390 + silver proof £5 crown Limited black boxed edition, 500 serials 000151 to 000650.	130
C174	**£20** Lowther **QC50** B386 + gold proof £5 crown Limited boxed edition, 100 serials 000151 to 000250.	*1350
C175	**£5 £10 £20 QC50** + three £5 crowns as C172/3/4 Set of three values. Limited wooden cased edition, 100 serials within range 000001 to 000150.	*1400

C174 QC50

In addition to the range marketed by Debden Security Printing and later by the Royal Mint, Debden Security Printing also prepared three issues for the Westminster Collection.

QUEEN MOTHER'S BIRTHDAY 2000 UNC

W100 **£5** Lowther **QM20** B380 + silver proof £5 crown 35
Limited edition, 500 covers franked with four royalty stamps (postmark 4th August 2000) serials 000001 to 000500.
Also: + Cupro-nickel £5 crown. Serials 000501 to 001500. 25

QUEEN VICTORIA CENTENARY 2001

W101 **£5** Lowther **QV20** B380 + Guernsey silver proof £5 crown 35
Limited edition, 500 covers franked with six first class stamps (postmark 29th January 2001) serials 000001 to 000500.

GOLDEN JUBILEE 2002

W102 **£5** Lowther **GJ20** B380 + silver proof £5 crown 35
Limited edition, 2,000 covers with five golden jubilee stamps (postmark 6th February 2002) serials 020000 (020567) and following.
Also as above but: + Guernsey £5 crown. 30

W100 QM20

Other individuals / manufacturers have produced covers/packs, too many to list here.

ERRORS

Considering the millions of banknotes that are in circulation, errors (spoils) are not common. Even so, collector interest means that examples of faulty printing, paper cutting, etc, are frequently spotted by the general public, so there has been a plentiful supply. However with modern printing/checking techniques, quality control has dramatically improved at the Banks' printing works in Debden, no errors having been seen so far on Series F. Polymer Series G banknotes seem to be easily altered, collectors should be wary of any errors being offered.

It is difficult to classify the full range of errors but in broad terms they can be divided into four categories: **Paper** - **Printing** - **Processing** - **Numbers**. Errors can be found with more than one of these categories. The most spectacular are those that involve the corner of a sheet being folded over (extra paper).

Extra Paper pair

A small section of the design can then be printed on the wrong side, and when opened after guillotining shows a blank area one side and misplaced printing the other. In practice there are dozens of minor variations, which a specialist could tabulate, the following classification is intended as a guide. Prices overall have been on the increase for errors over the past six years.

PRICE RANGE *FOR* ERRORS *FROM* 1948

			UNC
Paper	i	Paper Join (Paper join taped together)	300 *to* 700
	ii	Faulty or Misplaced Thread	100 *to* 400
	iii	Missing Thread	100 *to* 300
	iv	Paper Crease	100 *to* 300
	v	Watermark Missing or Misplaced	100 *to* 250
Printing	i	Missing Colours	300 *to* 900
	ii	Missing Colour or Foil (Part Missing)	250 *to* 750
	iii	Missing Signature	200 *to* 700
	iv	Printed One Side only (Uniface)	200 *to* 600
	v	Printed Twice	200 *to* 600
	vi	Offset Printing (Mirror Image)	150 *to* 500
	vii	Foreign Body on or in banknote	150 *to* 500
	viii	Design / Printing Missing, section/s	100 *to* 400
	ix	Misaligned Colour/s / Printing	100 *to* 400
	x	Excess Colour (Ink Runs, Blobs, Streaks, etc)	50 *to* 400
Processing	i	Extra Paper	150 *to* 900
	ii	Misguillotined	70 *to* 500
Numbers	i	Identical Prefix/Serials on a Pair of notes (or run)	200 *to* 850
	ii	Identical but Different Serials on Pair of banknotes	150 *to* 600
	iii	Top Prefix different from Bottom or Side Prefix	150 *to* 500
	iv	Prefix/Serial/s Missing	150 *to* 500
	v	Inverted or Misplaced Prefix/Serials	150 *to* 450
	vi	Prefix/Serial on Reverse	100 *to* 400
	vii	One Prefix/Serial Missing	100 *to* 350
	viii	Top Serial Different from Bottom or Side Serial	100 *to* 300
	ix	Doubled Prefix/Serial	50 *to* 250
	x	One Prefix/Serial Partly Missing or Misaligned	50 *to* 250

Prices can vary tremendously depending on the grade of the banknote, denomination, age and severity/attractiveness of the error. Add 25% if two or more categories of error on the same banknote, deduct 25% of price if error on reverse. Pre 1948 banknotes and White banknote errors will command a premium.

PAPER ERRORS

Faulty / Misplaced Thread

Paper Creases, after first print run

PRINTING ERRORS

Offset Printing, mirror image on reverse

Missing Colour, background

PRINTING ERRORS

Offset Printing, mirror image on reverse

Design / Printing Missing (Queens head)

PROCESSING ERRORS

Misaligned Printing

Foreign Body on banknote, part of a paper join

PROCESSING ERRORS

Over Inked, the last column sort

Misguillotined

PROCESSING ERRORS

Extra Paper + Missing Print

Extra Paper

NUMBERING ERRORS

Identical Prefix/Serial on a pair of banknotes

Misplaced Prefix/Serials

NUMBERING ERRORS

Prefix/Serials slightly misplaced, causing misguillotining?

Top prefix different from side prefix JK62 / AA00 (Specimen?)

Top prefix different from side prefix banknotes errors were created by being 'hand numbered' incorrectly, effectively operator error. The appearance of this type of error coincides with the absence of replacements at the start of Series E in 1990. Faulty banknotes were meant to be replaced with the same prefix/serial 'hand numbered' banknotes.

GENERAL INFORMATION FOR COLLECTORS

CONTROL BANKNOTES

Treasury £1 banknotes of the Third Issue from T16 applied a system whereby a Z prefix was printed on the bottom right corner banknote of each sheet, regardless of the prefix on the rest of the sheet. It has not been ascertained as to why this was done and it is an assumption that it was a method of stock control. Control Notes are priced separately in the catalogue, traced first and last prefixes listed.

T35 Control Note First Z1/78

REPLACEMENT & COLUMN SORT BANKNOTES

Collectors are divided on the existence of a recognisable replacement system for Treasury banknotes. The most tenable theory on the Bradbury First Issue is that the banknotes with double letter prefixes and a four number serial were used as replacements. This seems doubtful in view of the speed with which they were printed and the high wastage making it improbable that replacements were needed.

Bank of England replacement banknotes (known as 'star' banknotes by the printers) are used to make up a bundle where one or more banknotes have been damaged or misprinted ('spoils' in printers' terms). In fact the original 'star' banknotes were first produced for the Birmingham branch in 1844 as a means of measuring the annual average life of an issue in circulation, the experiment lasted until 1846 (Byatt: 'Promises to Pay').

B263 Replacement First 01A

When the Bank was preparing for the 1928 issue, it became clear that mass production would require some method of replacing faulty banknotes. The records show that on 20th January 1928 an invention for numbering single banknotes to replace spoils in production was patented by the Bank. Unfortunately the relevant patent no longer exists in the Bank's records, so it is still not possible to identify specific replacement banknotes until the blue £1 B250 S--D - S--E - S--H and the mauve 10s B252 T--D. After the war the --A prefix was set aside for Peppiatt Britannia threaded 10s and S--S - S--T for the £1.

B274 Replacement First S01T

Starting with the Portrait Series, the Bank adopted the letter M as the designated prefix, and as more replacement banknotes were required, the M was used in combination with other letters. The serials of these replacement banknotes do not fit into the numerical sequence that they are replacing. So, for example, you could be looking at a run from C52 834561 to C52 834573 in which there were two replacement banknotes in the middle carrying the prefix/serials M01 232889 and M01 232890. The existence of lengthy runs of some later replacements suggests that bundles of unused stock may have been released into general circulation.

B383 Replacement First LL01

The long running 'star' banknotes were finally discontinued in 1981 soon after the Bank had installed high-speed Crossfield counting machines. These were programmed to eliminate spoilt banknotes after guillotining the sheets, which the examiners marked with an orange/yellow phosphor pen, then make up bundles to the required quantities. At the same time all the prefix/serials were stored on computer, print spoils were not substituted so those specific prefix/serial banknotes were never issued.

It is possible, though unusual, for damage to occur or mistakes to be spotted (e.g. a fold in the paper) after the banknotes have been bundled and in this instance the faulty banknotes were taken out and replaced by handset numbered banknotes with the same prefix/serial. In practice there is no way for collectors to identify replacements from 1981 to 1993.

Starting in 1993 as well as the original type of replacements or 'star' banknotes a new system was introduced, known as 'B Ream' or 'Column Sort', a means of recovering 'good' banknotes from partly faulty sheets. So there are different ways of describing variations of the same process: getting the maximum number of 'good' banknotes from a given production run. The prefix/serial used on the substitute banknotes depends on where and how the spoils occurred. If, for example the error is constant in the same place on the same banknote on every sheet, a pack of replacements will be used. If there are random errors in one or more of the eight columns on a (8 x 5) sheet, then these will be marked, cut off and sent for destruction, the 'good' banknotes stacked until such time as they are numbered as 'Column Sort' using different prefix/serials.

B358cs Gill Column Sort First A71

Column Sort numbering had two applications. The first involved prefixes above the numerical limit of the sheet size. For example A01 to A80 would be the normal run and A81 to A98 would be column sort. The second used in presentation packs by Debden Security Printing sometimes asking for a column sort runs with the prefix 99 rather than trying to earmark 80 for instance, from the main run. Column Sorts have their prefix systems identified in the catalogue, which have settled down to L for the £50 and L in combination for the three lower values. For instance Bailey's are: EL for the £5 - EL and HL for the £10 - BL and AL for the £20.

B382cs EL01 Lowther First Column Sort

The Bank has been using LL for replacements, 1993 B365 saw the first LL replacement, these are given the same status (with separate catalogue numbers) as the old M replacements. The M prefix was also used by D.S.P. (in their commercial capacity) mainly to test cash machines. Z was set aside for specific ranges of banknotes that an organisation (e.g. a clearing bank) wished to monitor. These are listed as Experimental Issues.

B399 Bailey First Replacement LL46

The Bank has prioritised quality control as of 2010 as a consequence no new replacements or column sorts have been sighted on paper or polymer banknotes. The absence of any paper error banknotes over this period also points to this tightening of quality control.

SIGNATURE SEQUENCE PAIRS

Bank of England banknotes with errors prior to the Portrait Series C are sparse, but when reel-fed printing started in the 1960s the occurence is of a higher frequence. Fforde and Page Series C banknotes are also found with each cashier's signature on consecutively numbered banknotes (sometimes longer runs). These are not errors as such but were the result of a shortage of new signature blocks available when Page took up office. As things stand there are at least sixty-two £1 signature sequence pairs in fifteen prefix combinations:

B305p

S89L	T31D	T36D	T78D	T80D	T28H	T38H	T55H	T63H	T20K
T52K	T70L	U02B	U24B	U22C	U25C	U06D	U12D	W41A	W36B
W47B	W49B	W54B	W55B	W56B	W57B	W63B	W64B	W65B	W68B
W85B	W86B	W89B	W99B	W01C	W43C	W50C	W85C	X13B	X39B
X22C	X30C	X32C	X33C	X34C	X37C	X38C	X40C	X41C	

B306p Replacements

R44M	R51M	R52M	R53M	S32M	S35M	S51M	S57M	S59M	S61M
S63M	S72M	S78M							

The above list does not imply that only one linked signature sequence pair exists in each prefix. In a consecutively numbered run of twenty banknotes (W43C) formerly in Vincent Duggleby's collection, the signature changed no fewer than five times.

B314p Fforde / Page Pair

£5 Fforde/Page pairs prefix: 34D - 95D - 44E - 01H / 08M - 10M - 13M and £10 Fforde/Page pairs prefix: A92 - A95 have been logged. Pairs may still be made when un-numbered sheets (or part sheets) are used up from stock bearing a previous Chief Cashier's signature as happened with: £10 Page/Somerset B330p - £5 Gill/Kentfield B357p - £20 Gill/Kentfield B358p - £20 Lowther/Bailey B386p.

PRESENTATION FOLDERS

The Bank of England has continued to issue banknotes in presentation format since the Mahon Parchment Pair B214. These leather folders consisting of first prefix low serial banknotes have been filtering out onto the marketplace over recent years. A £10 Hollom A01 000005 B299 appeared on the market in 1990, followed by a group prefix/serial A01 000100 consisting of O'Brien 10s and £1, Hollom £5, Fforde £20 and Page £5 (Wellington) banknotes. Folders presented to designer Harry Eccleston, prefix/serial A01 or AN01 all 000010: Fforde £20, Page £1, £5 and £10 and Somerset £1 and £50. The most recent was Hollom's folders: B286 10s A01 000034, £5 B297 and £10 B299 A01 000015, £5 B297 and £20 B318 A01 000013 plus two first prefix serial 000001 (not in folders). Many more must have been presented to VIP's and will, no doubt, turn up on the collectors' market in the years to come.

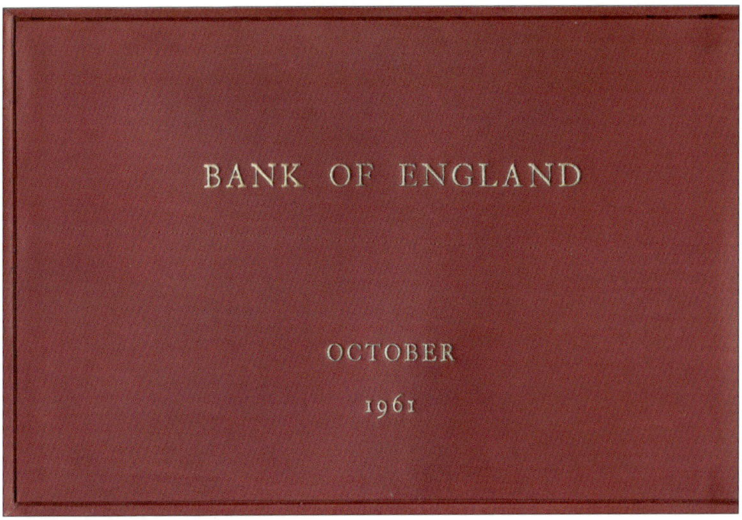

Presentation Folder 10s B286 (inside)

TEST NOTES

Test Notes are produced for testing machinery that use banknotes, prior to testing with the genuine article: (ATM's (automatic telling machines) - Paper money counting machines - Machines that accept or dispense paper money - Counterfeit detection equipment - etc) and are made in the research and development of new banknotes: (Paper/Polymer testing - Anti forgery devices - Printing techniques - Inks - New security innovations - etc). As printers became aware that polymer banknotes would become reality for many countries, they designed and prepared polymer test notes well in advance.

Nelson test note found in various sizes, designs and colours.

Sir John Everett Millais polymer test note, first produced in 1980 by De La Rue. Design variations exist.

Kentfield polymer test note, purposely miscut, variations exist.

Isaac Newton, solar system and apples polymer test note.

FORGERIES

Over the years many imitations of Bank of England banknotes have been produced. Some have been merely frivolous others have had serious intent. Forgery became a serious problem in the early 19th century during the Bank Restriction period. Some six hundred and eighteen people were sentenced to death for forgery between 1797 and 1829, it was not until 1832 that the death sentence was finally abolished and transportation for life was substituted. Forgery Acts were drafted in 1861, 1870 and 1913.

In 1914, within days of the first Treasury banknotes being issued, the Government commissioned a report from Mr Seymour Bennett on how to combat forgery. Mr Bennett had already advised the governments of Egypt and India, his report was submitted on 18th August. Some rare proofs and colour trials from the Treasury period, which were sold at auction some years ago originally came from his estate.

The first person to be charged with forging a £1 Treasury banknote was a music hall artist called Arthur Lloyd who appeared at the Old Bailey on 11th September 1914. A piece of paper had been found with a tracing on it, which the defendant had offered in a pub 'as a joke'. The prosecution offered no evidence, the Judge threw the case out.

During the second reading of the Currency and Banknotes bill on 27th August 1914 Lloyd George commented: "The simpler a design is the more difficult it is to forge, just as the simpler a signature is the more difficult it is to forge. If you have a simple signature like that on the Bank of England banknote it is the most difficult thing in the world for the forger. It is much more difficult to imitate simplicity than it is to imitate flourishes and special adornments. That is the principle on which we have proceeded."

B201g £5 Forged Hase 1812

In January 1915 a Treasury memorandum stated that the number of forgeries of the new £1 banknote which had come under review was 3,700. Of these the most dangerous were the work of a body of forgers in Tottenham whose activities had been recently terminated. "3,700 does not represent the total quantity put into circulation but a calculation based on the serials suggests that the quantity is unlikely to exceed 12,000. The number of forgeries of the 10s banknotes is extremely small (100 all told) and they are poor imitations. It is therefore considered they may be ignored." Nonetheless, fear of forgery was an important consideration in proceeding with the Third Issue banknotes which used colour and much more intricate engraving. According to a report in The Times on 10th August 1922 there had been thirty different efforts at forging the £1 “and it is a significant commentary on the technical efficiency of Germany that the best forgery ever circulated came from there..... the great majority of forgeries come from country towns and midland race courses.”

In ‘Promises to Pay’, Derrick Byatt devotes a good deal of space to the Bank of England’s battles against the forgers, and the comments on the Britannia banknotes are of particular interest. Today it is an offence for anyone knowingly to purchase, receive from any person, or have in his custody or possession a forged banknote regardless of its age or country of origin. Collectors should familiarise themselves with the provisions of the Forgery and Counterfeiting Act 1981 (which superseded the Forgery Act 1913). This states, inter alia, that “it is an offence for any person, unless the relevant authority has previously consented in writing, to reproduce on any substance whatsoever, and whether or not on the correct scale, any British currency banknote or any part of a British currency banknote.” This clearly covers both photographing and photocopying banknotes.

All forgeries are liable to confiscation by the Bank of England if presented for verification and this still applies to the Second World War forgeries produced by concentration camp prisoners for the Nazis at Sachsenhausen. The story is fully chronicled by Bryan Burke in ‘Nazi Counterfeiting of British Currency during World War II’ and ‘Promises to Pay’ reveals much inside information from the Bank’s records on operation ‘Andreas’ (or Andrew) and operation ‘Bernhard’ (named after the SS officer in charge, Bernhard Krueger). What is clear from reading Byatt is that there is no single guaranteed method of detecting the forgeries. Correspondence with the Swiss National Bank refers to the ultra violet test where the genuine banknotes emit light bluish light; slightly shinier and less weighty paper detectable by ‘feel’; the blackness of the ink; the thickness of a lines and the size of a stop. Different banknotes may fail a test for different reasons as the Germans developed their technical expertise. The Bank could also consult it’s white banknote ledgers, which show whether and when the banknote in question was paid.

Issued banknote with forged zero serials

Burke lists twenty-eight different ways in which to distinguish the forgeries, with accompanying photographic detail. Collectors should focus on two or three areas of the vignette and get used to looking at them. I suggest the eyes, spear head and shaded area to the left of the spear shaft, note the clarity of engraving on a genuine banknote as opposed to a forgery.

Pam suggests you look for an earring on her right ear (*to left*), a genuine banknote has one, whereas the forgery does not. The orbs around the sum block, on a genuine banknote all a constant size, the orbs in the corners may differ in size, but, are still circular On a forgery they are uneven in size and circularity, the orbs in the corners are distorted. The hook at the lower right of the vignette, on a genuine banknote has a tail inwards, on a forgery it turns the corner with no tail. Look on the website for more detailed information, under News & Info where you will find tables of known forgeries. All this leaves collectors with a cleft stick. Keeping the banknote, knowing it to be forged, is an offence. By checking it with the Bank, you risk losing it.

Genuine

Forgery

Although the number of modern counterfeits is relatively small, by 1994 the Bank had become so concerned about the risk to the public of being defrauded that they launched a campaign to increase awareness of the main security features of its banknotes. Despite their efforts, it took four years to crack the largest counterfeiting operation ever seen in Britain. The full story came out when the gang was tried and convicted at Winchester Crown Court in 1999. The ring was uncovered in a surveillance exercise known as 'Operation Mermaid'. It started with a police raid in the Isle of Wight in August 1998 when £2 million of fake £20 banknotes were found. The court was told that the forgeries were excellent and came complete with foil strip and watermark. Up to £50 million had been produced and at least £29 million worth was put into circulation from 1994-98, forcing the Bank to introduce new security measures including the foil hologram. Interestingly the main feature which the gang had ignored was intaglio printing which gives the raised feel to the words 'Bank of England' at the top of the banknotes. Further details can be found in newspaper reports, especially The Times for 23rd December 1999 and the story was also featured in a Channel Four television programme on 1st July 2004 called 'Behind the Crime'.

As already stated, it is an offence to photocopy or publish photographs of banknotes without specific written authorisation. In 2016 the Bank issued updated guidelines for the reproduction of Bank of England banknotes in advertisements and illustrations. One important concession regarding old banknotes (ie: banknotes issued before 1960 which do not contain a portrait of the Queen) is that they no longer need to be overprinted 'SPECIMEN'. Anyone, however, wishing to illustrate any Bank of England banknote of any period is most strongly advised to obtain the guidelines.

SKIT NOTES

Skit notes fall into four main categories: Campaigning - Propaganda - Satirical - Advertising. One of the earliest and best known is the anti-hanging note produced by George Cruickshank in 1818 and aimed at ending the death penalty for passing forged banknotes. Propaganda notes are often produced in wartime and should not be confused with forgeries designed to deceive the enemy. Most skit notes have been of the latter two categories, the aim being to sail as close to the wind as possible without infringing the Bank's copyright or breaking the law. Skits are not confined to paper items and a comprehensive collection will include many other artefacts: badges - bookmarks - bow ties - buttons - scarves - keyrings - dishes, moneyboxes - lighters - cigarette cases - ashtrays - etc.

Advertising skit £1 Lee on Solent Air Day 1958

PRODUCTION DEFECTS

Printers Waste sometimes comes onto the market, not strictly an error but spoils from the printing processes. Pieces seen are mainly from the Treasury period, usually having been marked with blue crayon.

T3-3 Printers' Waste, three signatures and two prefix/serials

One of the most remarkable errors was the omission of the Chief Cashier's signature in 1981 on a run of D.H.F. Somerset £5 B343a. The exact circumstances have not been officially disclosed and most of the packets were retrieved either before distribution or direct from the clearing banks before entering circulation.

An error in the copyright on the new Darwin £10 occurred in 2000 B388 when the plates were prepared with the wording 'The Governor and the Company of the Bank of England'. This was subsequently corrected to omit the second 'the' B390 but in this instance financial considerations dictated that both versions should be released into circulation.

The same applied when the Elizabeth Fry £5 banknotes B393 were issued in May 2002 and almost immediately withdrawn because the prefix/serial could be rubbed off. Apparently no one realised the printing ink might not stick to the uncoated paper. After various experiments the problem was solved by heating the banknotes, they were then re-issued. The cut halo around the Britannia resolved the issue B395.

Contrary to their usual policy of not formally admitting to printing errors (and after some banknotes had appeared on an online auction site), the Bank issued a press release on the 4th November 2005 which stated that: Up to four hundred and fifty £20 banknotes with major printing defects have been inadvertently delivered to a very small number of clearing bank cash machines this week..... There are two defects. One is a complete absence of the raised printing on the front of the banknote. The other is very poor quality raised printing. An initial investigation of the incident by the Bank's printer, De La Rue, indicates that sheets of partly printed banknotes containing the defects, which were intended to be destroyed, were accidentally included with 'good' banknotes and packed for distribution. A full investigation by the Bank and De La Rue is underway.'

SPECIMEN & CANCELLED BANKNOTES

Treasury issuing policy for Specimen and Cancelled banknotes seems haphazard and arbitrary. Certainly they were under great pressure in wartime and the banknotes were hurriedly distributed for comments to civil servants in the Treasury and Inland Revenue, who were part of the decision making process. The First and Second Issues were so short lived that it seems doubtful that many were sent out to the Commercial Banks for reference, still less to foreign governments. Cancelled banknotes' purpose was to provide an official record of the banknote as issued. The fact that no Specimen examples have yet turned up for the Third Issue Bradbury onwards suggests that Cancelled banknotes may have been used instead of Specimens in official distributions.

Specimen twice in solid black

Bank of England banknotes overprinted Specimen carry special prefix/serials, the most common being A00 000000. They are issued by the Bank mainly for publicity purposes and to provide means of verification for foreign central banks. As a matter of course the Bank required specimens to be returned on demand, but judging from the number coming on to the market, overseas and retired officials do not see themselves as bound by the undertaking.

PAPER MAKER'S NOTCH

To avoid using the wrong denomination watermarked paper, Portals created a notch in the right edge of the sheet, (2 x 1 *horizontal pair*, cut to give one straight edge and three deckled edges), angled top corner for the £5, placed in specific positions to matching the denomination. This facilitates the printers' selecting the correctly watermarked paper for the value to be printed. Therefore 50% of white banknotes up to 1944 have a paper maker's notch.

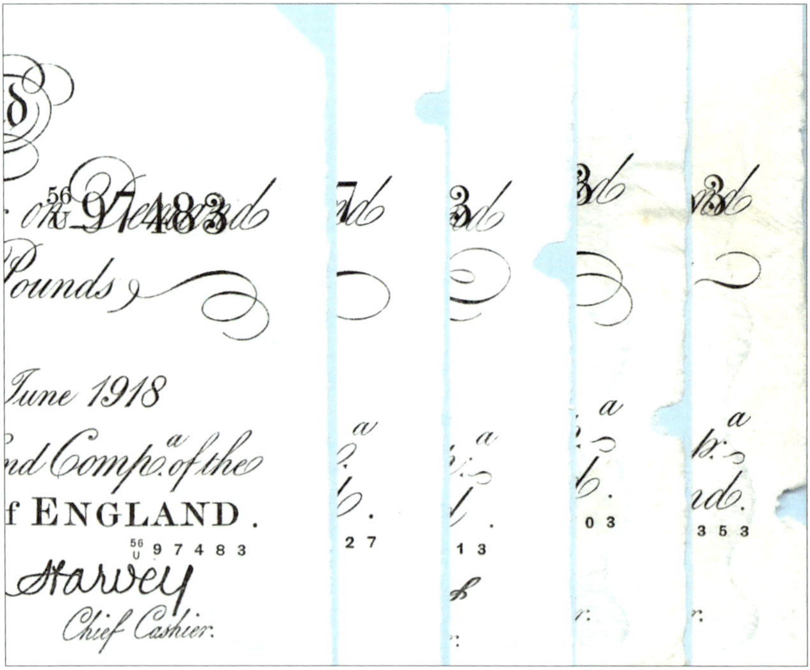

Paper Maker's Notches for: £5 - £10 - £20 - £50 - £100